£38 £30.40

Illicit Trafficking of Cultural Properties in Arab States

Illicit Trafficking of Cultural Properties in Arab States

Anas Al Khabour

Archaeopress Archaeology

ARCHAEOPRESS PUBLISHING LTD
Summertown Pavilion
18-24 Middle Way
Summertown
Oxford OX2 7LG
www.archaeopress.com

ISBN 978-1-80327-338-9
ISBN 978-1-80327-339-6 (e-Pdf)

This book is available direct from Archaeopress or from our website www.archaeopress.com

Contents

List of figures, tables and maps

Foreword

Illicit trafficking of cultural properties and the destruction of archaeological sites is an acute problem in many parts of the world. Illegal trade of cultural objects has for long been a profitable way for organized crime to make a living. In comparison to most other parts of the illegal sector, the risk for the persons involved in illicit trafficking of cultural properties are low. Law enforcement in different parts of the world has had other types of crimes in focus. But this is hopefully about to change.

One of the most tireless champions in the struggle against illicit trafficking of cultural objects is Dr. Anas al Khabour, the author of this report. The report highlights the huge challenges that relate to combatting illicit trafficking of antiquities in the Arab States. This is something that is connected not only to law enforcement and the heritage sector, but it is also something that needs to be dealt with in all parts of society. The problem must be dealt with by both preventing the suppliers to plunder heritage sites, and by combating the consumers want for new objects. Just like combatting climate change, the problems of illicit trafficking of cultural properties can only be solved by joint efforts in many parts of the society and in many parts of the world.

This is also something that is highlighted in the report. It is also the latest effort in a long run against illicit trafficking that Dr. Anas al Khabour has pursued, both as previously being head of the Archaeological Museum in Raqqa, Syria, and in his role as researcher at universities in Spain, Belgium and Sweden. In his current position at the Department of Archaeology and Ancient History at Lund University, Sweden, Dr. al Khabour has broadened the perspectives and knowledge of students and staff in this respect. His work has been presented and discussed at seminars. We are happy that this important report now has been finalized. It will hopefully have an impact of the struggle against illicit trafficking of cultural properties.

Dr. Martin Hansson
Associate Professor in Historical Archaeology
Head of Department
Department of Archaeology and Ancient History
Lund University, Sweden

Acknowledgments

It is my honor to begin these lines with a sincere gratitude to Lund University, my colleagues at the Department of Archaeology and Ancient History and the Department of Heritage Sciences, in special Dr. Björn Magnusson Staaf, for their unending inspiration.

I extend my gratitude to the INTERPOL, Works of Art Unit as well as the Carabinieri in special to BG Roberto Riccardi, Lt. Col. Luigi Spadari and Lt. Alfio Gullotta for facilitating access to the data.

I would like to express my deepest gratitude to Fria Larsdotter Lundgren for her contribution in measuring the Swedish Market. I am grateful to the Swedish authorities in special the Swedish Police Authority. A great friend and expert, Dr. Samuel Andrew Hardy provided fundamental support for this research; Dr. Morag Kersel for her advice on Middle East legislative framework. Additionally, thanks should also go to Prof. Håkan Karlsson, Prof. Didier Vivier and Prof. Joaquin Cordoba for the wise advise on the topic.

Lastly, my thanks must go to SAR network represented by Robert Quinn and to all my colleagues and friends in museums and antiquities authorities alongside of Arab States who have been an invaluable source of security and guarantor of my work. I cannot mention all the names, but I should mention Prof. Ahmed Maouloud Eida El-Hilal and Prof. Mamoun Abdul Karim.

الإتجار غير المشروع بالممتلكات الثقافية في الدول العربية

ملخص

يهدف هذا البحث إلى تقديم نظرة شاملة عن ظاهرة الإتجار غير المشروع بالممتلكات الثقافية وإلى أن يكون علامة مرجعية للحكومات ووكالات إنفاذ القوانين والمنظمات الدولية والأطراف المؤثرة والمنظمات المدنية. المنطقة الجغرافية المستهدفة هي العالم العربي المكون من دول الشرق الأوسط وشمال إفريقيا والقرن الإفريقي. يوجد هناك غياب لمنهج شامل حول الموضوع في تلك المنطقة.

يبحث هذا العمل في طبيعة الإتجار غير المشروع بالممتلكات الثقافية ووسائل وتأثير الأنشطة غير المشروعة والجرائم المرتكبة ضد المواقع الأثرية والمتاحف. يحاول أيضا سد فجوة المعرفة حول ظاهرة الإتجار غير المشروع بالممتلكات الثقافية استنادا على معلومات محدثة، قائمة على بيانات بحثية قوية، وتتبع طرق الإتجار غير المشروع، وتحليل الوضع الفعلي للمنطقة المستهدفة مع التركيز على تنفيذ الاتفاقيات الدولية. وبهذا نهدف إلى التحقيق في حلول مجدية ممكنة لمكافحة الإتجار وتحديد أولويات واحتياجات هذه المنطقة.

نتوقع ترجمة نتائج هذا العمل إلى توصيات واضحة حول تحدي الإتجار غير المشروع بالممتلكات الثقافية في المنطقة العربية، وتعزيز طرائق مشاركة البيانات، وتشجيع مراجعة الأنظمة والممارسات التشريعية والقضائية المرتبطة بالإتجار غير المشروع بالممتلكات الثقافية. وأخيرًا، تشجيع التنسيق بين الأطراف المؤثرة واستخدام التقدم التكنولوجي لإنجاز هذه المهمة الصعبة.

Abstract

The present edited research aims to capture a bird's-eye view of the phenomenon of illicit trafficking of cultural properties and to serve as a reference point for governments, enforcement agencies, international organizations, stakeholders, and civil societies. The targeted geographic region is the Arab World, the countries in the Middle East, Arabic Gulf, Horn of Africa and North Africa. There is absence of a holistic approach on the topic in this region.

The present work investigates the nature of illicit trafficking of cultural properties, means and impact of illicit activities and crimes perpetrated against archaeological sites and museums. It attempts to fill a gap of knowledge on the phenomenon of illicit trafficking of cultural properties. Through up-to-date information, grounded on a solid research data, tracing the routes of illicit trafficking, analyzing the actual situation of the targeted region with an eye over the implementation of the international conventions, we aim to investigate possible firm responses to illicit trafficking and determine the priorities and needs of this region.

We expect to translate the outcomes of this work into visible recommendations on the challenge of illicit trafficking of cultural properties in Arab region, to promote modalities for sharing data, and to encourage reviewing the legislative and judicial systems and practices connected to illicit trafficking of cultural properties. And finally, encourage coordination of stakeholders and using technological advances to fulfill this monumental duty.

Abrégé: Le trafic illicite de biens culturels dans les États arabes

Le présent rapport édité vise à donner une vue d'ensemble sur le phénomène du trafic illicite des biens culturels et à servir de point de référence aux gouvernements, aux forces de l'ordre, aux organisations internationales, aux parties prenantes et aux sociétés civiles. La région géographique ciblée est le monde arabe, les pays du Moyen-Orient, du Golfe arabe, Corne de l'Afrique et de l'Afrique du Nord. Il n'existe pas d'approche holistique sur le sujet dans cette région.

Le présent travail étudie la nature du trafic illicite des biens culturels, les moyens et l'impact des activités illicites et des crimes perpétrés contre les sites archéologiques et les muséums. Il tente de combler les lacunes sur les connaissances du phénomène du trafic illicite des biens culturels. Grâce à des informations actualisées, fondées sur des données de recherche solides, en retraçant les itinéraires du trafic illicite, en analysant la situation actuelle de la région ciblée tout en regardant la mise en œuvre des conventions internationales, nous voulons étudier les réactions radicales possibles face au trafic illicite et déterminer les priorités et les besoins de cette région.

Nous espérons traduire les résultats de ce travail en recommandations concrètes sur le défi du trafic illicite des biens culturels dans la région arabe. Nous espérons également promouvoir les modalités de partage des données et encourager la révision des systèmes législatifs et judiciaires qui traitent sur les pratiques liées au trafic illicite de biens culturels. Enfin, nous espérons encourager la coordination des différentes parties prenantes ainsi que l'utilisation des avancées technologiques pour accomplir ce devoir monumental.

خلاصة

أصبحت مكافحة الإتجار غير المشروع بالممتلكات الثقافية إحدى أولويات المجتمع الدولي، وتم وضع معاهدات واتفاقيات مختلفة لهذا الغرض. لقد مضى ما يقرب من 50 عامًا منذ عقد اتفاقية منظمة الأمم المتحدة للتربية والعلم والثقافة اليونسكو لعام 1970 بشأن وسائل حظر ومنع الاستيراد والتصدير غير المشروع ونقل ملكية الممتلكات الثقافية. كان التنسيق بين اليونسكو ومختلف المنظمات والسلطات الوطنية والإقليمية والمنظمات غير الحكومية والأطراف المؤثرة مثمرًا، إلا أن التحدي لا يزال ضخمًا ويطلب توحيد كل القوى للتخفيف من عواقب الإتجار غير المشروع بالممتلكات الثقافية. بكل الأحوال، فقد تأثرت الدول العربية إلى حد كبير بالإتجار غير المشروع، وأصبحت الحاجة إلى إدراك طبيعة الإتجار غير المشروع في المنطقة العربية وتقييم التدابير والأطر التشريعية والسياسات من أهم الأولويات. تم تصميم هذا البحث لإعطاء رؤى أفضل حول التحدي.

يتناول هذا البحث في الأنشطة غير المشروعة والجرائم التي تُرتكب بحق المواقع التراثية لاستكمال الصورة المجزأة لظاهرة الإتجار غير المشروع. وبذات الوقت يجمع أحدث الأدلة والمعلومات المتاحة ويركبها، بما يتعلق بالتهديدات على المواقع والأشياء التراثية، ويتتبع الطرق المحتملة المستخدمة لغرض الإتجار غير المشروع، ويحلل حالة المنطقة المدروسة مع التركيز على تنفيذ الاتفاقيات الدولية والمعاهدات والقوانين والتشريعات الوطنية. من خلال استخدام المنهجية المناسبة، نهدف إلى تحديد الثغرات وتشخيص الجوانب الضعيفة لسياسات الدول العربية تجاه التراث، وتحديد احتياجات التنمية وتحديات مكافحة الإتجار غير المشروع في المنطقة المدروسة.

كان المنهج المستخدم للإجابة على هذه الأسئلة من خلال:

- فحص نتائج البحث بالاعتماد على التقنيات الجديدة مثل صور الأقمار الصناعية.
- الاطلاع على البيانات المتوفرة عن سوق الآثار عبر الإنترنت والأسواق الإلكترونية.
- مقارنة الأطر التشريعية في الدول العربية.
- التحقيق في أنواع القطع المعرضة لخطر النهب في كتالوجات الآثار في أحد الأسواق الأوروبية من حيث: المواد والمنشأ والنوع وتفاصيل المصدر والقيمة النقدية.
- رسم خرائط لطرق الإتجار غير المشروع بناء على ضبط الآثار في الدول العربية.

تشمل **نتائج البحث** ما يلي:

وضحت **التكنولوجيا الجديدة ونظام المعلومات الجغرافية وصور الأقمار الصناعية** أنشطة نهب واسعة النطاق ألحقت أضرارًا بالمشهد الأثري وخاصة في مناطق النزاع. لقد وفرت صور الأقمار الصناعية فهماً للمشهد الأثري قبل الصراع وبعده، كما أشارت إلى تورط معظم أطراف الصراع في أنشطة غير مشروعة. وبالمقابل، كشف انتشار أعمال النهب والسرقة للممتلكات الثقافية أن الحكومات غير قادرة على حماية مواقعها بسبب الافتقار إلى الموارد المالية والبشرية. من الواضح أن القطع المنهوبة تحاول إيجاد طريقها إلى المشترين المحتملين من خلال القنوات التقليدية أو الأسواق عبر الإنترنت. نفترض أن جزءًا كبيرًا من المواد المنهوبة يتم تداولها في السوق السوداء، في انتظار لحظة غسيلها ودمجها في السوق المشروعة في السنوات القادمة.

ساعد انتشار **الأسواق الرقمية عبر الإنترنت** والتطورات التكنولوجية والاستخدام الواسع للإنترنت ووسائل التواصل الاجتماعي على تسهيل التواصل بين البائع والمشتري. تشير مراقبة الممتلكات الثقافية المعروضة للبيع على منصات الآثار عبر الإنترنت إلى أن العناصر منخفضة القيمة هي العناصر الأكثر مبيعاً. من ناحية أخرى، وخلافًا للافتراضات السائدة، فإن شبكة الأنترنيت العامة او السطحية (Surface Web) هي المكان الأفضل للتداول في الآثار من الشبكة المظلمة (Dark Web)، نظرًا للعدد المحدود من البائعين الذين يستخدمونها، ولصعوبة العثور على الأشياء الثقافية لصعوبة تصنيفها، وللخصوصية التي لا تسمح بإقامة علاقة ثقة بين البائع والمشتري. بالإضافة إلى ذلك، تم استخدام (Facebook) و(Telegram) و(eBay) و(WhatsApp) و(Viber) وغيرها من التطبيقات المماثلة على نطاق واسع لإنشاء جهات اتصال ولعرض العناصر المنهوبة. تتم المعاملات المالية بالدفع المباشر بين البائع والمشتري بعد أن يتواصلوا عن طريق وسائل التواصل الاجتماعي وتطبيقات الهاتف المحمول.

بالنسبة إلى **القطع الأثرية المنهوبة** (الأشياء المهددة بالخطر) من الدول العربية **في سلسلة الإتجار**، فقد أظهرت دراسة موجزة لسوق المواد الثقافية في المملكة السويدية أن أقل من 6 ٪ من هذه القطع تم التأكد منها في قاعدة بيانات القطع الفنية المسروقة. تقدم الدراسة بحثا يشير إلى أن أكثر من نصف القطع لم يكن لها تاريخ مسجل في أوروبا قبل عام 1995 وأن أكثر من 72٪ منها ليس لها مصدر محدد. هذا مؤشر مقلق ويتطلب مزيدًا من البحث.

فيما يتعلق برسم **خرائط طرق الإتجار غير المشروع** فإن معظم الدول العربية تتأثر بالإتجار غير المشروع بدرجات مختلفة، سواء كانت دول مصدر للقطع المنهوبة أو دول عبور لها أو كليهما. يفحص البحث 18 دولة عربية أبلغت عن مصادرة ممتلكات ثقافية ويحدد بعض المسارات المحتملة. تعد دول العبور الرئيسية هي الإمارات العربية المتحدة وإسرائيل.

تنتقل الآثار الليبية عبر تونس ومصر، وهي ثلاث دول عانت من عدم الاستقرار السياسي والسرقة والنهب بشكل ملحوظ. كما يُلاحظ المسار المصري السعودي أيضا، ويلعب الطريق العراقي السوري إلى بلد العبور التقليدي تركيا دورًا أساسيًا في التهريب. كما تم تأكيد طريق آخر بين اليمن وجيبوتي من خلال عمليات المصادرة وتكرار محاولات تهريب الممتلكات الثقافية اليمنية. لا ننسى الطريق اللبناني الأردني الإسرائيلي، فبمجرد وصول القطع إلى الأردن يتم نقلها إلى إسرائيل، أو «جنة الإتجار غير المشروع «. بالإضافة إلى ذلك، يقدم البحث مواقع الخروج والمعابر الحدودية المعرضة للخطر داخل الدول العربية. في الواقع، تتطلب مكافحة الإتجار غير المشروع بالممتلكات الثقافية إدارة صارمة للحدود في البلدان التي يعوقها الفساد وعدم الكفاءة بين المسؤولين.

كما يؤكد البحث على **ارتباط الإتجار غير المشروع بالممتلكات الثقافية بالجريمة المنظمة** من خلال تدمير المواقع المحمية دوليًا والنهب والسرقة والاستيلاء على الممتلكات الثقافية. ترتبط هذه الجرائم ارتباطًا مباشرًا بجرائم لا تقل خطورة عنها بما في ذلك تمويل الإرهاب. كانت الجماعات الإرهابية مثل الدولة الإسلامية في العراق والشام (داعش) عاملاً مدمراً للتراث والهوية الوطنية والعلم والمعرفة الإنسانية. أما بالنسبة لتقدير حجم أرباح داعش من الإتجار غير المشروع بالآثار فقد تعذر الحصول على إجابة وبقي هذا سؤالا مفتوحا بسبب عدم وجود مصادر موثوقة ومحايدة بعيدة عن الدعاية السياسية. كما أشار البحث إلى انتشار المنتجات المقلدة والمزورة والنسخ في أسواق القطع الثقافية من الدول العربية.

يقدم البحث بعد ذلك، نظرة عامة حول **حجم وتصنيف الممتلكات الثقافية التي يتم الإتجار بها بشكل غير مشروع** بالإضافة إلى **الأدوات المستحسن استخدامها لمكافحة هذه الظاهرة**. تحتوي قاعدة بيانات الإنتربول على 4929 قطعة مسروقة تم الإبلاغ عنها على أنها مسروقة أو مفقودة. علما أن بعض الدول العربية لم تبلغ الإنتربول عن أية سرقة، بينما أبلغت دول أخرى. كانت حصة الأسد من نصيب العراق بـ 2786، وسوريا بـ 1118، وثالثا مصر بـ 514 قطعة مسروقة مسجلة. أما فيما يتعلق بأنواع الأشياء التي يتم الإتجار بها بشكل غير مشروع، فعادة ما تكون الأشياء الصغيرة المحمولة، التي يصعب

تتبعها ويسهل بيعها هي الأكثر شيوعًا في الإتجار، مثل العملات المعدنية والتماثيل والمخطوطات. إلى جانب ذلك، هناك أشياء مفضلة من كل منطقة مثل الأختام الأسطوانية والألواح المسمارية والتماثيل الصغيرة من العراق وسوريا الأدوات الحجرية والمستحاثات من المغرب. كما يتناول البحث **شبكات تهريب الممتلكات الثقافية** ومجرى عملية التهريب ابتداء من بلدان المصدر إلى بلدان العبور والوجهة أو السوق. ثم يقدم البحث بعد ذلك قائمة بالأدوات المستحسن استخدامها والتي توفرها المنظمات الدولية في سبيل مكافحة الإتجار غير المشروع مثل القوائم الحمراء الصادرة عن المجلس الوطني للمتاحف (ICOM) وبطاقة تعريف القطع الثقافية وشهادة التصدير النموذجية المعتمدة لدى اليونسكو وكذلك قواعد البيانات والتطبيقات ذات الصلة مثل قواعد بيانات المنظمة الدولية للشرطة الجنائية الإنتربول وقوات الدرك الوطني الإيطالي (Carabinieri).

وأخيراً، يبحث البحث في مجموعة **الاتفاقيات والمعاهدات الدولية المكرسة لمكافحة الإتجار غير المشروع والإطار التشريعي للدول العربية**. هناك نقص ملحوظ في التعاون وتناقض في القوانين فضلاً عن محدودية الاتفاقيات الثنائية. تم إجراء مقارنة بين القوانين في ظل تنفيذ اتفاقية اليونسكو لعام 1970 وكذلك اتفاقية المعهد الدولي لتوحيد القانون الخاص يونيدروا UNIDEROIT لعام 1995، حيث قام البحث بتحليل الآثار المترتبة على هذه القوانين وتحديد الثغرات في قوانين الآثار الوطنية في 20 دولة عربية. استثنيت الصومال وجيبوتي لعدم توفر إطار تشريعي للآثار. كما ناقشت الدراسة الوضع الإسرائيلي مع الدول الأخرى التي تسمح ببيع وشراء ونقل ملكية الممتلكات الثقافية والتحديات التي تواجه مكافحة الإتجار غير المشروع بسبب هذه الممارسات.

التوصيات

بناءً على تحليل الأدلة والوثائق والبيانات التي تم الرجوع إليها، فقد أحصى البحث عدة توصيات لمكافحة الإتجار غير المشروع بالممتلكات الثقافية في الدول العربية وهي:

- إنجاز قوائم جرد وطنية لمجموعات المتاحف الموجودة ورقمنة المخزون وتسهيل الوصول إليه والرجوع إليه بسهولة. من المهم اعتماد معايير تخزين عالمية على سبيل المثال معيار هوية القطعة (Object ID standard).
- جرد جميع المواقع التراثية والأماكن الدينية والمواقع الأثرية.
- إنشاء قواعد بيانات وطنية عن القطع الأثرية المسروقة باستخدام سجل المتحف وتقارير التنقيب والمنشورات الأكاديمية والصور والرسومات لإعطاء أقصى قدر من البيانات المتاحة عن القطع المفقودة وتسهيل التعرف عليها واستعادتها عند ظهورها في المستقبل. بالنسبة للمخطوطات والكتب الدينية، فإن التعاون مع الكنائس والأوقاف وكذلك المحفوظات ضروري لتضمين البيانات ذات الصلة في قاعدة البيانات.

ينبغي مشاركة قواعد البيانات هذه من خلال السلطات المختصة مع قاعدة بيانات دولية مثل قاعدة بيانات الإنتربول للأعمال الفنية المسروقة.

- تشكيل لجان وطنية برعاية جامعة الدول العربية تختص بتقريب وجهات النظر في مناطق النزاع لجلب الأطراف المتحاربة إلى اتفاقيات تحييد المواقع التراثية وعدم استخدامها من قبل أي طرف تحت أي ظرف من الظروف.
- إنشاء هيئات متخصصة «مفرزة التراث» لتحديد القطع الثقافية المسروقة والمنقولة بطريقة غير مشروعة، للتعامل مع الجرائم المتعلقة بتهريب الآثار وتعزيز التعاون الدولي مع الدول الأخرى في المنطقة العربية وخارجها.
- اعتماد لوائح جديدة على مستوى الدول العربية مخصصة لمنع استخدام الإنترنت والأسواق الإلكترونية للاتجار بالممتلكات الثقافية، ومنع استخدام أجهزة الكشف عن المعادن، ونشر مجموعة أدوات مرجعية باللغة العربية حول الممارسات الجيدة، والعناية الواجبة، ومدونة الأخلاقيات.

- تعزيز التعاون الثنائي بين الدول العربية للسيطرة على المنافذ الحدودية لضمان قدرتها على مكافحة التهريب. يجب مصادرة القطع الثقافية التي ليس لها أوراق رسمية قبل مغادرة حدود الدول العربية. فالقطعة المهرَّبة وبمجرد دخولها داخل أوروبا، ستكون في منطقة حرية الحركة وسيكون من الصعب مصادرتها.
- مواءمة تشريعات الآثار في الدول العربية وتنظيم التصدير والاستيراد والملكية ووثائق المنشأ وفق المعايير الدولية.
- الاستفادة من شهادة التصدير النموذجية للقطع الثقافية التي أصدرتها اليونسكو ومنظمة الجمارك العالمية. يسهل هذا المعيار كلاً من التداول القانوني للسلع المصدرة وكشف الحركة غير القانونية لهذه المواد من قبل الشرطة والجمارك.
- تشكيل لجنة تمثيلية للدول العربية لمعالجة قضايا الاسترداد.

يجب أن تتكون من خبراء من خلفية قانونية ومدربين تدريباً جيداً للاستفادة من الاتفاقيات الدولية.

- استهداف دول الطلب في سوق الإتجار للتعاون في قطع سلسلة العرض والطلب. تمت مناقشة العلاقة بين الطلب في بلدان السوق والإمداد في بلدان المصدر جيدًا وتم قبولها في الوسط الأكاديمي.
- يجب على المجتمع الدولي وضع تدابير لتجريم الإتجار غير المشروع بالممتلكات الثقافية بناءً على الاتفاقيات الدولية مثل اتفاقية (باليرمو) لعام 2000 وقرار مجلس الأمن رقم 2199 (2015) و2347 (2017). بالنظر إلى أن الإتجار بالآثار يستكمل عناصر الجريمة المنظمة: التي ترتكبها جماعة إجرامية منظمة وتمارس غسيل الأموال، والفساد، والتهرب الضريبي، والإرهاب.

إن قضية ملاحقة أحمد الفقيه المهدي المسؤول عن جريمة تدمير التراث الثقافي في تمبكتو في مالي عام 2012 والتي اعتبرت جريمة حرب هي قضية ملهمة لتجريم الإتجار غير المشروع بالممتلكات الثقافية.

- تشجيع الدول العربية على التصديق على الاتفاقيات الدولية مثل اتفاقية اليونسكو لعام 1970 والمعهد الدولي لتوحيد القانون الخاص يونيدروا 1995.
- (إجراء خاص بالدول العربية في حالة النزاع).

النظر في إمكانية نقل مجموعات المتاحف، أو القطع الأكثر أهمية، من المتاحف في مناطق النزاع إلى الدول العربية الآمنة الأخرى وضمان استعادتها عند انتهاء النزاع.

إذ أن التجربة الإسبانية خلال الحرب الأهلية 1939-1936 خير مثال على ذلك، عندما أخلت إسبانيا أعمال الفن الإسباني وأودعتها في فرنسا ثم أعيدت بعد انتهاء الحرب. إن تطبيق هذه التجربة في الدول العربية من شأنه أن يصون متاحفها ويضمن سلامة الممتلكات الثقافية من السرقة والإتجار غير المشروع.

- تعزيز التعاون في مجال إنفاذ القانون في الدول العربية في مراقبة دور المزادات وصالات العرض والموانئ الحرة، وتبادل البيانات مع المنظمات ذات الصلة مثل مكتب الأمم المتحدة المعني بالمخدرات والجريمة ومنظمة الجمارك العالمية والإنتربول.
- رفع الوعي ونشر أفلام الرسوم المتحركة والحملات الإعلامية العامة حول أهمية التراث والعقوبات المرتبطة بالإتجار غير المشروع بالممتلكات الثقافية.

في السويد على سبيل المثال، وبالتعاون مع (United4Heritage#)، تم إطلاق حملة كبيرة في المطارات والمعابر الحدودية والتلفزيون وأقيمت المعارض في المتاحف لهذا الغرض.

- زيادة احتمالات منح المهنيين فرص عمل وحماية اجتماعية، كما يعد توظيف المزيد من الحراس في المواقع التراثية أمرًا بالغ الأهمية لحماية المواقع الأثرية من النهب.
- تعزيز دور التعليم وإشراك جيل الشباب في حماية التراث الثقافي والحفاظ عليه والتدريب والرقمنة والتأكيد على مهمة المتاحف في الحفاظ على التراث الثقافي للأجيال القادمة في العصر الرقمي.
- اعتماد «القانون الإرشادي للمحافظة على الآثار العربية وحمايتها» المقدم من البرلمان العربي عام 2020.

Summary

Combating illicit trafficking of cultural properties has become one of the priorities of the international community; various treaties and conventions have been developed for this end. Almost 50 years have passed since the establishment of the UNESCO Convention of 1970 on the Means of Prohibiting and Preventing the Illicit Import, Export and Transfer of Ownership of Cultural Property. The coordination between UNESCO and different organizations, national and regional authorities, NGOs, and stakeholders has been productive, but still the challenge is monumental and requires uniting all forces to mitigate the consequences of illicit trafficking of cultural properties. However, Arab States have been disproportionately affected by illicit trafficking and the need to perceive the nature of illicit trafficking in Arab region and evaluate measures, legislative frameworks and policies has become a first-concern duty. This research is designed to give better insights into the challenge.

The research investigates illicit activities and crimes perpetrated against heritage sites to complete the fragmented image of the phenomenon of illicit trafficking. Likewise, it gathers and synthesizes the available up-to date evidence and information on threats to heritage sites and objects, traces potential routes used for illicit trafficking, and analyzes the situation of the studied region with an eye on the implementation of the international conventions and treaties, national laws and statutes. By employing suitable methodology, we aim to determine gaps and diagnose weak aspects of Arab States' policies towards heritage, identify development needs and challenges to combat illicit trafficking in the studied region.

The **method** used for responding these questions was through:

- Examining the results of research based on new technologies, for example satellite imagery.
- Consulting the available data on the antiquities market online and internet marketplaces.
- Comparing the legislative framework in Arab States.
- Investigating types of objects subject to risk of looting in catalogues of antiquities in one European market in terms of material, origin, type, provenance details and monetary value.
- Mapping routes of illicit trafficking, based on seizures of antiquities in Arab States.

The research's **outcomes** include:

New technology, GIS and satellite imagery provided evidence of large-scale looting activities and damage to the archaeological landscape, in particular in conflict zones.

Satellite imagery provided understanding of the pre- and post-conflict archaeological landscape. It also pointed to the involvement of most of conflict parties in illicit activities. Similarly, the spread of looting and theft of cultural properties revealed that governments are unable to protect their sites, owing to the lack of financial and human resources. Obviously, looted objects try to find their way out to potential purchasers through traditional channels or online marketplaces. We assume that a considerable quantity of looted objects are circulating in the black market, waiting for their moment to be laundered and integrated in the licit market in the coming years.

Online marketplaces, technological developments and the wide use of internet and social media has facilitated networking and connection between seller and buyer. Observing cultural properties offered for sale on antiquities online platforms indicates that low value items are predominant. On the other hand, and contrary to widespread assumptions, the Surface Web is the preferred place to trade in antiquities rather than the Dark Web, which has a limited number of sellers using it, difficulties in finding cultural objects classified in an easy way, and anonymity which does not allow a relationship of trust between seller and purchaser. Additionally, Facebook, Telegram, eBay, WhatsApp, Viber, and similar applications have been used widely to create contacts and present looted objects. Transactions occurred directly, payment being based on establishing regional contacts by means of social media and mobile applications.

Looking at **looted archaeological objects (risk objects)** from Arab States in the trafficking chain, a brief study of the Swedish market demonstrated that less than 6% of those objects were checked against a stolen art database. The research indicates that more than half of the objects had no recorded history in Europe prior to 1995 and that over 72% of them had no named provenance. This is a worrying indication and requires further research.

As to **mapping illicit trafficking routes**, most Arab States are affected by illicit trafficking to different extents, being source countries, transit countries or both. The research examines 18 Arab States that have reported seizures of cultural properties and identifies a few potential routes. The main transit countries are the United Arab Emirates and Israel. Libyan antiquities move through Tunisia and Egypt, three countries that have suffered political instability and remarkable theft and looting. The Egyptian-Saudi route is noted, as well as the Iraqi-Syrian route to the typical transit country, Turkey, which also played essential role. Another route between Yemen and Djibouti was confirmed through seizures and the repeated intention to smuggle Yemeni cultural properties. A Lebanese-Jordanian-Israeli route is possible: once objects arrive in Jordan, they are transported to Israel, the 'paradise of traffickers'. The research identifies exit locations and vulnerable border crossings within Arab

States. Combating illicit trafficking of cultural properties requires rigorous border management in countries hampered by corruption and inefficiency among officials.

The research has emphasized the **connection of illicit trafficking of cultural properties to organized crime** through destruction of internationally protected sites, looting, theft, and fraudulent appropriation of cultural properties. These offences are directly connected to more serious crimes, including financing terrorism. Terrorist groups such as ISIS has been a destructive factor to heritage, national identity and to science and human knowledge. As to estimating the scale of benefits from illicit trafficking of antiquities in ISIS territory, it was not possible to obtain and this is still an open question owing to the lack of reliable politically neutral sources. The research pointed to the dissemination of fakes, forgeries, reproductions, and copies in the art market of objects from Arab States.

Thereafter, a general view on the **measure, typology of illicitly trafficked cultural properties, and recommended tools to** combat this phenomenon is presented. The INTERPOL database contains 4929 stolen objects reported as stolen or missing. Some Arab States have not reported any theft to INTERPOL, while others did: the highest number was Iraq with 2786, Syria with 1118 and thirdly Egypt with 514 registered stolen objects. As to the types of illicitly trafficked objects, usually, small portable objects, difficult to trace and easy to sell are the most popular for trafficking; for example, coins, figurines and manuscripts. Additionally, there are preferred objects from each region such as cylinder seals, cuneiform tablets and small statues from Iraq and Syria, lithic artefacts, and fossils from Morocco. The research investigates **smuggling networks** of cultural properties and a smuggling process within source, transit and destination or market countries. Next, we present a list of recommended tools offered by international organizations to combat illicit trafficking, such as the ICOM Red Lists, Object ID and Model Export Certificate, as well as relevant databases and applications for this end such as the INTERPOL and the Carabinieri databases.

Finally, the research investigates the set of **international conventions** and treaties dedicated to combatting illicit trafficking and examines the legislative framework of Arab States, finding a notable lack of cooperation, discrepancy of laws as well as very limited bilateral agreements. A comparison between the implementation of the UNESCO Convention of 1970 and the UNIDEROIT Convention of 1995 was realized; the report analyzes the implication of these laws and identifies gaps in the national antiquities laws of 20 Arab States, since Somalia and Djibouti do not provide the relevant legislative framework. The Israeli situation is discussed with other states that permit sell, buy and transfer of ownership of cultural properties, and the challenges to the fight against illicit trafficking due to these practices are set out.

Recommendations

Building on the analysis of the evidence, documents and consulted data, the research puts forward several recommendations to combat illicit trafficking of cultural properties in Arab States:

- Realizing national **inventories of the existing museums' collections**. Digitizing the inventory and making it accessible and easily consultable. It is important to adopt inventory standards for example Object ID standard.
- Realizing an **inventory of all heritage sites**, religious places, and archaeological sites.
- Realizing national **databases on stolen artefacts** using the museum register, excavation reports, academic publication, images, and drawings in order to give the maximum available data about the lost object and facilitate its identification and recovery when it shows up in the future. For religious manuscripts and books, cooperation with churches and *awqaf* (endowment) as well as archives are necessary to include the relevant data in the database.
- These databases should be shared through the competent authorities with international databased such as the INTERPOL database of stolen works of art.
- Creating national committees under Arab League auspices, dedicated to the convergence of views in conflict zones to bring fighting parties to agreements to **neutralize heritage sites**, not allowing their use by any party under any circumstances.
- Setting up specialized '**heritage squad**' bodies to identify stolen and illegally removed cultural objects, to deal with crimes related to antiquities smuggling and enhance international cooperation with other states in the Arab region and beyond.
- Adopting new regulations at an Arab State level dedicated to preventing **internet and online marketplaces** for cultural properties, preventing the use of **metal detectors**, and publishing a **'toolkit'** in Arabic on good practices, due diligence and code of ethics.
- Enhancing bilateral collaboration between Arab States to control **border crossing points** to ensure their capacity to combat smuggling. Cultural objects without proper paperwork should be seized before leaving the frontier of Arab States. Once a smuggled object reaches Europe, it is in a region of free movement, and is more difficult to be seized.
- Harmonizing antiquities **legislation of Arab States**: regulating export and import, ownership and provenance documents in accordance with the international standards.
- Utilizing the UNESCO-WCO ***export certificate.*** This standard facilitates both legal circulation of exported items and the detection of illegal movement of such items by police and customs.
- Creating a representative committee of Arab States to tackle **restitution** matters. It should consist of experts of a jurist background, well-trained to make use of the international conventions.

- Targeting demand in the market countries to cooperate in cutting the **chain of supply and demand.** The connection between demand in market countries to supply in source countries is well discussed and accepted in academic milieu.
- The international community should develop measures to **criminalize illicit trafficking of cultural properties** based on international conventions like the Palermo Convention of 2000, UNSCR 2199 (2015) and 2347 (2017). This, given that antiquities trafficking meets the elements of organized crime: it is perpetrated by an organized criminal group, involving money laundering, corruption, tax evasion and terrorism. The prosecution of Al Mahdi with the war crime of directing the destruction of cultural heritage in Timbuktu in 2012 is an inspiring case in criminalizing the illicit trafficking of cultural properties.
- Encouraging the Arab States to ratify international conventions like UNESCO Convention of 1970 and UNIDROIT 1995.
- (Special measure for Arab States in conflict situations).

Considering the possibility of **transferring museum collections**, or the most representative objects, from museums in conflict zones to other safe Arab States and guaranteeing their recovery when the conflict is finished.

The Spanish experience during the civil war of 1936-1939 is a good example, when Spain evacuated Spanish art and it deposited in France; after the war it was returned. Applying this experience in Arab States would safeguard their museums and guarantee the integrity of cultural properties from theft and illicit trafficking.

- Strengthening law enforcement collaboration in Arab States in monitoring **auction houses, galleries, and free ports**, and sharing the data with potential organizations UNODC, WCO and INTERPOL.
- **Raising awareness** through animated films and public information campaigns of the importance of heritage and penalties associated with illicit trafficking of cultural properties. In Sweden, for example, in collaboration with #United4Heritage, a large campaign was launched in airports, border crossings, TV and exhibitions in museums.
- Increasing possibilities to give access to professionals to **employment** and social protection. Employing more guards on heritage sites is crucial to protect archaeological sites from looting.
- Enhancing the role of **education**, engaging the younger generation in the protection and preservation of cultural heritage, training, digitization and emphasizing the mission of museums to preserve cultural heritage for future generations in the digital age.
- Adopting the '**Guiding Law for the Preservation and Protection of Arab Antiquities**' presented by the Arab Parliament, in 2020.

Résumé

La lutte contre le trafic illicite de biens culturels est devenue l'une des priorités de la communauté internationale, d'ailleurs divers traités et conventions ont été élaborés à ce propos. Près de 50 ans se sont écoulés depuis l'établissement de la Convention de l'UNESCO de 1970 qui concerne les mesures à prendre pour interdire et empêcher l'importation, l'exportation et le transfert de biens culturels de façon illicite. La coordination entre l'UNESCO et les différentes organisations, les autorités nationales et régionales, les ONG et les parties prenantes a été productive, mais le défi reste monumental et demande d'unir toutes les forces pour réduire les conséquences du trafic illicite de biens culturels. Malheureusement, les États arabes ont été largement touchés par le trafic illicite. De ce fait, la nécessité de percevoir la nature de ce trafic dans leur région, d'évaluer les mesures, les cadres législatifs et les règles est devenue un devoir de première importance. Ce rapport est conçu pour donner un meilleur aperçu de ce défi.

Ce rapport enquête sur les activités illicites et les crimes perpétrés contre les sites patrimoniaux pour compléter l'image fragmentée du phénomène du trafic illicite. De même, il rassemble et synthétise les preuves et les informations actualisées disponibles, les menaces qui pèsent sur les sites et les objets du patrimoine, et trace les routes potentielles utilisées à des fins de trafic illicite. Il analyse la situation de la région étudiée en tenant compte de la mise en œuvre des conventions et des traités internationaux, des lois et des statuts nationaux. En employant une méthodologie appropriée, nous visons à déterminer les lacunes et à diagnostiquer les points faibles des règles en matière de patrimoine dans les États arabes. Nous visons également à identifier les besoins de développement et les défis à relever pour lutter contre le trafic illicite dans la région étudiée.

La **méthode** utilisée pour répondre à ces questions est la suivante :

- L'examen des résultats des recherches basées sur les nouvelles technologies, par exemple l'imagerie satellitaire.
- Consulter les données disponibles sur le marché des antiquités en ligne et sur les marchés de l'Internet.
- Comparer le cadre législatif dans les États arabes.
- L'étude des types d'objets sujets au risque de pillage dans les catalogues d'antiquités d'un marché européen en termes de matériau, d'origine, de type, de détails de provenance et de valeur monétaire.
- Cartographier les routes du trafic illicite, sur base des saisies d'antiquités dans les États arabes.

Les **résultats** du rapport sont les suivants:

Les **nouvelles technologies, les SIG et l'imagerie satellite** ont permis d'identifier les activités de pillage à grande échelle et les dommages causés au paysage archéologique, en particulier dans les zones de conflit. L'imagerie par satellite a permis de comprendre le paysage archéologique avant et après le conflit. Elle a également mis en évidence l'implication de la plupart des parties au conflit dans des activités illicites. Par ailleurs, l'augmentation du pillage et du vol de biens culturels a révélé que les gouvernements sont incapables de protéger leurs sites, en raison du manque de moyens financiers et humains. De toute évidence, les objets pillés tentent de trouver leur chemin vers des acheteurs potentiels par le biais des canaux traditionnels ou des marchés en ligne. Nous supposons qu'une partie considérable des objets pillés circule sur le marché noir, attendant le moment d'être blanchis et intégrés au marché licite dans les prochaines années.

Les **marchés en ligne**, les développements technologiques et la large utilisation d'Internet et des médias sociaux ont facilité la mise en réseau et la connexion entre le vendeur et l'acheteur. L'observation des biens culturels proposés à la vente sur les plateformes en ligne d'antiquités indique que les objets de faible valeur sont les objets dominants de la vente. D'autre part, et contrairement aux idées reçues, le Surface Web est le lieu de prédilection pour le commerce d'antiquités par rapport au Dark Web, en raison du nombre limité de vendeurs qui l'utilisent, des difficultés à trouver des objets culturels classés de manière simple et de l'anonymat qui ne permet pas d'établir une relation de confiance entre vendeur et acheteur. En outre, Facebook, Telegram, eBay, WhatsApp, Viber et d'autres applications similaires ont été largement utilisés pour créer des contacts et exposer des objets pillés. Les transactions ont donné lieu à un paiement direct basé sur l'établissement de contacts régionaux au moyen des médias sociaux et des applications mobiles.

En ce qui concerne **les objets archéologiques pillés (objets à risque)** provenant des États arabes dans la chaîne de trafic, une brève étude du marché suédois a démontré que moins de 6 % de ces objets ont été vérifiés dans une base de données sur l'art volé. Le rapport fournit une preuve qui indique que plus de la moitié des objets n'avaient pas d'historique enregistré en Europe avant 1995 et que plus de 72% d'entre eux n'avaient pas de provenance nommée. Il s'agit d'une indication inquiétante qui nécessite des recherches plus approfondies.

En ce qui concerne la **cartographie des itinéraires du trafic illicite**, la plupart des États arabes sont touchés par le trafic illicite à des degrés divers, qu'il s'agisse de pays sources, de pays de transit ou des deux. Le rapport examine 18 États arabes qui ont signalé des saisies de biens culturels et identifie quelques itinéraires potentiels. Les principaux pays de transit sont les Émirats arabes unis et Israël. Les antiquités libyennes transitent par la Tunisie et l'Égypte, trois pays qui ont connu une instabilité politique et des vols et pillages remarquables. La route égypto-saoudienne a aussi été repérée. De plus, la route irako-syrienne vers la Turquie, pays de transit typique, a également joué un rôle essentiel. L'autre route entre le Yémen et Djibouti a été confirmée grâce à des saisies et à l'intention répétée de faire passer des biens culturels yéménites en contrebande. La route libanaise jordano-israélienne est une route potentielle. Une fois arrivés en Jordanie, les objets sont transportés en Israël, le 'paradis des trafiquants'. Le rapport indique les lieux de sortie et les passages frontaliers vulnérables dans les États arabes. La lutte contre le trafic illicite de biens culturels exige une gestion rigoureuse des frontières dans les pays où la corruption et l'inefficacité des fonctionnaires font obstacle.

Les recherches ont mis en évidence le **lien entre le trafic illicite de biens culturels et le crime organisé**, par la destruction de sites protégés au niveau international, le pillage, le vol et l'appropriation frauduleuse de biens culturels. Ces infractions sont directement liées à des crimes plus graves, notamment le financement du terrorisme. Les groupes terroristes tels qu'ISIS ont été un facteur de destruction du patrimoine, de l'identité nationale et de la science et des connaissances humaines. Quant à l'estimation de l'ampleur des bénéfices du trafic illicite d'antiquités sur le territoire d'ISIS, elle n'a pas pu être obtenue et reste une question ouverte en raison du manque de sources fiables, neutres par rapport à la propagande politique. Le rapport a permis de relever la diffusion de faux, de contrefaçons, de reproductions et de copies sur le marché de l'art d'objets provenant d'États arabes. Nous détaillons ci-après une vue générale sur **la mesure, la typologie des biens culturels faisant l'objet d'un trafic illicite, et les outils recommandés** pour lutter contre ce phénomène. La base de données d'INTERPOL contient 4929 objets volés signalés comme volés ou disparus. Certains États arabes n'ont signalé aucun vol à INTERPOL, tandis que d'autres l'ont fait. Le nombre le plus élevé est celui de l'Irak avec 2 786, de la Syrie avec 1 118 et de l'Égypte avec 514 objets volés enregistrés. En ce qui concerne les types d'objets faisant l'objet d'un trafic illicite, ce sont généralement les petits objets portables, difficiles à tracer et faciles à vendre qui sont les plus populaires, comme les pièces de monnaie, les figurines et les manuscrits. En outre, il existe des objets préférés selon la région, tels que les sceaux cylindriques, les tablettes cunéiformes et les petites statues d'Irak et de Syrie, les artefacts lithiques et les fossiles du Maroc. Le rapport examine **les réseaux de contrebande** de biens culturels et le processus de contrebande dans les pays d'origine, de transit et de destination ou de marché. Ensuite, le rapport dresse une liste de recommandations proposée par les organisations internationales pour lutter contre le trafic illicite tels que les listes rouges de l'ICOM, Object ID, Model Export Certificate ainsi que les bases de données et applications pertinentes à cette fin telles que les bases de données d'INTERPOL et des Carabiniers.

Enfin, le rapport étudie l'ensemble des **conventions et traités internationaux** consacrés à la lutte contre le trafic illicite et examine le cadre législatif des États arabes. Il existe un manque notable de coopération, une divergence entre les lois ainsi que des accords bilatéraux très limités. Une comparaison avec la mise en œuvre de la Convention de l'UNESCO de 1970 ainsi que de la Convention d'UNIDEROIT de 1995 a été réalisée, le rapport analyse l'implication de ces lois et identifie les lacunes dans les lois nationales sur les antiquités de 20 États arabes, la Somalie et Djibouti ne fournissant pas de cadre législatif. La situation en Israël et dans d'autres États arabes, où la vente, l'achat et le transfert d'antiquité sont pratiqués, constitue un défi à relever pour lutter contre le trafic illicite de biens culturels.

Recommandations

Sur base de l'analyse des preuves, des documents et des données consultées, le rapport a compté plusieurs recommandations pour lutter contre le trafic illicite de biens culturels dans les États arabes :

- Réaliser des **inventaires nationaux des collections des musées existants.** Numériser l'inventaire et le rendre accessible et facilement consultable. Il est important d'adopter des normes pour les inventaires, par exemple la norme Object ID.
- Réaliser l'**inventaire de tous les sites patrimoniaux**, des lieux de culte et des sites archéologiques.
- Réaliser des bases de données nationales sur **les objets volés** en utilisant le registre du musée, les rapports de fouilles, les publications universitaires, les images et les dessins afin de fournir le maximum de données disponibles sur l'objet perdu et de faciliter son identification et sa récupération lorsqu'il réapparaît dans le futur. Pour les manuscrits et les livres religieux, la coopération avec les églises et les awqaf (dotations) ainsi que les archives est nécessaire pour inclure les données correspondantes dans la base de données.

Ces bases de données devraient être partagées par les autorités compétentes avec des bases de données internationales telles que la base de données INTERPOL sur les œuvres d'art volées.

- Créer des comités nationaux sous les auspices de la Ligue arabe, chargés de faire converger les points de vue dans les zones de conflit afin d'amener les parties en conflit à s'entendre sur **la neutralisation des sites du patrimoine** et sur le fait qu'aucune partie ne doit les utiliser, quelles que soient les circonstances.
- La mise en place d'organes spécialisés '**brigade du patrimoine**' pour identifier les objets culturels volés et enlevés illégalement, pour traiter les crimes liés à la contrebande d'antiquités et pour renforcer la coopération internationale avec d'autres États de la région arabe et au-delà.
- Adopter de nouvelles réglementations au niveau des États arabes afin d'empêcher l'utilisation d'Internet et des **marchés en ligne** pour les biens culturels, empêcher **l'utilisation de détecteurs de métaux** et publier une '**boîte à outils**' en arabe sur les bonnes pratiques, la diligence raisonnable et le code d'éthique.

- Renforcer la collaboration bilatérale entre les États arabes pour contrôler **les points de passage frontaliers** afin de garantir leur capacité à lutter contre la contrebande. Les objets culturels dépourvus des documents requis doivent être saisis avant de quitter la frontière des États arabes. Un objet de contrebande, une fois qu'il se trouve en Europe, se trouve dans une région de libre circulation et il serait difficile de le saisir.
- Harmoniser **la législation sur les antiquités des États arabes**, réglementer l'exportation et l'importation, la propriété, les documents de provenance conformément aux normes internationales.
- Utiliser le ***certificat d'exportation*** **UNESCO-WCO**. Cette norme facilite à la fois la circulation légale des objets exportés et la détection des mouvements illégaux de ces objets par la police et les douanes.
- Créer un comité représentatif des États arabes pour traiter les questions de **restitution.**

Il devrait être composé d'experts de formation juridique et bien formés à l'utilisation des conventions internationales.

- Cibler la demande dans les pays du marché pour coopérer à la réduction de la **chaîne de l'offre et de la demande.** Le lien entre la demande dans les pays du marché et l'offre dans les pays sources est bien discuté et accepté dans le milieu universitaire.
- La communauté internationale devrait élaborer des mesures visant à **criminaliser le trafic illicite de biens culturels** sur base de conventions internationales telles que la Convention de Palerme de 2000 et les résolutions 2199 (2015) et 2347 (2017) du Conseil de sécurité des Nations unies étant donné que le trafic d'antiquités répond aux éléments du crime organisé : perpétré par un groupe criminel organisé, blanchiment d'argent, corruption, évasion fiscale et terrorisme.

Le cas de la persécution d'Al Mahdi accusé de crime de guerre pour destruction du patrimoine culturel à Tombouctou en 2012 est un cas inspirant pour criminaliser le trafic illicite de biens culturels.

- Encourager les États arabes à signer les conventions internationales telles que la Convention de l'UNESCO de 1970 et UNIDROIT de 1995.
- (Mesure spéciale pour les États arabes en situation de conflit).

Envisager la possibilité de **transférer les collections des musées**, ou les objets les plus représentatifs, des musées situés dans les zones de conflit vers d'autres États arabes sûrs et garantir leur récupération lorsque le conflit est terminé.

L'expérience espagnole pendant la guerre civile de 1936-1939 est un bon exemple, lorsque l'Espagne a évacué l'art espagnol et l'a déposé en France, après la guerre, il a été restitué. L'application de cette expérience dans les États arabes permettrait de protéger leurs musées et de garantir l'intégrité des biens culturels contre le vol et le trafic illicite.

- Renforcer la collaboration entre les services répressifs des États arabes pour surveiller les **salles de vente aux enchères, les galeries et les ports francs**, et partager les données avec les organisations potentielles que sont l'ONUDC, l'OMD et INTERPOL.
- **Sensibiliser, diffuser** des films d'animation et des campagnes d'information du public sur l'importance du patrimoine et les sanctions associées au trafic illicite de biens culturels.

En Suède par exemple, en collaboration avec #United4Heritage, une vaste campagne a été lancée dans les aéroports, aux postes frontières, à la télévision et dans les expositions des musées.

- Augmenter les possibilités d'accès des professionnels à **l'emploi** et à la protection sociale. Il est essentiel d'employer davantage de gardes sur les sites du patrimoine pour protéger les sites archéologiques contre le pillage.
- Renforcer le rôle de **l'éducation**, engager la jeune génération dans la protection et la préservation du patrimoine culturel, la formation, la numérisation et mettre l'accent sur la mission des musées de préserver le patrimoine culturel pour les générations futures à l'ère du numérique.
- Adopter la '**loi d'orientation pour la préservation et la protection des antiquités arabes**' présentée par le Parlement arabe, en 2020.

List of abbreviations

ICC:	International Criminal Court
ICCROM:	International Centre for the Study of the Preservation and Restoration of Cultural Property
ICOM:	International Council of Museums
ICPRCP:	Intergovernmental Committee for the Promoting the Return of Cultural Property to their Country of Origin or its Restitution in the Event of Illegal Appropriation.
INTERPOL:	International Criminal Police Organization
ISIS:	Islamic State of Iraq and the Levant
NGO:	Non-governmental organization
UNESCO:	United Nations Education, Scientific and Cultural Organization
UNIDROIT:	International Institute for the Unification of Private Law
UNODC:	United Nations Office on Drugs and Crime
UNSC:	United Nations Security Council
UNTOC:	United Nations Transnational Organized Crime Convention 2000
WCO:	World Customs Organization

Chapter One
Introduction

Background

To celebrate the 50th anniversary of the 1970 Convention on Means of Prohibiting and Preventing the Illicit Import, Export and Transfer of Ownership of Cultural Property, we aimed to conduct this research to capture a bird's-eye view of illicit trafficking of cultural properties. There is a need to share data from a representative and reachable organization such as UNESCO and ICOM, in order to coordinate efforts and address the challenge of combating illicit trafficking. This research will serve as a reference point for governments, law enforcement agencies, international organizations, civil society organizations and other stakeholders.

This research's geographical focus is the Arab States, an aggregation of the countries in the Middle East, Arabic Gulf, African Horn and North Africa. There is a gap in knowledge that hinders efforts to establish a comprehensive assessment of illicit trafficking in the Arab World. This is caused by the lack of transparency and reliability of domestic databases on illicit trafficking of cultural properties as well as connectivity to others in Arab World. These are caused by political and legal inconveniences that hinder efforts to create a holistic approach to the topic in this region, plus discrepancies in matters of ownership among the various national regulations. Where trafficking is licit, and where it is illicit, is still an open debate in the Arab World – and it is an issue that seriously needs to be discussed.

First, this report will study the nature of illicit trafficking of cultural properties; investigate illicit activities and crimes committed against archaeological sites and museums; and piece together the fragmented image of the phenomenon of illicit trafficking. **Second**, it will cover up-to-date information; trace routes of illicit trafficking; analyze the actual situation of each and every country in the region, according to the implementation of national laws and statutes and international conventions and treaties. **Finally**, it will investigate possible firm responses to illicit trafficking through collaboration between multiple stakeholders; assess the concrete needs of each country in the region; and determine the needs and priorities of the region. Obviously, these responses will require enhanced cooperation at the national, regional and international levels – and indeed on a global scale.

We expect to translate the outcomes of this work into clear suggestions for solutions to the challenge of illicit trafficking of cultural properties in the Arab region; to encourage revisions of the legal frameworks connected to illicit trafficking of cultural properties in terms of domestic laws and statutes, alternative measures, and international conventions; and, finally, to encourage coordination among stakeholders.

Objectives and research questions

The research aims to:

1. develop a common holistic understanding of illicit trafficking of cultural properties in Arab States;
2. develop methods for investigation of illicit trafficking, plus its threats to and effects on archaeological sites and museums in the region;
3. trace routes used for illicit trafficking;
4. examine the implementation of the international conventions;
5. determine the region's needs;
6. publish a sophisticated study on illicit trafficking of cultural properties to be shared with stakeholders; and
7. suggest recommendations at the national, regional and international levels.

Terminology

To avoid any kind of misinterpretation, it is important to establish clear definitions of the concepts discussed in this study.

Arab States

According to the League of Arab States (LAS), they comprise 22 countries: Algeria, Bahrain, Comoros, Djibouti, Egypt, Iraq, Jordan, Kuwait, Lebanon, Libya, Mauritania, Morocco, Oman, Palestine, Qatar, Saudi Arabia, Somalia, Sudan, the Syrian Arab Republic, Tunisia, the United Arab Emirates and Yemen.[1]

Source countries

They are the starting point of the supply chain, characterized by rich heritage, yet poor or corrupt authorities and/or exceptional conditions such as war, conflict and political unrest, which problematize efforts to control looting and theft. Looters are typically opportunists and 'subsistence diggers' (e.g. Egypt, Libya and Iraq).

Transit countries

They have weak or corrupt border control, free trade agreements and/or flexible antiquities laws (e.g. the United Arab Emirates and Bulgaria). Here, items are laundered onto the legal market or transported to market countries. Various countries have

[1] https://arab.org/directory/league-of-arab-states/

been identified as common transit routes: Turkey for material from Arab States, Pakistan and post-Soviet states for Central and South Asian antiquities, or Belgium for material from West Africa.[2] Usually, smuggled items are laundered onto the legal market.

Market countries

They are usually wealthy countries, where the smuggled cultural properties end up in galleries, museums or private collections (e.g. the United States, the United Kingdom and Japan).

Source-market countries

In many cases, source countries are also market countries, such as the United States, where there is a demand for the cultural properties of its indigenous communities.

Source-transit countries

In these countries, looted objects can pass through the grey market in the hands of local dealers, who legitimize such objects, so that they are ready to be transferred to market countries. The best example of these cases is Israel.

Due diligence

The concept was articulated in the 1995 UNIDROIT Convention. It is an obligation that a buyer of a cultural property secures the necessary legal documentation and complies with legal standards. Due diligence is the prerequisite of legal authorities for accepting an assertion of good faith ('*bona fide*') in the case of a legal claim.[3]

Illicit trafficking or illicit trade

As characterized in the 1970 UNESCO Convention, this comprises the import, export or transfer of ownership of property contrary to the provisions of the domestic legal norms of the jurisdiction in which the import, export, or transfer occurred and/or any applicable international legal norms.[4]

Good faith ('*bona fide*')

This legal term – which dates back to Ancient Rome, when '*bona fide*' was used when a buyer of a stolen object acted in good faith (in other words, was unaware of its illicit status) – serves as a form of protection in most nations. In many nations, a good

---

[2] Hardy 2016.
[3] Anderson 2017: 83–84
[4] http://www.unesco.org/culture/en/natlaws/db/database_glossary_e_2009.pdf

faith buyer is entitled to reimbursement if the work is returned to other party. Both UNESCO's 1970 Convention and UNIDROIT's 1995 Convention protect the good faith purchaser.[5]

Cultural properties

Also known as cultural goods, these are all objects that are of archaeological, historical, artistic, and cultural importance for a nation's heritage and collective identity. States identify such goods as belonging to their cultural heritage, and their protection as of public interest, and these definitions lead to protective regulations (protective restrictions, non-availability, export prohibition, special criminal provisions, etc.).[6]

The UNESCO's definition is: Cultural property or object is a property which, on religious or secular grounds, is of importance for archaeology, prehistory, history, literature, art or science.[7]

Trafficking

This covers any movement, transport, import, export, possession or commerce in goods that is carried out in violation of the rules governing ownership or circulation of those goods or their status.[8]

This includes both tangible objects (e.g. humans, narcotics and antiquities), intangible objects (e.g. digital identities and services) and money transfers (e.g. money laundering, illicit financial flows, tax avoidance and informal economies). In this research we will address the illicit trafficking of cultural properties.

Looting

Also known as illegal excavation, this criminal activity aims to extract antiquities from on the surface, underground or underwater. This always involves excavation and happens in locations where looters believe that they can find antiquities.

Theft

Also known as larceny, this broader term involves the felonious taking of another's personal property with the intent of depriving the true owner of the stolen good.[9] This term is typically used to identify illegal removal that does not involve excavation

---

5 Anderson 2017: 83–84

6 The European Commission Directorate-General Home Affairs published in 2011 a report titled 'Study on preventing and fighting illicit trafficking in cultural goods in the European Union': European Commission, CECOJI-CNRS — UMR 6224. 2011. *Study on preventing and fighting illicit trafficking in cultural good*: 18. Brussels: European Commission. Available at https://op.europa.eu/en/publication-detail/-/publication/ca56cfac-ad6b-45ab-b940-e1a7fa4458db

7 https://unesdoc.unesco.org/ark:/48223/pf0000146118

8 European Commission 2011: 18

9 http://www.unesco.org/culture/en/natlaws/db/database_glossary_e_2009.pdf

and that targets known artefacts in open archaeological sites, museums, collections and other locations.

In contrast to looting, objects that have been removed through theft can more easily be repatriated or restituted to the country of origin, since they have been documented and inventoried, so their illegal appropriation can more easily be demonstrated.

Black Market

Here, transactions are both illegal and clandestine.

Gray Market

Here, illegal items are sold relatively openly; at the same time, legal transactions may be conducted in private.

White Market

Here, transactions are legal and conducted openly.

Geographic region of the study

The region is a wide geographical area that spans the Middle East, the Arab Gulf, the African Horn and North Africa. In general terms, this region is influenced by Islam and, thus, Arabic is the official language there. The League of Arab States (LAS) is a regional organization of Arab states in the Middle East and North Africa, formed in Cairo on March 22, 1945, following the adoption of the Alexandria Protocol in 1944. The founding member states were Egypt, Syria, Lebanon, Iraq, Transjordan (now Jordan), Saudi Arabia and Yemen. Other members are Libya (1953); Sudan (1956); Tunisia and Morocco (1958); Kuwait (1961); Algeria (1962); Bahrain, Oman, Qatar, and the United Arab Emirates (1971); Mauritania (1973); Somalia (1974); the Palestine Liberation Organization (PLO; 1976); Djibouti (1977); and Comoros (1993). [10]

Due to research needs and to the similarities in conventions, when addressing heritage and geography, this work will include the new state on Palestinian territory, Israel. These countries according to the LAS are shown on Map 1.

[10] https://arab.org/directory/league-of-arab-states/

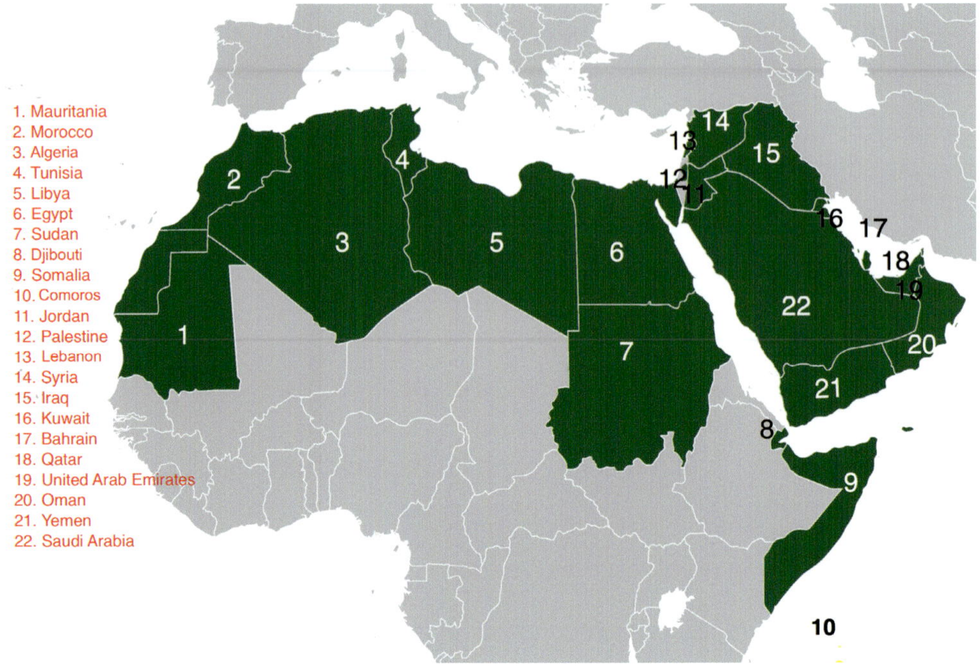

Map 1. Map of Arab States (from the Arab League)

Structure of this research

The first chapter is a general introduction to the work and the geographical scope of the research (Chapter 1). The second chapter establishes a methodology and describes the collection of data that have been used to assess the challenge of illicit trafficking in the region (Chapter 2). The third chapter studies the online market in detail (Chapter 3). The fourth chapter is a contribution by Frida Larsdotter Lundgren, who is an expert in analyzing risk markets, who assesses the presence of objects from Arab States in Nordic countries, in order to give an estimation of the scale and nature of the problem (Chapter 4). The fifth chapter maps trafficking routes in each country of the Arab States in detail (Chapter 5). The sixth chapter analyses correlations between illicit trafficking of cultural properties and other illegal activities, organized criminal activity and harm to knowledge (Chapter 6). The seventh chapter examines the outcomes and analyzes the findings in terms of trafficking stages and the international tools to combat illicit trafficking (Chapter 7). The implementation of conventions and treaties and national responses to fight illicit trafficking in Arab States are analyzed in (Chapter 8). The last chapter includes the final conclusion and recommendations (Chapter 9). There are also three annexes, where references (Annex 1), antiquities laws of Arab States (Annex 2) and seizures in Arab States are recorded (Annex 3).

References

Anderson, M. 2017. *Antiquities: What Everyone Needs to Know.* Oxford: Oxford University Press.

European Commission, CECOJI-CNRS — UMR 6224. 2011. *Study on preventing and fighting illicit trafficking in cultural goods in the European Union.* Final report October 2011. Brussels: European Commission. Viewed 30 August 2022. https://op.europa.eu/en/publication-detail/-/publication/ca56cfac-ad6b-45ab-b940-e1a7fa4458db

Hardy, S.A. 2016: Illicit trafficking, provenance research and due diligence: The state of the art. Paris: UNESCO. Viewed 30 August 2022. https://conflictantiquities.wordpress.com/2017/02/15/illicit-trafficking-provenance-research-and-due-diligence-and-confidence-and-risk/

League of Arab States. Viewed 30 August 2022. https://arab.org/directory/league-of-arab-states/

UNESCO. UNESCO Database of National Cultural Heritage Laws. Viewed 30 August 2022. http://www.unesco.org/culture/en/natlaws/db/database_glossary_e_2009.pdf

UNESCO. *Legal and practical measures against illicit trafficking in cultural property: UNESCO handbook.* Viewed 30 August 2022. https://unesdoc.unesco.org/ark:/48223/pf0000146118

Chapter Two

Methodology

Studies of illicit trafficking of antiquities mostly focus on the trafficking chain, source countries, transit countries, and destination or market countries. This research attempts to employ diverse approaches, since no single method is able to provide a complete picture of the phenomenon of illicit trafficking.

This research will employ two methods to tackle the challenge:

A. The **essential method** that consists of tracing changes in the archaeological landscape with new technologies, examining the online market, and investigating the legal framework and its effect on illegal activity.
B. The **complementary method** that consists of analyzing risk markets, plus applying the 'End Destination' concept and mapping the routes of seizures of cultural properties in Arab States.

As to the essential method, **firstly**, this study will examine the results of research that used new technologies, including Geographic Information Systems (GIS) and satellite imagery. This will assist in identifying the looting of archaeological sites. This also enables the comparison of the past and present of sites in regions that have witnessed power shifts, political instability, loss of control of borders and conflicts such as Syria, Iraq, Libya and Yemen. **Secondly**, by consulting the available data on the online antiquities market, this study will examine the typology of artefacts that are commonly demanded by those markets. **Thirdly,** by considering the implications for law enforcement and national-level responses to illicit trafficking in the Arab Region, this study will help to determine the specific needs of the region, accounting for national differences in terms of conditions and political challenges.

Regarding the complementary method, it will be applied from two perspectives, in both source countries and market countries. **Firstly**, it will target the types of 'risk objects' that are at high risk of looting. By examining the data in antiquities catalogues in terms of material, origin, type, provenance details and monetary value, we hope to create an image of the market for Arab States' antiquities. **Secondly**, by mapping routes of illicit trafficking through seizures of antiquities in the process of being smuggled, it will provide a clearer image of relevant ports and borders, as well as pinpoint smuggling hotspots and smuggling destinations.

By conducting a mixed-methods analysis, we can validate the results and extend our knowledge of the nature, means and impact of illicit trafficking of cultural properties in Arab Region.

Data collection

The research explores relevant data on the challenge of illicit trafficking of cultural properties in Arab States from sources such as databases of international bodies such as UNESCO, ICOM and INTERPOL; reports of national law enforcement agencies such as police services and customs agencies; publications and discussions of academics; reports by NGOs; and other material from other pillars of civil society. Then, it makes recommendations, based on reliability and applicability. It particularly focuses on Arabic-language data, as material in the main language of the region, and a range of European languages, namely English, French, German, Spanish and Swedish.

There was some difficulty in collecting data, particularly for Somalia, Djibouti and Mauritania. The political situation was reflected in the availability of information on cultural heritage in general and on illicit trafficking of cultural properties in particular. For example, Somalia is divided into three administrations and none of these *de facto* states has the capacity to prioritize cultural heritage needs. Likewise, the online data about Djibouti and Mauritania is extremely sparse and generic. Other Arab States displayed varying degrees of transparency in terms of accurate statistics on theft and looting in their territories.

Mapping trafficking routes

To understand the phenomenon of illicit trafficking in Arab States, there is need to investigate the routes that are used in each one of those states; their relationship to border crossings, neighboring countries and socio-political contexts; their connection to organized crime and the routes used in drugs trafficking, arms trafficking, people smuggling, etc. The seizures that have been recorded in these countries can be useful in drawing an outline of these factors and their connection to illicit trafficking of cultural properties. This research dedicates a chapter to trafficking routes, according to the available data, collected from official sources, non-governmental analyses and media reports. The map that was produced by the Antiquities Coalition was inspirational when preparing this analysis.

Satellite imagery

Analysis of high-resolution satellite imagery is an efficient tool for the assessment of the damage that is caused by looting and destruction of heritage sites, especially in conflict zones. Logically, when satellite imagery documents looting of archaeological sites, looted objects must find their way to antiquities markets.

The European policy considered the potential of algorithmic development, satellite technology, and remote sensing in protecting threatened cultural heritage and landscapes. These included the Valletta Convention 1995[1], the Florence Convention 2000[2] and the INSPIRE Directive[3], among others. In 2003 the UNESCO and European Space Agency (ESA) launched an 'Open Initiative on the Use of Space Technologies to Support the World Heritage Convention'[4]. This international collaboration was strengthened by using the Copernicus Emergency Management Service[5] to provide satellite imagery of cultural heritage at risk in order to document and protect heritage, quantify and identify risks to heritage sites such as lack of maintenance and looting. More complementary *in situ* techniques and methods have contributed to better interpretation of satellite imagery to provide inputs for calibration, assessment and interpretation of the results, such as the ground-penetrating radar (GPR), field surveying, periodical observation of changes to the archaeological landscape, surface magnetometer, geometric and electromagnetic induction and spectroradiometer.[6]

Numerous institutions have published mapping resources that reveal looting, destruction, construction in archaeological sites and other earthmoving. One of these initiatives is the Antiquities Coalition, whose interactive satellite image map shows destruction by ISIS. In collaboration with Hexagon, the Antiquities Coalition created the Culture Under Threat Map, which provides high-resolution satellite imagery maps and displays the destruction of heritage sites across the Arab region. The map only includes places targeted by non-state armed groups such as ISIS. Currently, nearly 700 heritage sites throughout the Arab League states have been damaged: 209 UNESCO World Heritage Sites and Tentative World Heritage Sites, 34 of which are in Syria and Iraq; 230 other damaged or destroyed sites; and 277 museums.[7]

Various other initiatives, such as those of the American Schools of Oriental Research (ASOR), have used satellite imagery to trace destruction and looting.[8] Further efforts by archaeologists and heritage professionals who have joined the international movement to assess damage to heritage sites include the present study's author's previous assessment of 177 sites in three Syrian governorates – Raqqa, Deir ez-Zor and Hasake – by means of Google Earth maps.[9]

Other initiatives have been undertaken in other countries of the Arab region. For instance, satellite imagery on Google Earth has been used to assess damaged sites across Egypt.[10]

1 Council of Europe. https://www.coe.int/en/web/culture-and-heritage/valletta-convention
2 Council of Europe. https://www.coe.int/en/web/landscape/the-european-landscape-convention
3 European Commission. https://workshop.copernicus.eu/sites/default/files/content/attachments/ajax/copernicus_cultural_heritage_workshop_report.pdf
4 Unesco.
5 European Commission 2017.
6 Hadjimitsis *et al* 2020.
7 Antiquities Coalition Releases 'Culture Under Threat' Mapping Resource https://www.prnewswire.com/news-releases/antiquities-coalition-releases-culture-under-threat-mapping-resource-300251043.html
8 Casana 2015: 150–151.
9 Al Khabour 2015.
10 Parcak 2015.

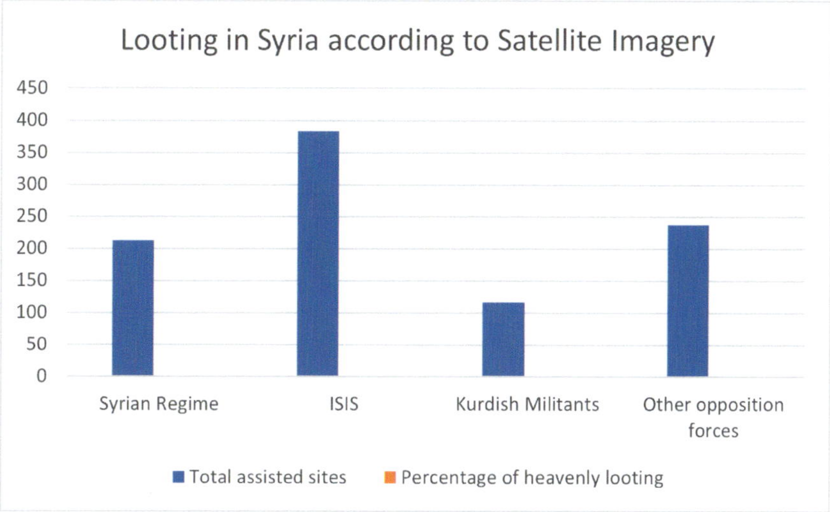

Table 1. Looting in Syrian sites by dominant forces according to Satellite Imagery (evidence based on Casana 2015: 152)

Interestingly, in conflict zones such as Syria, satellite imagery has demonstrated, in contrast to what was expected, that looting has involved not only the jihadists of the Islamic State (ISIS), but also other actors such as Syrian state forces, since numerous mounds were looted while occupied by them in 2012 and 2013. Even more surprisingly, among assessed sites in Syria, 17% of sites in regime areas had been looted, 21% of sites in ISIS areas had been looted, 27% of sites in opposition-held areas had been looted and 28% of sites in Kurdish areas had been looted (Figure 2).

Risk markets

In the prevention of trafficking of stolen or archaeologically looted artefacts, the 'risk market' or 'end destination' methodology is an approach that takes its data from where the artefact is generally last seen – the seller.

This method was first applied in a study in Sweden in 2018 by Frida Larsdotter Lundgren, a jurist and art historian who wrote 'The Swedish market for cultural objects from war and conflict zones: A risk analysis'.[11,12]

[11] https://www.raa.se/app/uploads/2020/02/Swedish-market-for-cultural-objects-from-war-and-conflict-zones-A-risk-analysis.pdf

[12] The project, 'The Swedish market for cultural objects from war and conflict zones: A risk analysis', was developed between 2016 and 2018. It was a collaboration between the Swedish Police Department of National Operations, the Swedish National Heritage Board and the National Museums of World Culture. The study was developed by: Lars Korsell, Research Consular at the Swedish National Council for Crime Prevention; Frida Larsdotter Lundgren, Researcher; and Maria Ellior, Chief Superintendent at the Cultural Heritage Crime Unit, Swedish Police. The present study's author assisted with the examination of Arabic objects, except for coins, during my work at Gothenburg University and as a Curator of the Ancient Middle East Collection at the National Museums of World Culture, Sweden. https://www.raa.se/app/uploads/2020/02/Swedish-market-for-cultural-objects-from-war-and-conflict-zones-A-risk-analysis.pdf

This study applies this method in a preliminary probe by Lundgren in Chapter 4. It searches for so-called 'conflict antiquities'. It has now been expanded to weigh more individual risk factors, such as due diligence and recorded provenance, and widened to apply to archaeological goods from all of the Arab States.

References

Al Khabour, A. 2015. *El conflicto armado en Siria y su repercusión sobre el Patrimonio Cultural: Vol. III: Inventario del Patrimonio Cultural afectado en la provincia de Hasakeh (marzo 2011-marzo 2015)*. Viewed 30 August 2022. https://www.academia.edu/15115500/El_conflicto_armado_en_Siria_y_su_repercusi%C3%B3n_sobre_el_Patrimonio_Cultural_Vol_III_Inventario_del_Patrimonio_Cultural_afectado_en_la_provincia_de_Hasakeh_marzo_2011_mazro_2015_

Casana, J. 2015. Satellite Imagery-Based Analysis of Archaeological Looting in Syria. *Near Eastern Archaeology, Special Issue: The Cultural Heritage Crisis in the Middle East* 78(3): 142–152.

Council of Europe. Convention for the Protection of the Archaeological Heritage of Europe (revised) (Valletta, 1992). Viewed 30 August 2022. https://www.coe.int/en/web/culture-and-heritage/valletta-convention

The Antiquities Coalition. Antiquities Coalition Releases 'Culture Under Threat' Mapping Resource. Viewed 30 August 2022. https://www.prnewswire.com/news-releases/antiquities-coalition-releases-culture-under-threat-mapping-resource-300251043.html

The European Landscape Convention (Florence, 2000). Viewed 30 August 2022. https://www.coe.int/en/web/landscape/the-european-landscape-convention

European Commission. Copernicus Support Office for European Commission - DG GROW (2017) Copernicus For Cultural Heritage Workshop. Viewed 30 August 2022. https://workshop.copernicus.eu/sites/default/files/content/attachments/ajax/copernicus_cultural_heritage_workshop_report.pdf

INSPIRE Directive. Viewed 30 August 2022. https://inspire.ec.europa.eu/inspire-directive/2

Hadjimitsis, D.G., K. Themistocleous, B. Cuca, A. Agapiou, V. Lysandrou, R. Lasaponara, N. Masini, and G. Schreier. 2020. *Remote Sensing for Archaeology and Cultural Landscapes Best Practices and Perspectives Across Europe and the Middle East*. Springer International. Viewed 30 August 2022. https://doi.org/10.1007/978-3-030-10979-0

Parcak, S. 2015. Archaeological Looting in Egypt: A Geospatial View (Case Studies from Saqqara, Lisht, and el Hibeh). *Near Eastern Archaeology, Special Issue: The Cultural Heritage Crisis in the Middle East* 78(3): 196–203.

Swedish Police Authority. 2019. *Swedish market for cultural objects from war and conflict zones: A risk analysis*. Published by The Swedish Police Authority. Stockholm. Viewed 30 August 2022. https://www.raa.se/app/uploads/2020/02/Swedish-market-for-cultural-objects-from-war-and-conflict-zones-A-risk-analysis.pdf

UNESCO. UNESCO and Partners Demonstrate Space Technologies for Monitoring World Heritage. Viewed 30 August 2022. https://whc.unesco.org/en/news/293

Chapter Three

Online platforms and auctions: online trafficking of cultural properties

The internet and its technologies are used in parallel to sell antiquities. These tools have different levels of secrecy regarding the identity of users and can be used to arrange various stages of antiquities trafficking within the supply chain. The use of the internet typically starts early in the trafficking process, soon after looting. Sometimes, it even starts during or before the looting process, while the item is still *in situ*. Then, it continues throughout the trafficking process, as the goods pass through intermediaries, brokers and smugglers to dealers and collectors in the destination market.

The international organizations, such as UNESCO, INTERPOL[1] and ICOM, have raised awareness about the seriousness of the online trade for countries of origin and destination countries as well.[2] Various researchers have addressed the issue of online trafficking and selling of cultural properties as well. Nevertheless, there is limited evidence to support the estimations of the size of the online market. This chapter discusses the Internet platforms that are used to coordinate illicit trafficking of cultural properties. Likewise, it sheds light on the use of the Dark and Deep Web for antiquities sales, as well as the use of other open online markets and messaging platforms such as eBay, Facebook, Telegram, WhatsApp, Viber, etc.

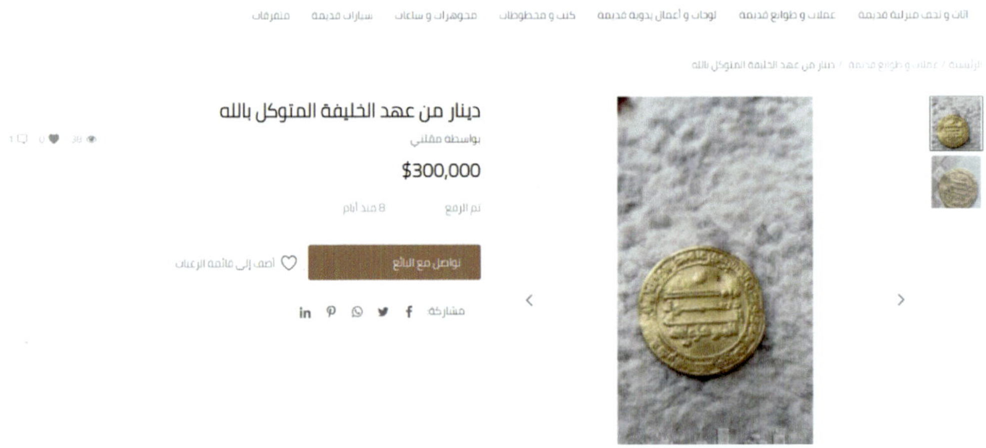

Figure 1. Omayyad golden coin on Alathar sale

1 https://www.interpol.int/News-and-Events/News/2020/101-arrested-and-19-000-stolen-artefacts-recovered-in-international-crackdown-on-art-trafficking

2 E.g. Basic Actions concerning Cultural Objects being offered for Sale over the Internet. https://en.unesco.org/sites/default/files/basic-actions-cultural-objects-for-sale_en.pdf

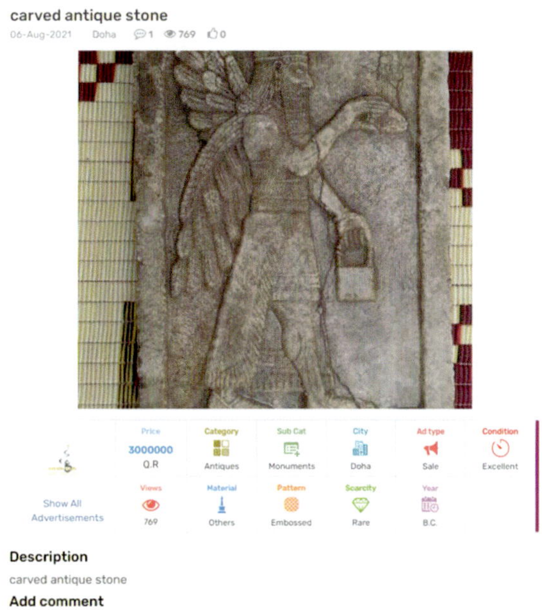

Figure 2. An artifact from Iraq posted on Mzad Qatar on August 6, 2021[3]

Figure 3. An artifact from Yemen posted on Mzad Qatar on August 6, 2021[4]

3 https://en.mzadqatar.com/products/14181927
4 https://en.mzadqatar.com/products/14558063

عمولة الموقع بعد بيع المقتنيات

هى عمولة لإستمرار خدماتنا التسويقية لمقتنياتكم الاثرية ونشرها لمحبى المقتنيات الأثرية

العمولة يدفعها المعلن وهى أمانة فى ذمته بعد البيع اذا كنت لست راضى عن هذه العمولة يرجى عدم نشر الاعلان لدينا.

موضح قيمة العمولة كالتالى:

العملة	من سعر	الى سعر	نسبة العمولة	طريقة حساب العمولة
دولار امريكى	1	100	مجانى	عند بيع اى مقطعه اثريه من 100 دولار و أقل سوف يكون ذلك مجانى بدون اى عمولة للموقع
دولار امريكى	اعلى من 100	1000	%1	طريقة حساب العمولة : مبلغ البيع * 0.1 = الناتج عمولة الموقع
دولار امريكى	اعلى من 1000	100.000	%075	طريقة حساب العمولة : مبلغ البيع * 0.075 = الناتج عمولة الموقع
دولار امريكى	اعلى من 100.000	1000.000	%050	طريقة حساب العمولة : مبلغ البيع * 0.050 = الناتج عمولة الموقع
دولار امريكى	اعلى من 1000.000	∞	%040	طريقة حساب العمولة : مبلغ البيع * 0.040 = الناتج عمولة الموقع

Figure 4. Commission on advertising on the site of Athar Sale in Saudi Arabia

Online markets exist in numerous Arab States, for example the website of Athar Sale (antiquities sale in Arabic) based in Saudi Arabia, it offers for sale ancient items such as the recently posted Islamic coins from Omayyad period (Figure 1).[5] Another site base in Qatar, named Mzad Qatar (Auction Qatar) offered for sale more objects. For instance, one sculpture was typical of 9th century BC Nimrud (figure 2). Another carving was from approximately the same time period in Yemen (figure 3). At the same time, it is important to bear in mind that forgeries and fakes have flooded online marketplaces.

It is worth mentioning that some sites take a commission from the advertiser when an item is sold (Figure 4).[6] For instance, through Athar Sale,

- on an item that is sold for 100 USD or less, there is no commission;
- for between 100 USD and 1,000 USD, the commission is 1%;
- for between 1,000 and 100,000 the commission is 0.75%;
- for between 100,000 and 1,000,000 the commission is 0.50%; and
- for more than 1,000,000, the commission is 0.40%.

Several Arab States have online marketplaces that sell antiquities, including Algeria, Jordan, Kuwait, Morocco, Oman, Tunisia and the United Arab Emirates. Again, fakes and forgeries are flooding those markets.

5 https://tinyurl.com/2zn5nwrt

6 https://tinyurl.com/y5ndxj59

Deep and Dark Web and antiquities sales

Firstly, it is necessary to explain the differences in the terms that are used, to understand the rumors surrounding the use of the Dark and Deep Web in illegal activities, including in this study's focus point, the sale of antiquities.

Janssen (2021)[7] explains that the surface web, the deep web and the dark web are parts of the internet. Therein,

- The internet is a worldwide network.
- The web is a communication tool that uses the internet network.
- The web consists of the surface web, deep web, and dark web.

The surface web, along with the deep web, is the internet we use every day, we access it through regular browsers such as Chrome, Safari and so on.

The surface web is the part of the web that can be reached easily through a search engine such as Google.

To gain access to deeper layers, we need a username and password. This is the deep level of the internet.

The deep web is the biggest part of the internet, estimated to make up between 90 and 95% of the entire worldwide web. It consists of pages and databases that are only meant for a certain group of people within an organization. Google does not display pages on the deep web. Examples of pages on the deep web are the private data of companies, universities, libraries, hospitals, governments, international organizations, etc.

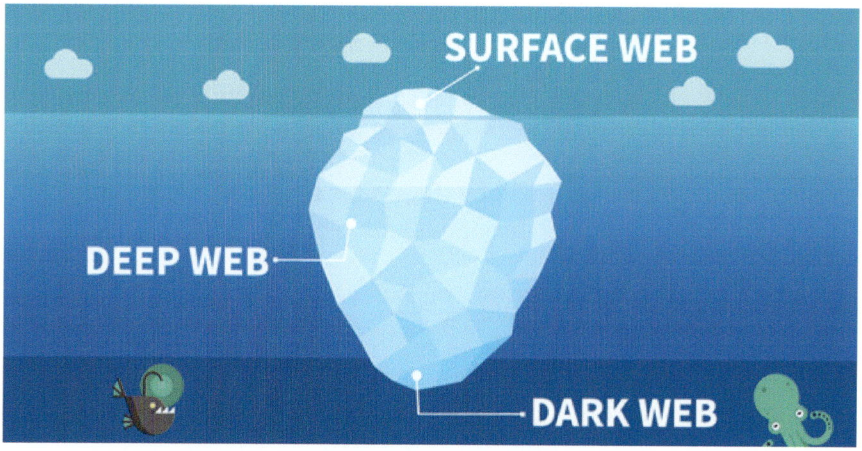

Figure 5. The three parts of the Internet (from Janssen 2021)

[7] Janssen 2021

The dark web is part of the deep web, yet it is even harder to reach. The dark nets that form the dark web are only accessible through browsers such as TOR (The Onion Router). It is impossible to reach the dark web through an everyday web browser such as Chrome (Figure 5).

The dark web is the most unregulated part of the internet. No organization, business or government oversees it. This is exactly the reason why the dark web is commonly associated with illegal activities and is a home to many black marketplaces.

The Silk Road was one of the first well-known black markets on the dark web. Now there are many different ones competing to be the next. In Russia, for instance, the dominant marketplaces are Hydra and, more recently, RAMP (Russian Anonymous Marketplace). As for payment methods, almost everything is paid for in cryptocurrencies, like Bitcoin. These cryptocurrencies are online currencies in worldwide use. So, there is criminal activity on the dark web.

However, what criminal activity in the antiquities market is conducted through the Deep and Dark Web? According to Sargent *et al.* (2020): '*Unlike other illicit goods, such as drugs and weapons, antiquities attract relatively little regulatory scrutiny or enforcement attention, so there is often little need for traffickers to hide their activities*'. Traffickers prefer legal online markets to dark web and hidden online markets. The report by the RAND Cooperation, demonstrated through sophisticated searches by Sixgill, an Israeli company that specializes in Dark Web analytics, that there was evidence that the Deep and Dark Web marketplaces were used to traffic weapons and illegal drugs, yet there was little evidence that these marketplaces were used to traffic antiquities.[8] The report proposed various explanations:

- The Dark Web limits the size of audience that sellers can reach by requiring that they access a site with specific browsing software and a specific connection protocol.
- Many Dark Web sites are not indexed and searchable, so potential buyers cannot easily find the goods that they are looking for unless they know where to look.
- The anonymity that is afforded by these sites limits the establishment of trust between buyers and sellers through identity-based reputations.[9]

Online marketplaces: eBay, Telegram and Facebook

eBay

Some states have chosen to combat illegal online antiquities markets of antiquities through agreements with brokerage websites such as eBay. In October 2006, the

[8] Sargent *et al* 2020: 44
[9] Ibid: 44–47

United Kingdom signed an agreement concerning trade in archaeological goods from the UK. A team formed by the Portable Antiquities Scheme (which is funded by the Museums, Libraries and Archives Council and run by the British Museum) monitors the sales of antiquities.[10] For this reason, eBay launched an Antiquities Buying Guide.[11]

Completed antiquities sales on eBay indicated that very few transactions were made in the Arab States. Logically, in-person transactions are the most common within the region.[12]

Telegram

Based on the assumption that Telegram is widely used to sell antiquities, the RAND Cooperation compared the Sixgill database with Telegram posts. The research revealed that both the value of antiquities and the frequency of postings for sale were low. In contrast to the 20,000 postings for weapons, there were only 4 for ancient coins. Consequently, Telegram was judged not to be a significant online platform for antiquities trafficking.[13]

Facebook

Facebook is an easily-accessible and popular digital platform to communicate, to exchange ideas and information and to buy and sell various products, including antiquities. Facebook's users can post antiquities; join groups that specialize in selling antiquities; share images and videos of posted items; send and receive messages; and ask for information, ask for evaluations, auction artifacts and arrange payment methods. As a result, this platform has also hosted criminal groups that are dedicated to illicit trafficking, including illicit trafficking of antiquities.

Through research on Facebook, the Antiquities Trafficking and Heritage Anthropology Research (ATHAR) Project investigates online trafficking and its connections to terrorism financing and organized crime, with a particular focus on the illicit trafficking of Syrian antiquities during the ongoing conflict.[14]

As for completed online purchases, investigations revealed that, in contrast to eBay users, who make remote payments, Facebook users conduct transactions directly in person, after regional contacts have been established. Still, the value is low in comparison to that of the overall international market.[15] And, in June 2020, Facebook banned the trading of antiquities.[16]

[10] CNRS: 115. https://op.europa.eu/en/publication-detail/-/publication/ca56cfac-ad6b-45ab-b940-e1a7fa4458db
[11] https://pages.ebay.co.uk/buy/guides/antiquities/
[12] Sargent *et al* 2020: 44–47
[13] Ibid: 49–51
[14] https://atharproject.org/
[15] Sargent *et.al* 2020: 49–51
[16] https://www.bbc.com/news/world-middle-east-53140615

To sum up, online platforms for selling antiquities, social media and technological development have brought together a wide range of collectors, in contrast to the typical physical galleries. The Internet has facilitated such business, particularly in low-value objects, which do not need expensive locations for storage and protection or special conditions to ensure their preservation.[17] As such, there is a need to control electronic platforms and social media to ensure they are not facilitating illicit trade in antiquities, and vendors linked to terrorism are not involved in stealing and destroying the past. This is a shared responsibility that requires the efforts of everyone involved to combat illicit trafficking.[18]

There are overestimations about the size and value of sales of antiquities from Arab States through the internet, but dealers do use (primarily) the Surface Web and the Deep Web, plus (rarely) the Dark Web, to conduct their business. Still, the range of avenues for selling antiquities online is one of the negative factors that affect cultural properties in the Arab States and around the world.

The next chapter examines 'risk markets' within a region of Europe, in order to have a general view of the online market.

References

Athar Project. Viewed 30 August 2022. https://atharproject.org/

Athar Sale. Coins online. Commissions online Market. Viewed 30 August 2022. https://tinyurl.com/2zn5nwrt https://tinyurl.com/y5ndxj59

Brodie, N. 2015. The Internet Market in Antiquities, in F. Desmarais (ed.) *Countering Illicit Traffic in Cultural Goods: The Global Challenge of Protecting the World's Heritage*. Paris: ICOM. Viewed 30 August 2022. https://traffickingculture.org/app/uploads/2016/01/2015-Brodie-ICOM-Internet.pdf

eBay. Antiquities Buying Guide. Viewed 30 August 2022. https://pages.ebay.co.uk/buy/guides/antiquities/

European Commission. 2011. *Study on preventing and fighting illicit trafficking in cultural good*: 18 Brussels. CECOJI-CNRS (2011) Study on preventing and fighting illicit trafficking in cultural goods in the European Union. Viewed 30 August 2022. https://op.europa.eu/en/publication-detail/-/publication/ca56cfac-ad6b-45ab-b940-e1a7fa4458db

INTERPOL. 6 May 2020. 101 arrested and 19,000 stolen artefacts recovered in international crackdown on art trafficking. Viewed 30 August 2022. https://www.interpol.int/News-and-Events/News/2020/101-arrested-and-19-000-stolen-artefacts-recovered-in-international-crackdown-on-art-trafficking

Janssen, D. 2021. The Dark Web: What is it Exactly and What can you Find There? VPNoverview. Viewed 30 August 2022. https://vpnoverview.com/privacy/anonymous-browsing/the-dark-web/

[17] Brodie 2015

[18] Mackenzie 2002

Mackenzie, S. 2002. Organised Crime and Common Transit Networks. *Trends and Issues in Crime and Criminal Justice* 233 (July 2002). Australian Institute of Criminology

Mazad Qatar. Viewed 30 August 2022. https://mzadqatar.com/products/14181927 https://en.mzadqatar.com/products/14558063

Sargent, M., M. James, A. Evans, L. Bilyana, E. Nemeth and S. Dalzell. 2020. *Tracking and Disrupting the Illicit Antiquities Trade with Open Source Data*. RAND Corporation: Santa Monica CA.

Swan, S. BBC News. 23 June 2020. Facebook bans 'loot-to-order' antiquities trade. Viewed 30 August 2022. https://www.bbc.com/news/world-middle-east-53140615

UNESCO. Basic Actions concerning Cultural Objects being offered for Sale over the Internet. Viewed 30 August 2022. https://en.unesco.org/sites/default/files/basic-actions-cultural-objects-for-sale_en.pdf

Chapter Four

Risk markets and the 'end destination' concept

This chapter was prepared by Frida Larsdotter Lundgren, based on her research in 2016-2018.

Introduction

Frida Larsdotter Lundgren is a jurist and art historian, who has worked for the Art Crime Unit at the Swedish Police's National Operations Unit as well as worked as an art crime researcher at the Swedish National Council for Crime Prevention and as a legal consultant for Sweden's National Museums of World Cultures. She has given many lectures on, and taught the subject of, cultural property law at several Swedish universities. Between 2016 and 2018, she was the primary researcher for a project on '*The Swedish market for cultural objects from war and conflict zones: A risk analysis*', where a variation of the methodology that is discussed in this chapter was first applied.

Methodology: quantified risk analysis for looted objects on art markets

The phrase '*follow the money*' applies, of course, to art crime. If one, in search of illicit or suspicious artefacts, chooses to focus on the seller – the market actor – rather than the buyer (as the latter's identity is often protected by multiple clauses in auction houses' non-disclosure and privacy contracts), there are a variety of methods to pursue. On the surface, the most straightforward method is in-person visits to antique sellers (auction houses and boutiques), with more or less conspicuous inquiries about a particular object's provenance.[1] Whether the visitor is looking for archaeologically looted, illicitly trafficked or stolen objects or not, this method typically plays out in more or less the same way: the reliability and/or knowledge of the seller is questionable, at best; the time frame stretches inquiries about only a dozen objects into hours and the resulting data is still virtually impossible to verify. If the question is put differently, however – not '*Are there looted objects on this (nation's, city's, individual) market?*' but '*Are there items typically at risk of being looted on the market – and, in that case, which types of objects, from what cultural origin, on which types of markets or vendors, at what prices – and have these risk objects increased over time?*' one is able to get hard, and *very* usable, data. It should be noted that the question of 'items typically at risk of being looted' is not a problematic

[1] In a brief article, "The Scholar and the Market" (Swedish Archaeologists on Ethics, ed. Håkan Karlsson, 2004), Dr. Staffan Lundén actually made an attempt at tracing the provenance of a few selected Chinese objects on sale in Swedish antique stores through in-store interviews. Although the article is most informative and in-depth on the problem of looting and trafficking, it contains little to no hard data. While some may argue that the validity of a provenance can be determined by what is listed in an auction catalogue, this is highly doubtful. As can be seen, a seller may dispute a previously given oral provenance but be held legally accountable by what is written in a catalogue, in an advertisement or on a website.

one. The International Council of Museums ICOM has compiled extensive lists of such objects in their 'Red Lists'.[2] Thus, the main tool for this methodology is the construction of three '*reference catalogues*': these are created for (1) the chosen geographical area of origin for the risk objects and its cultural history past the modern name of the country or countries; (2) types of objects called 'risk objects', which are at particular risk of being looted, and (3) the chosen geographical area for the 'end destination' or market study. Any type of seller of art and antiques is given a code based on such things as its location, whether it is a generalist or a specialist and whether it is an auction house, a boutique or a website for the trading of works of art between individuals.

Every detail of data is quantified and coded in these three reference catalogues – origin, material, object type, market type, provenance details, market type, market location, monetary value, etc. It is given a code and added to the database, where any question – such as 'What is the total market value of ancient Babylonian coins on the specialist numismatic market?' or 'Have artefacts of Iraqi origin increased or decreased in number and/or price since the invasion in 2003?' – can be answered. The typological process allows statistical data to be processed and presented more easily and patterns in risk groupings – such as the risk ratio of object types to market types – to be discovered and analysed more easily. The numbers presented in a report can vary from the number of risk objects found on the market, to their monetary value in any chosen currency, to the numerical distribution of both object types and market types. In addition to this, a five- and ten-year comparison of objects' appearance on the market is studied from past catalogues, to see if any increase – due to changes in tastes, increased illicit export or conflicts – have changed the market situation.[3] Finally, one 'control group' is selected to be examined by museum experts, to determine whether the items could be forgeries or if their geographical/cultural attributions could be wrong. Each object type can be placed in a large number of categories: country/area of origin, material, chronology, etc. An internal system for coding these objects is necessary. This is as follows:

- Country or historical culture of origin;
- Material (e.g. metal);
- Material, sub-category (e.g. silver);
- Object category (e.g. coins);
- Chronology, with a sub-category of local chronology (e.g. precisely-dated kingdom, precisely-dated culture);
- Checks performed against any stolen art database;
- Provenance (number of named previous owners);
- Data concerning the object's history in the West.

Each of these categories is provided with a heading number. For example, Syria-> metal-> precious metal-> gold -> coins is thus presented as 2.1.1.2.3. This may seem

2 https://icom.museum/en/resources/red-lists/

3 In the case of potential conflict antiquities on the market in Sweden, the situation had changed. See pages 32–33 in "The Swedish market for cultural objects from war and conflict zones: A risk analysis" (2019).

cumbersome; but, since the number of object types, including sub-categories, is very large, it would otherwise be difficult to match the collected data against the market and present it in a form that is easy to grasp. These two code schemes, for the type of object and for the market, are then added to the codified register for each object, thus building a database of an entire market.

The 2018 Swedish study

A study based on this methodology was performed on the risk object category of *conflict antiquities*[4] on the entire Swedish art and antiquities market in 2017.[5] Five countries of origin where 'conflict antiquities trafficking' could be verified were chosen and archaeological items from these cultures[6] were meticulously traced in stores, in generalist and specialist auction houses and on online peer-to-peer auction and sales sites. Then, a market alert was set up with 41 key phrases relating to the cultures, countries and archaeology, as well as 13 categories (such as 'Archaeological'). It sent an e-mail every time an object matching a key word or category was listed for sale (in this case, about 50-75 times a day; about 5-10 of those involved risk objects). When the object was seen and classed as a risk object, it was entered into the database.[7]

During a **six-month** period, **1,642** objects classified as 'risk objects' were found and registered on the Swedish market. In total, the objects had an estimated value (based on sale price, or starting bid price if found at an auction), of **€116,000 ($136,450)**. This establishes Sweden, internationally, as a comparatively *low-risk market* for looted Middle Eastern Antiquities. However, according to a ten- and twenty-year analysis of objects' appearance on the market, there had been a steep rise in the appearance of the selected risk object category when compared to the years 2007 and 1997, respectively.[8] In the research for this report, the study covered the international market for archaeological artefacts of Arabic, North African and Middle Eastern origin.

---

[4] The term, coined by Dr. Sam Hardy of Det Norske Institutt i Roma, is applied to archaeological items looted in, and trafficked from, areas of war and/or conflict for the purpose of financing the conflict further, either via terrorist/ insurrection groups or governments.

[5] Published internationally under the title" The Swedish market for cultural objects from war and conflict zones: A risk analysis" (2019).

[6] Cultures that, of course, predate the countries themselves – such as Babylonian instead of Iraqi, and so forth.

[7] Following a presentation for various UN organs, at the request of UNESCO, the Security Council and other countries' police units, the study was also published internationally. https://www.raa.se/app/uploads/2020/02/Swedish-market-for-cultural-objects-from-war-and-conflict-zones-A-risk-analysis.pdf

[8] Ibid: 33

The 2021 preliminary probe

The Western art market is teeming with archaeologically looted objects – often openly for sale, in printed or online auction catalogues, or in shop windows. And the present chapter's author has explored high-risk markets of all kinds – higher- and lower-quality stores, (more and less) prestigious auction houses, peer-to-peer online sales (at more or less legitimate web sites): their risk calculations; their import/export practices; their commission fees; their legal documents (such as client confidentiality contracts) and their inner operations and workings. Thus, it is safe to say that, for a long criminal chain, which starts with either subsistence digging or organised looting and which is trafficked in several stages, it is of utmost importance to study the market as the looted object's *end destination* – where it ends up for a seemingly legitimate sale, often half a world away from its rightful home. With knowledge of where the artefact came from, and where it ended up, trafficking routes are more easily determined and points of inspection for customs can be adjusted. And it is necessary to study all of the larger European (both EU and non-EU) countries including those in Scandinavia and the wider Nordic region, plus the United States, Canada, Australia, New Zealand and preferably also Russia, in order to establish a comprehensive overview of the entire Western market with regards to risk objects of Arab and North African origin. In all of these countries, the full range of market types (generalist and specialist auction houses, generalist and specialist antique stores, plus peer-to-peer online auction and sales sites) should be considered.

This study sought to conduct a preliminary probe, expanding the term 'risk object' to encompass any archaeological artefact from the Arab States on the Western art market. As a very modest introductory comparison with the market for Middle Eastern antiquities in Sweden, as assessed in the 2018 Swedish Police's study, *one single European open-market, generalist antiques printed catalogue* for the autumn of 2021 held **292** Middle Eastern, Arab, Egyptian or North African archaeological artefacts and coins for the total estimate starting price (as the bidding for the auction had yet to begin) of **211,676** GBP (**293,701** USD).[9] Graphics quickly and clearly show the findings of this 'mini risk market study'.

2021 probe data

The preliminary probe assessed a European generalist auction house, which has been anonymised. Likewise, in the 2018 study, all market actors were anonymised and only identified by their respective market type and region. This was done to avoid any conflict or legal controversy by pointing the finger at one particular actor, as the purpose was to assess and quantify a risk. The Swedish Police could not, and should

[9] 'The Swedish market for cultural objects from war and conflict zones: A risk analysis' (2019). In the aforementioned six-month study of 2018, a comparative European study found, under the same time period, 705 risk objects were found in the catalogues of one single country's auction houses, with an estimated value of 53.4 million Euros (circa 74.5 million USD).

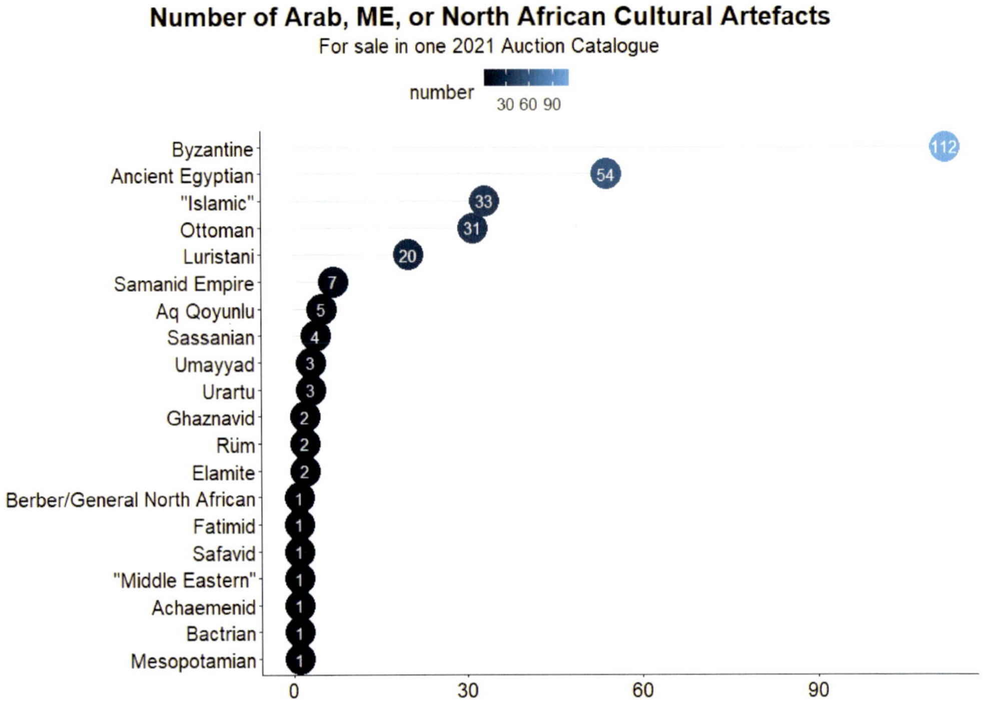

Figure 6. Number of Arab, ME or North African Cultural Artefacts in one 2021 Auction Catalogue

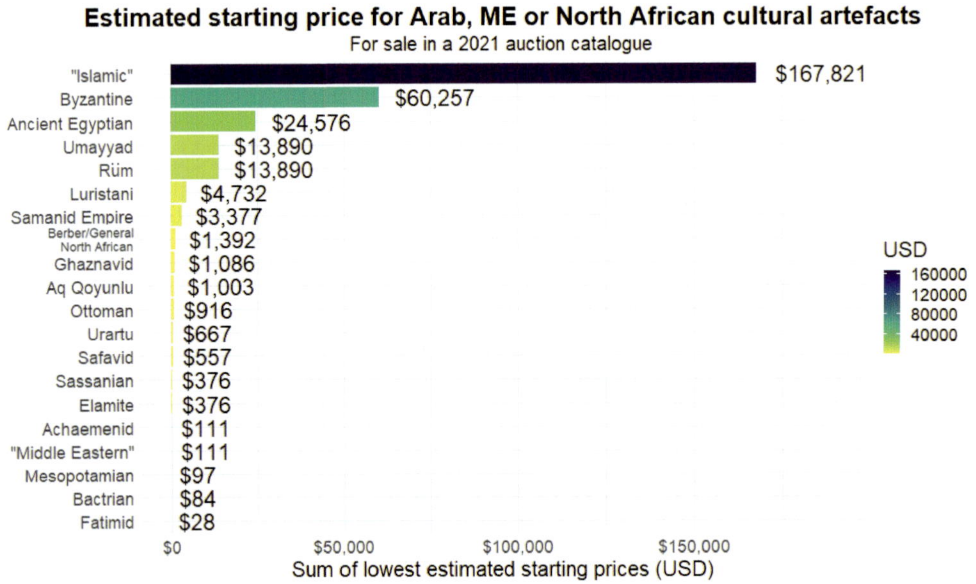

Figure 7. Estimate Starting Price for Arab, ME or North African Cultural Artefacts in one 2021 Auction Catalogue

not, name individual companies in a context such as terrorist financing without very solid evidence.

A few quantitative approaches from the 2018 study could not be performed in this probe. It only looked at *one* auction house and, therefore, could not generate any data with which to infer which market types could be considered 'risk markets'. Nor could it compare and contrast markets *geographically* – this European nation's auction house could not be used to infer the state of the entire Western art market. Nor could it infer developments in markets *historically*, as it did not have access to an auction catalogue from the same auction house for comparison. However, the 2021 probe expanded the fields of data in other aspects: provenance, checks against a stolen arts database and recorded time in Europe.

Cultural and geographical origin of the risk objects found

Figure 6 displays the *numbers* of objects found, and attributed to, ancient Middle Eastern, Arab or North African civilizations in the studied European catalogue.

Figure 7 represents the *sum of the lowest auction house estimate prices* for all risk objects that were found in the catalogue. The final prices, with the auction house's additional commission, would have varied from those. The sheer number of items in the catalogue is not necessarily the primary risk factor when assessing the risk of cultural heritage being damaged or destroyed – it is the individual items' importance to their respective nation's heritage that matters in when it comes to assessing damage in a context of heritage destruction. Unfortunately, there is only one way that this can be quantified without knowing anything about provenance or background (which have been very sparse throughout the catalogue): price. The average price was **1,006 USD**, but the individual price estimates started as low as **28 USD** and ended at the extreme of **69,375 USD**.

Provenance

Then, the details of the object's background were explored. A named provenance should reasonably be more reliable than an anonymous one (as someone who is open about their identity can be expected to be held accountable for the legitimacy of their ownership). Named owners encompassed private collectors, families, museums and art galleries. As the overwhelming majority of objects for sale in this probe had no named provenance, it must be seen an increased risk factor.

Due diligence

Then, the probe considered the observance of due diligence – the effort of the auction house to ensure the legitimacy of the objects for sale. There are several competing 'stolen art registers' in the West – the largest of these is simply called

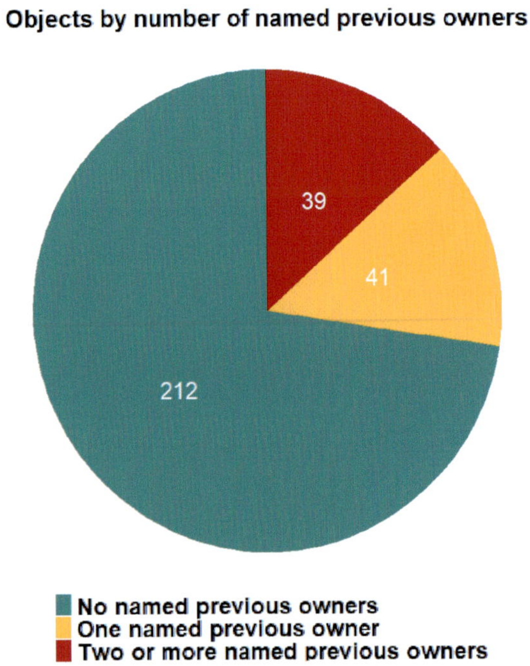

Figure 8. Objects by Number of Named Previous Owners

'the Art Loss Register' (the ALR) and is owned and run as a non-profit organization by IFAR.[10] It is considered part of an art dealer's 'due diligence' - ethically, if not legally - to check any acquisitions against the ALR or another stolen art database. However, at the time of writing, the ALR charged **95 USD** for a single check against their register[11] and with lower-value items it would not always be profitable – or even economically sustainable – to perform these checks. Antiquities also require a higher standard with regards to the information that the art dealer must supply to the ALR, due to the fact that they are considered to be at '*higher risk*' of having been stolen.[12] Only **16** of the **292** objects in the probe were stated to have been checked against the ALR. The minimum lowest estimate price of a checked object was **1,660 USD.** There were, however, antiquities with equal or higher estimate prices that were not stated to have been checked against the ALR. The highest of these prices was **2,495 USD.**

Price, however, isn't everything in this context. Some *cultural origins* must be considered to indicate a higher risk than others: for instance, origins in a country that is currently in a state of war or in a territory where there is material evidence – such as satellite imagery – of large-scale archaeological looting.

For instance, archaeological looting in Egypt is an established and known fact – the subject is discussed to some extent even in the general media. Yet, although the country had the highest representation of ALR checks, that constituted only **10** out of **54** Egyptian objects.

[10] The International Foundation for Art Research. https://www.ifar.org/

[11] https://www.artloss.com/search/. Larger dealers can opt to subscribe to the ALR's services for the fee of 1,800 USD for up to 50 checks per year.

[12] Ibid

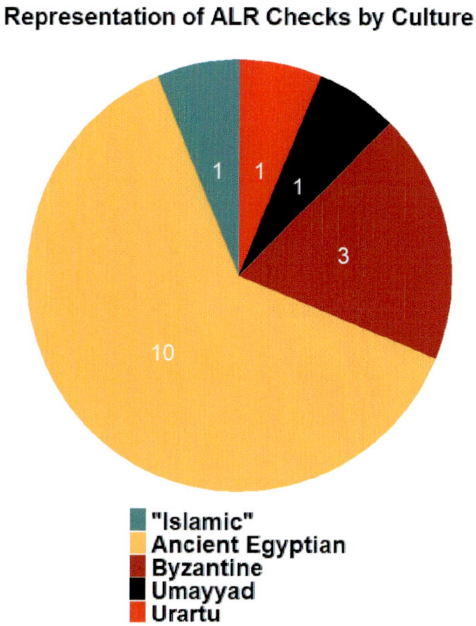

Figure 9. Representation of ALR Checks on Objects by Culture

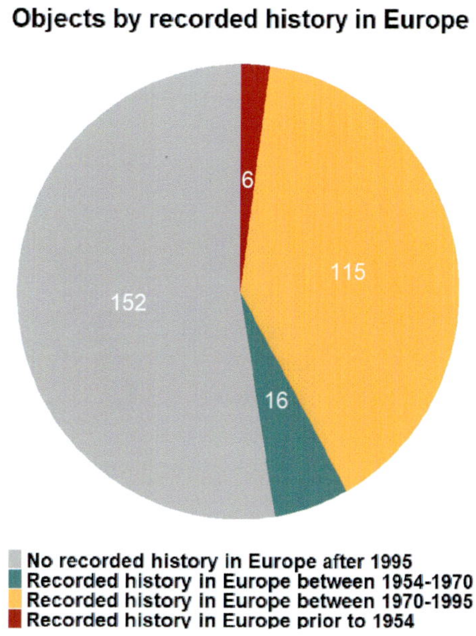

Figure 10. Objects by Recorded History in Europe

Recorded history in the West

Then, the probe explored the question of recent versus long-past looting. It is, of course, contemporary looting that seems most urgent; but the products of historical looting may still be illicit. Any assessment must consider all treaties and conventions that regulate and outright criminalize the theft of art in order to determine whether an object was removed from a country – or imported into another – illicitly or whether a demand for the return of an object is even legally possible.[13] Three highly-relevant conventions regulate the international theft of art: the 1954 Convention for the Protection of Cultural Property in the Event of Armed Conflict, the 1970 UNESCO Convention on the Means of Prohibiting and Preventing the Illicit Import, Export and Transfer of Ownership of Cultural Property and the 1995 UNIDROIT Convention on Stolen or Illegally Exported Cultural Objects. Different states chose to sign – or abstain from signing – these conventions at different points in time, of course, but the years of their establishment were used as reference points. The auction house, as stated, is European, so it made sense to see what was stated in the provenance records about how long the object had been in Europe.

[13] Neither the 1970 UNESCO Convention, the 1995 UNIDROIT Convention nor the 1954 Hague Convention can be retroactively applied.

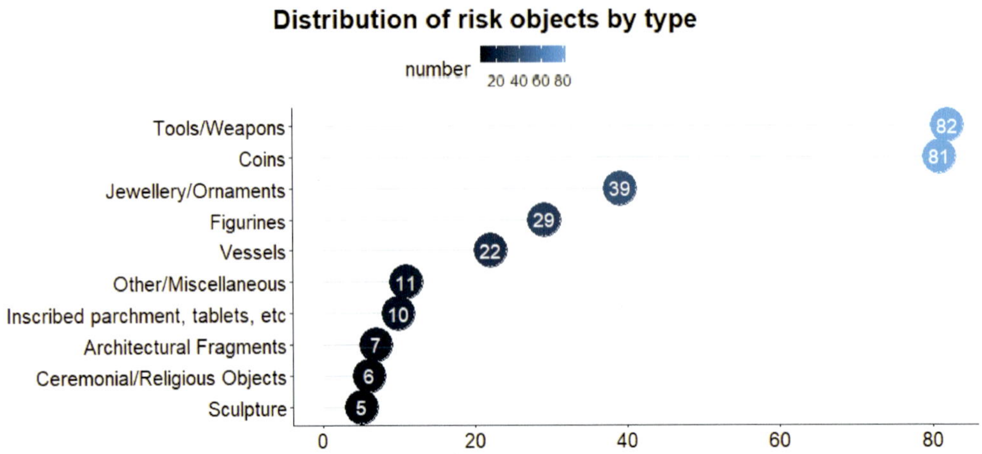

Figure 11. Distribution of Risk Objects by Type

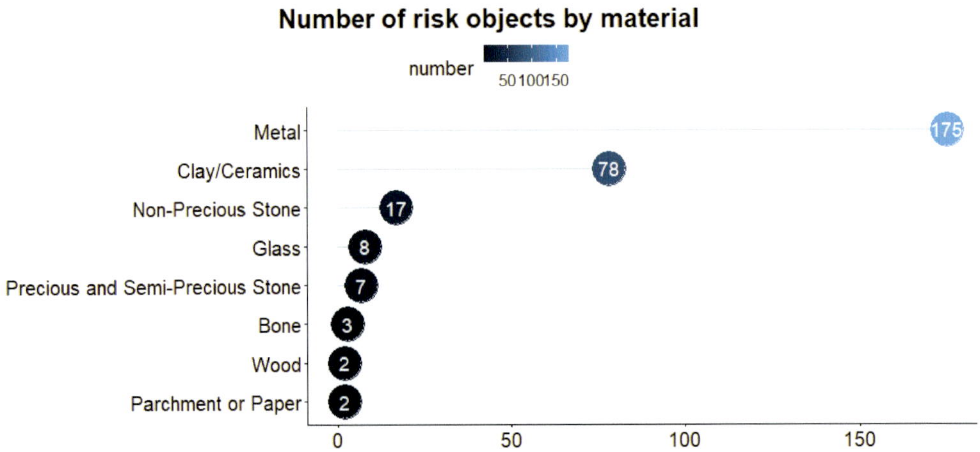

Figure 12. Number of Risk Objects by Material

Distribution of object types and materials

Determining the quantity of *different types* of risk objects is an important tool for customs offices of both source and destination countries. It should also be added that, with regard to the analysis of the data, coins have the advantage that they can be traced very accurately to a time period and geographical area of origin.

The distribution of the types of risk objects on the market and their cultural origins have been priorities since the 2018 study. A seemingly inconsequential detail, such as an over-representation of metals (especially precious metals) as a material in the

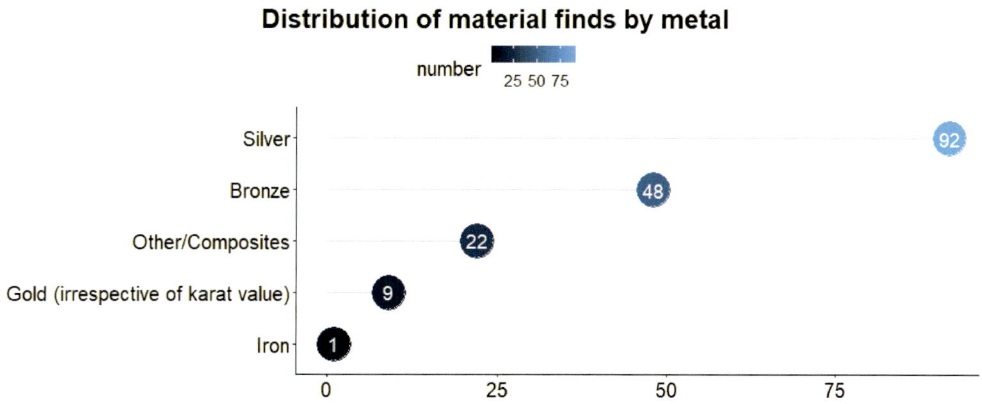

Figure 13. Distribution of Material Finds by Metal

identified risk objects, could be an indicator of the use of metal detectors (with an increasing ability to distinguish silver and gold from base metals) in their extraction and therefore a heightened risk that the objects had been looted relatively recently.[14]

Analysis: applications and practical uses for the methodology's data

To reiterate, this chapter's data is from a *very* small probe into the Western art market. Nonetheless, such hard data can be useful to the authorities, customs agencies, police services and international agencies such as INTERPOL, market actors and the public. Although the Swedish 'risk object' market was comparatively small, we found an extremely prominent market type and object type: peer-to-peer online sales and numismatics (antique coins), respectively. This may not reflect the market situation in other countries, but it still offers potential intelligence on how to target, prevent and combat the trafficking and sale of risk objects. Swedish customs laws have since been changed to require import licenses for a range of archaeological objects.[15]

The prime peer-to-peer online vendor site was invited to a conference and given a presentation of the data at hand. They stated that they understood how problematic the issue was – not only for themselves but also for the conflict zones that covered the source territories of the marketed objects – and that they would immediately review their policy on the marketing of archaeological goods. However, this was not and could not be the only course of action. The study's data was swiftly provided to the government, to market actors, to authorities (like customs agencies, national police and INTERPOL) and to museums. Targeted information campaigns for risk markets and collectors of risk objects are a necessity, although they have to be approached

[14] In addition to this, the rankings of most to least common of metals found in archaeological excavations is well-established. The most common is iron, followed by copper, lead, tin and then alloys of these (Lugan 2002).
[15] EU (2019/880 av den 17 april 2019).

with different methods – and with caution. In addition to this, it is necessary for such a study to keep figures on the number of sellers who actually list and describe an object's provenance, rather than just its origin.

Using the data for research – and for claims of repatriation

If a database for risk assessment of the Western market is created, it should be open-source. Verified researchers could be granted access to the database (and the reference catalogues with which it would be coded, with which the database's entries would be understood easily). An image of any object of interest could be sent on receipt of the item's code registration number. That would open up a great deal of possibilities: the image of the object could be analysed, compared to reference works and books, data-mined and tracked back geographically and historically. If an item was found that could be traced back to a site that had been looted, or to a theft, this study's authors could provide practical legal guidance for its return. Aside from a full, preventative risk analysis of the Western art market, this study's authors recommend the creation of a full step-by-step handbook[16] for the practical and legal means and methods of the return and repatriation of possibly illegally exported artefacts. It should reflect private and public, as well as national, international and transnational legislation on export and export licensing; bilateral and multilateral conventions; and international police and customs cooperation.

Using the data to work with risk markets

'Risk markets' is a term for a group of market actors that by category, selling practices or geographical location has been deemed by the study to be a risk in the sense that many archaeological items from the chosen origin are sold there, that the artefacts have little to no provenance recorded. Risk markets that repeatedly sell excavated artefacts without full and transparent provenance need a visit – or at the very least a strongly-worded letter – from a legal representative of the organization conducting the research and manages the database, which presents the various national and international import, export and trafficking laws and the financial and/or criminal penalties that lawbreakers may face. What is suggested as a starting point, however, is an offer of a collaborative approach to resolving issues. After all, all vendors are concerned with their public image and none wants to be associated with criminal activity – or, in the very worst cases, links to the financing of terrorist activities. As mentioned in *2021 Probe Data*, market/vendor anonymization was a legal necessity in the Swedish study, and this principle would likely also apply to any other Western country, so potential partners could manage their risk and their reputation by revising their practices.

[16] Lundgren 2020

Using the data to work with the public and buyers

Of course, a different approach is needed for potential buyers and other members of the public: information campaigns in close proximity to any antiques website, magazine, auction house or fair could be provided in the form of brochures or web adverts. They should not only appeal to the potential buyer's conscience, but also highlight potential legal ramifications based on national and international private law.

Using the data to work with legislators and government authorities

Government authorities could also help by putting limits on market actors, by introducing low-level regulations such as changes to practices in customs and pinpoint regulations of the necessary details in publications of provenance by sellers of archaeological objects. Naturally, the relevant authorities – and those authorities' powers – vary from state to state. Customs agencies are the first line of defence and, once high-risk categories of objects have been identified, easily-made brochures of risk objects can be supplied to improve their agents' responses. Customs agencies' technological capacity to identify risk objects is also developing at a striking rate.[17] Once targets at high risk of being looted are known, co-operation with police services and universities may lead to the establishment of an effective force on the ground.

When it comes to legislation, the Arab States need to work as a team to stem the flow of trafficked archaeological goods. Import must be as closely regulated as export, as the Arab states are neighbours – and, of course, the first transit country of a trafficked object is typically a neighbour of the source country.

Using the timeline data of increases or decreases in risk objects to understand and combat trafficking and looting

With data on changes in targeted countries, targeted cultures and consuming markets, it is also possible to trace changes in patterns of trafficking routes. This, of course, requires international cooperation; but, once routes can be identified, it may be possible to disrupt trafficking mid-chain – something that has long been exceptionally rare.

Conclusion

In brief, this preliminary probe has laid the groundwork for what we believe is a necessity in the study of the trafficking of looted objects from the Arab, Middle Eastern and North African World. The 'end destination' concept and the risk analysis method

[17] Red Arch Cultural Heritage Law and Policy Research, where dogs, already widely used in the search for narcotics and firearms in airports, are trained to also search for the distinguished scents of recently excavated archaeological goods. https://www.redarchresearch.org/K-9-Artifact-Finders.html

will provide solid data for research and prevention at every stage of the trafficking chain. Although the 2021 probe was meant merely to be a showcase of expanding the methodology, and was too small to be conclusive, its results are somewhat troubling. It is worrying that under 6% of the selected risk objects had been checked against a stolen arts database, that more than half of the objects had no recorded history in Europe prior to 1995 and that over 72% had no named provenance. It is still necessary to determine what types of different risk markets there are, how many risk objects are found on which markets and where in the West (geographically) efforts to find stolen artefacts should be focused.

Preparatory work to expand this study to cover the entire European market, the entire North American or, preferably, the entire Western market is nearly complete. It includes the production of all three reference catalogues, the design of the basic structure of the database and the design of the customized search engine. What remains is the collection and registration of market data, followed by a compilation of graphics and diagrams – and, if it is seen to be worthwhile, the compilation of an easy-to-follow, step-by-step guidebook on national, international and transnational law with the sole purpose of returning the objects to their rightful homes.

References

Art Loss Register (ALR) database. Viewed 30 August 2022. https://www.artloss.com/

EUROPAPARLAMENTETS OCH RÅDETS FÖRORDNING (EU) 2019/880 av den 17 april 2019 om införsel och import av kulturföremål. Viewed 30 August 2022. https://eur-lex.europa.eu/legal-content/SV/TXT/PDF/?uri=CELEX:32019R0880&from=PL

ICOM. Red Lists Database. Viewed 30 August 2022. https://icom.museum/en/resources/red-lists/

International Foundation for Art Research. Viewed 30 August 2022. https://www.ifar.org/

Lugan, J. 2002. Identifying Archaeological Metal. Canadian Conservation Institute (CCI) Notes 4/1. Originally published 2002, revised 2007. Minister of Public Works and Government Services Canada, 2007 Cat. Viewed 30 August 2022. https://www.canada.ca/en/conservation-institute/services/conservation-preservation-publications/canadian-conservation-institute-notes/identifying-archaeological-metal.html

Lundgren, F. 2020. Utredningsåtgärder För Museipersonal Vid Krav På Återlämnande Av Kulturföremål i Museets Ägo, (English title: '*Procedures of Investigation for Museum Staff at the Reception of a Claim of Repatriation of an Object in the Museum's Possession*') Swedish National Museum of World Cultures.

Red Arch Cultural Heritage Law and Policy Research. Viewed 30 August 2022. https://www.redarchresearch.org/K-9-Artifact-Finders.html

Swedish Police Authority. 2019. *Swedish market for cultural objects from war and conflict zones: A risk analysis.* Published by The Swedish Police Authority. Stockholm. Viewed 30 August 2022. https://www.raa.se/app/uploads/2020/02/Swedish-market-for-cultural-objects-from-war-and-conflict-zones-A-risk-analysis.pdf

Chapter Five

Mapping routes of illicit trafficking of cultural properties

Introduction

The main destination countries are the wealthy countries in Western Europe and North America plus Japan. Traffickers usually follow well-established trafficking routes, which are also used for the trafficking of humans, arms and drugs. Goods may be smuggled over land, by sea or by air or through a combination of those.

Trafficking structures and routes develop for geographical, social, historical, economic and cultural reasons. For example, 'Orthodox Christian icons are stolen from churches in Bulgaria to supply the regional market in Greece as well as the global market in Western Europe and North America'.[1] However, political developments, wars and conflicts also play vital roles in forming and structuring trafficking routes. The 1990s witnessed the outbreak of the Yugoslav wars in parallel to the civil war in Afghanistan. Social disorder and economic chaos led to the emergence of criminal gangs involved in illicit trafficking, including illicit trafficking of antiquities.[2] Likewise, after the fall of Gadafi, antiquities from Libya found their way to the illicit market through Egypt, which was in disorder after the January Revolution of 2011; and antiquities from Iraq found their way through Syria as well. In Bulgaria, under the former communist government, the Bulgarian Secret Service engaged in illicit trafficking through a front company named Kintex, which handled antiquities among other materials. Thus, Bulgaria became one of the main trafficking routes for antiquities smuggled from Arab States towards European transit countries like Switzerland and Germany and European market countries like Belgium and the United Kingdom.[3]

Research on trafficking routes in Arab States and neighboring regions highlighted that there were certain repeatedly-used routes such as Jordan, Turkey and the United Arab Emirates. These routes were confirmed through an investigation of the Spanish Historical Heritage Brigade (*Brigada de Patrimonio Historico*) in 2017. The smuggled antiquities followed two routes: overland from Libya through Egypt to Jordan, then by air to Barcelona or to the United Arab Emirates through Saudi Arabia. The second route diverged in Jordan, through the United Arab Emirates then Thailand,

[1] Hardy 2016

[2] UNODC. 2019. Opiate trafficking along the early stages of the Balkan route. https://www.unodc.org/documents/data-and-analysis/Studies/IFF_report_2015_final_web.pdf

[3] Campbell 2013: 123–125

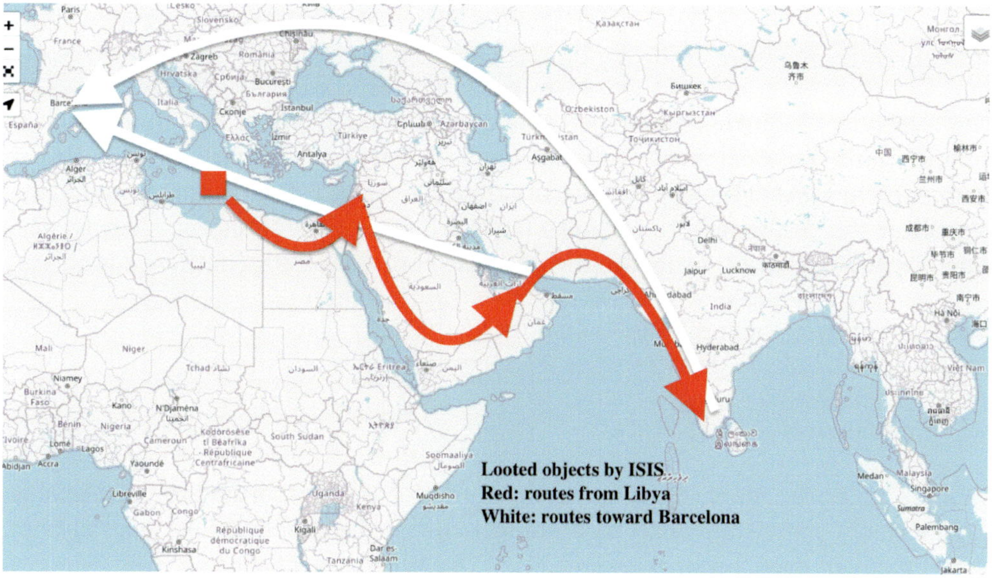

Map 2. Map of the routes taken from Libya to Spain (from ABC Spain)

to numerous European countries such as Russia, Germany, France and the United Kingdom, as shown on the map (Figure 1).[4]

Antiquities trafficking routes in Arab States

It is a monumental challenge to trace the flow of smuggled antiquities in Arab States, to identify the points of origin of these antiquities and to reconstruct all of the points and crossing points that they pass. The USA-based Antiquities Coalition offers a user-friendly database, with interactive maps on antiquities that have been seized around the globe, which may assist in this endeavour.[5]

Methodology

The data has been collected from primary and secondary sources. The primary sources are antiquities seizures by national police forces in Arab States that have been mapped by the Antiquities Coalition. However, their map includes data from only 13 of the 22 Arab States. These recorded states are Algeria, Tunisia, Libya, Egypt, Palestine (and Israel), Jordan, Lebanon, Syria, Iraq, Saudi Arabia, Kuwait, the United Arab Emirates and Yemen. Moreover, their data needs to be expanded and updated,

[4] Muñoz and Morcillo 2018.

[5] Antiquities Coalition. https://theantiquitiescoalition.org/antiquities-coalition-releases-cultural-piracy-mapping-antiquities-seizures-around-the-globe/ https://theantiquitiescoalition.org/multimedia-resources/interactive-maps/

as they list one seizure case in Algeria, while there have been more than 20, and the last case from anywhere in the region was uploaded in 2018.

The secondary sources are reports and other publications by international organizations, national organizations, media organizations and scholars. These sources fill in some of the gaps in the data from the maps. By combining primary and secondary sources, we aim to outline a holistic image of the situation. Likewise, the data may indicate exit locations and vulnerable border crossings in these countries.

Due to the large number of sources on seizures that took place in Arab States between 2000 and 2021, links to these seizures are recorded separately in Annex 3.

Mapping seizures in Arab States

Seizures have been mapped in alphabetical order of state, according to the available data. Notably, some states had high numbers of seizure cases while others did not report many or even any. It is assumed that this is because of a lack of transparency and a low level of data-sharing, which are among the most serious challenges in the region.

Collating primary sources, data seizures of cultural properties have been documented in 16 Arab States: Algeria, Egypt, Iraq, Jordan, Kuwait, Lebanon, Libya, Mauritania, Morocco, Oman, Palestine, Qatar, Saudi Arabia, Sudan, Syria, Tunisia, the United Arab Emirates and Yemen. While the rest did not report anything, compensatory data was sought in secondary sources.

1. Algeria

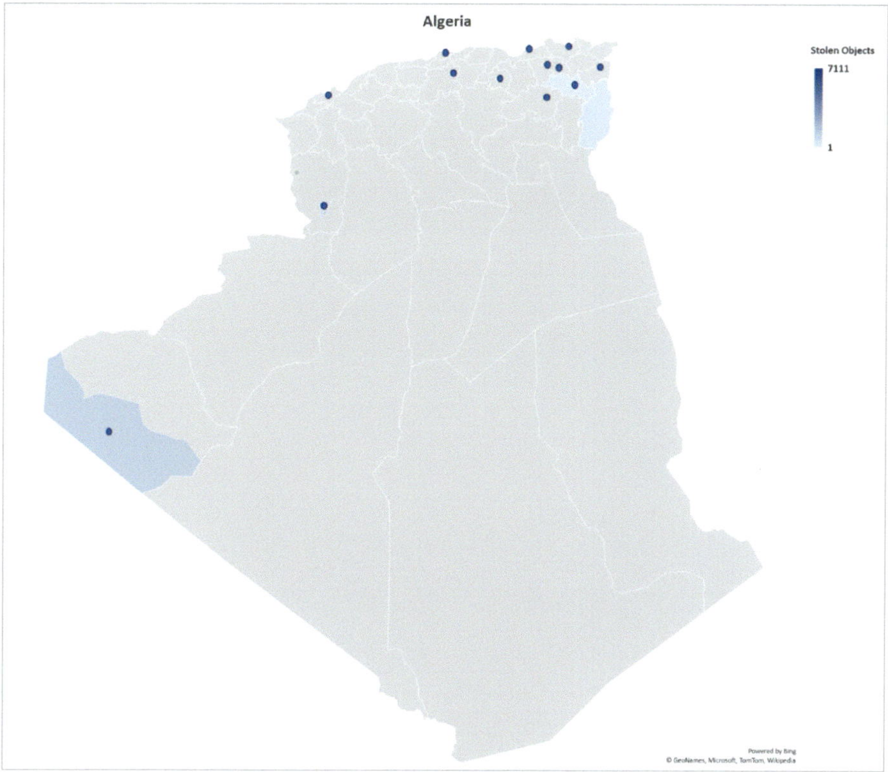

Map 3. Location of cultural properties seizures in Algeria

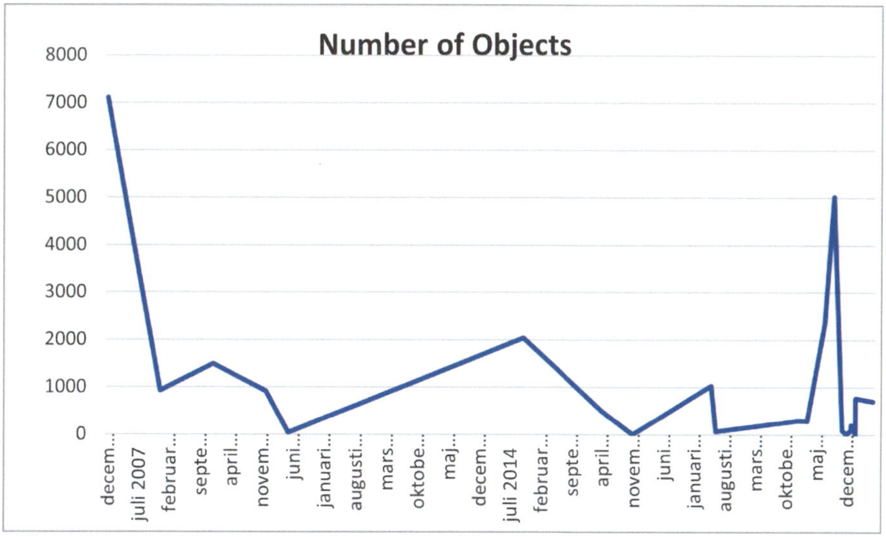

Figure 14. Date and number of seized objects in Algeria

2. Egypt

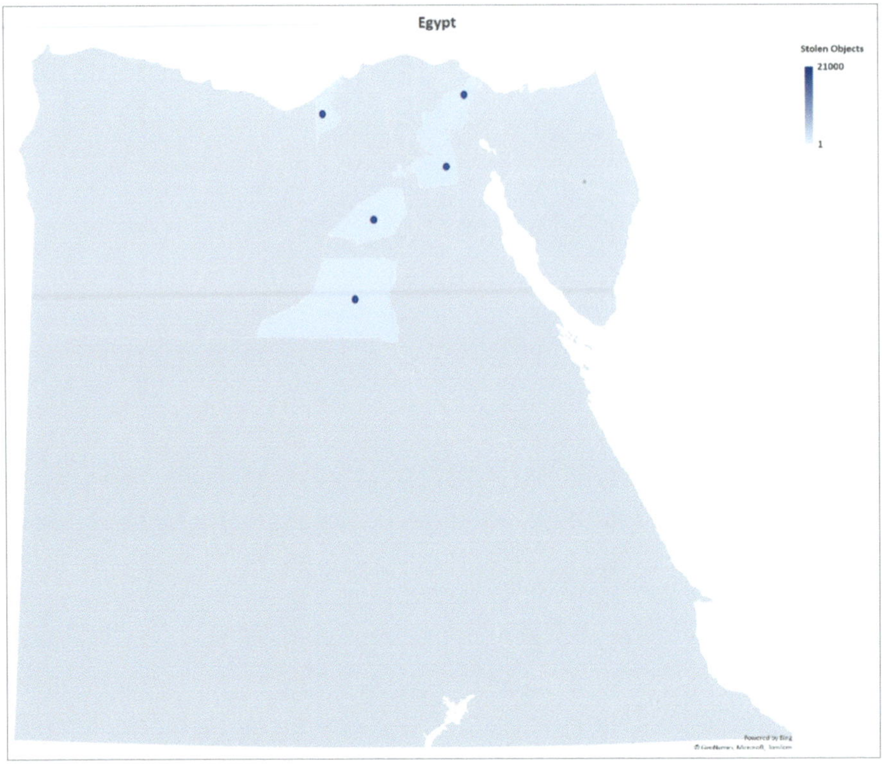

Map 4. Location of cultural properties seizures in Egypt

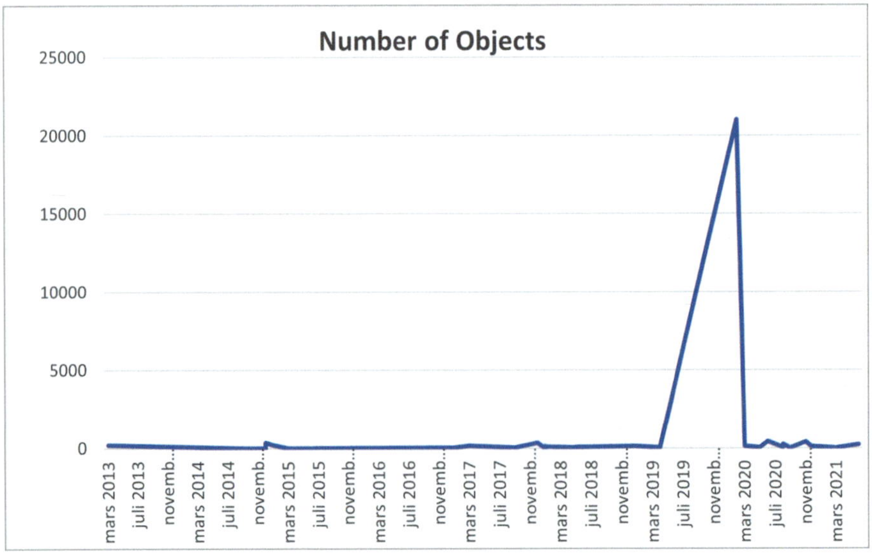

Figure 15. Date and number of seized objects in Egypt

3. Iraq

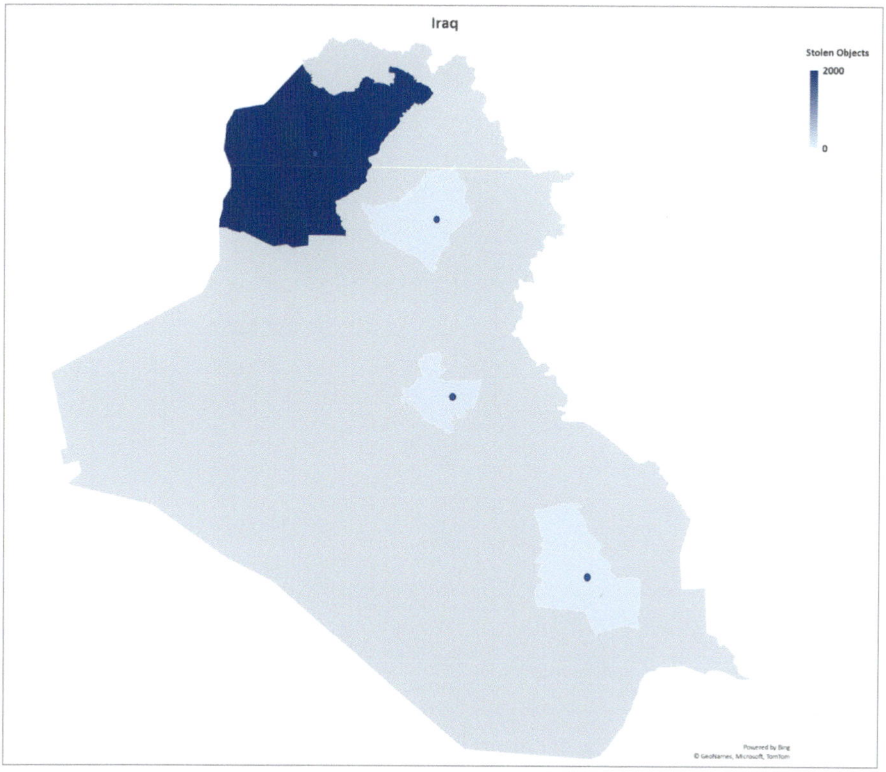

Map 5. Location of cultural properties seizures in Iraq

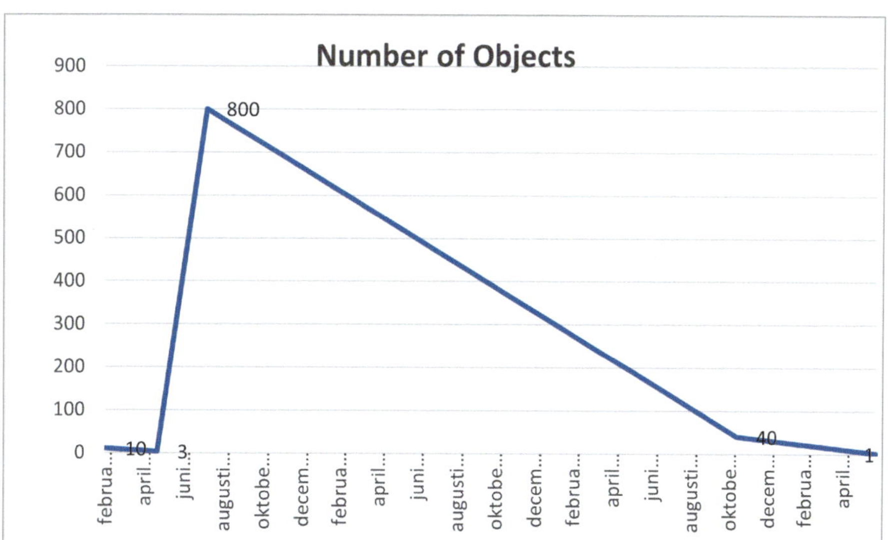

Figure 16. Date and number of seized objects in Iraq

4. Jordan

Map 6. Location of cultural properties seizures in Jordan

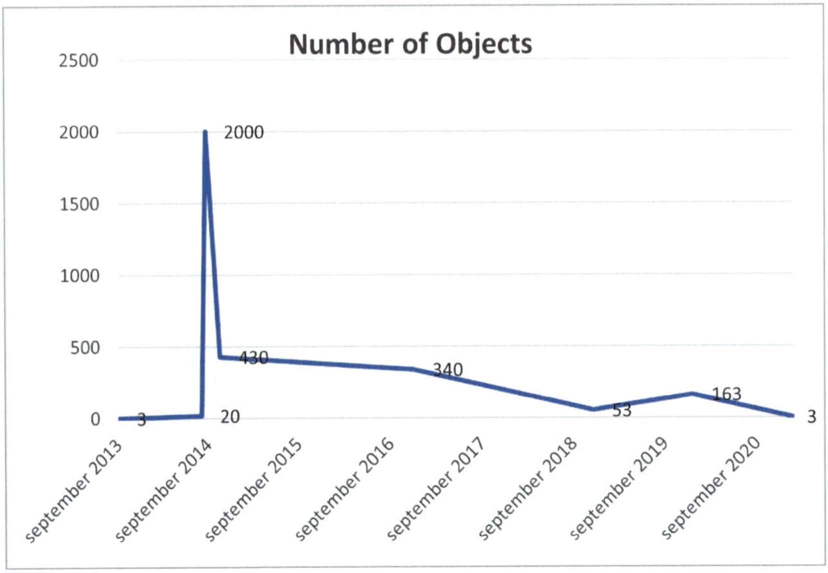

Figure 17. Date and number of seized objects in Jordan

5. Kuwait

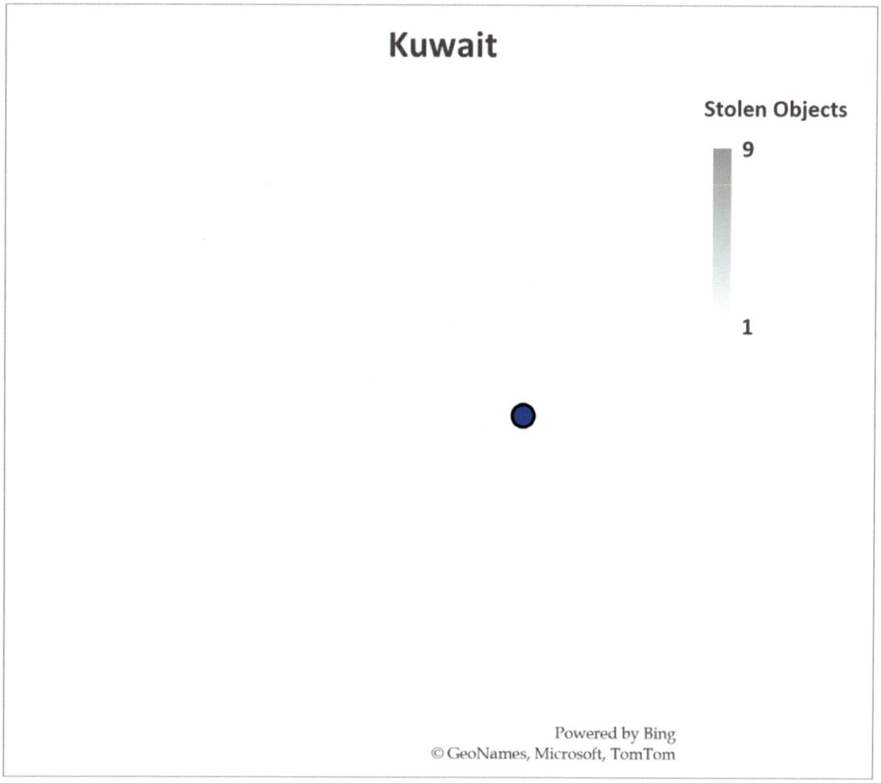

Map 7. Location of cultural properties seizures in Kuwait

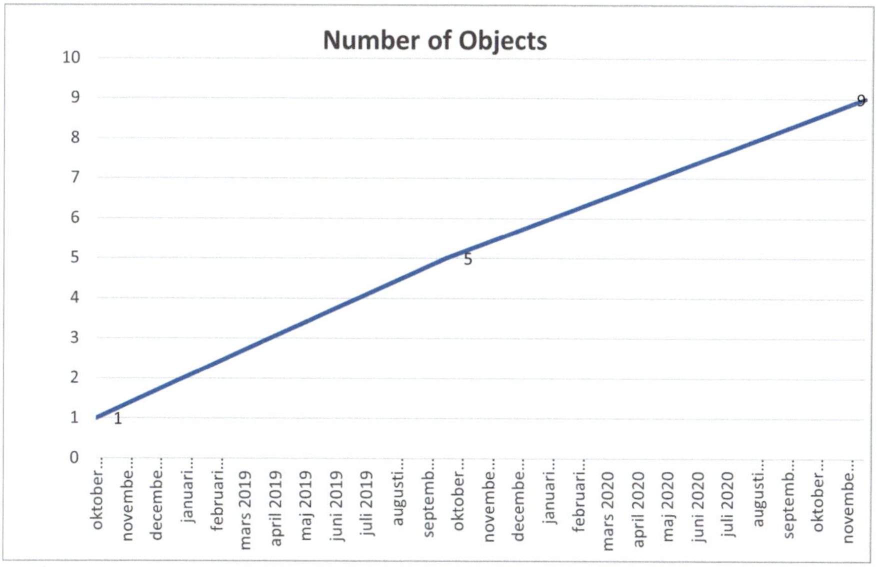

Figure 18. Date and number of seized objects in Kuwait

6. Lebanon

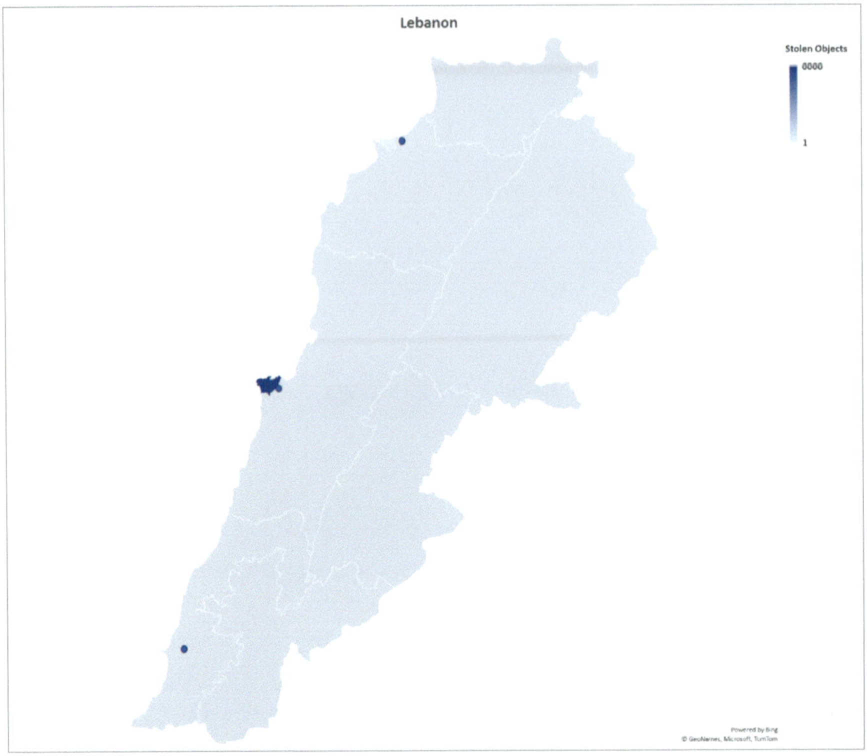

Map 8. Location of cultural properties seizures in Lebanon

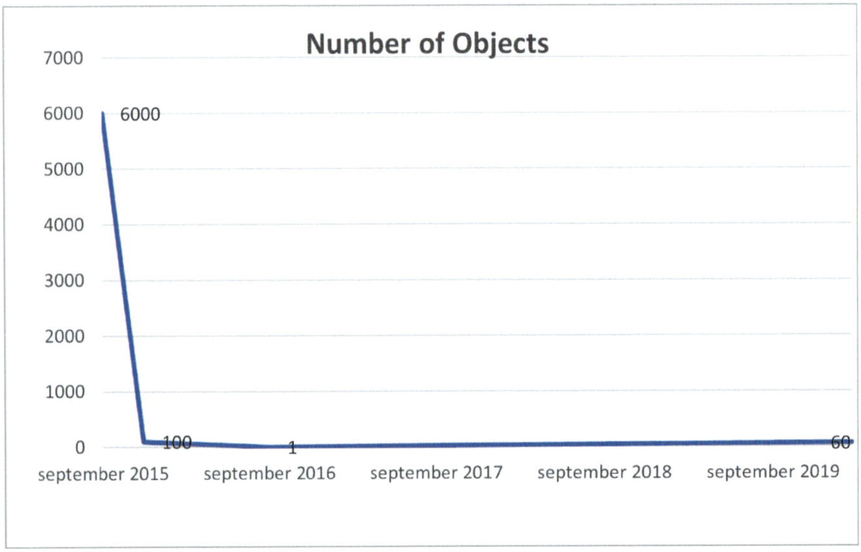

Figure 19. Date and number of seized objects in Lebanon

7. Libya

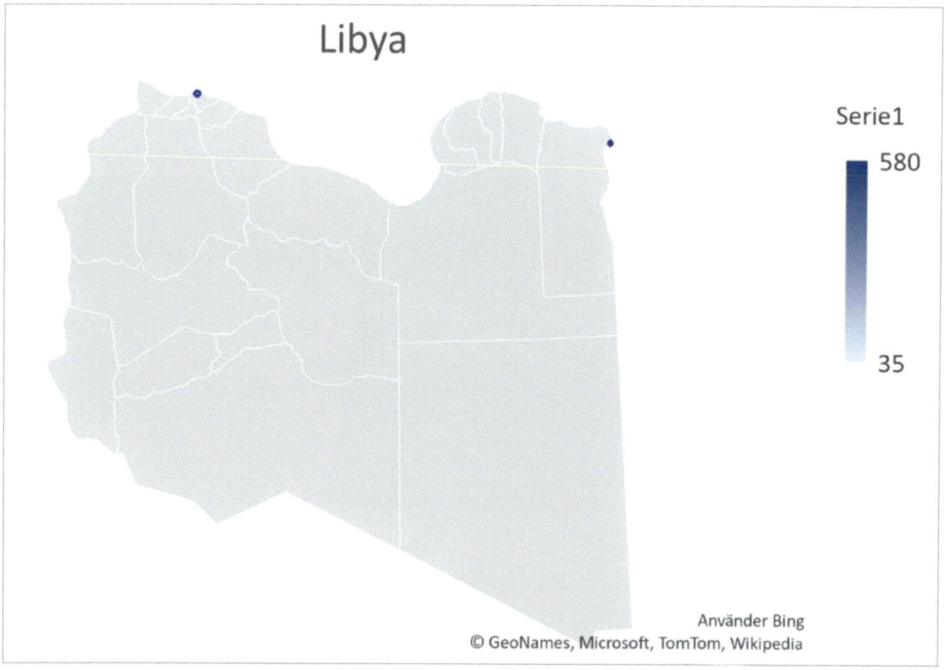

Map 9. Location of cultural properties seizures in Libya

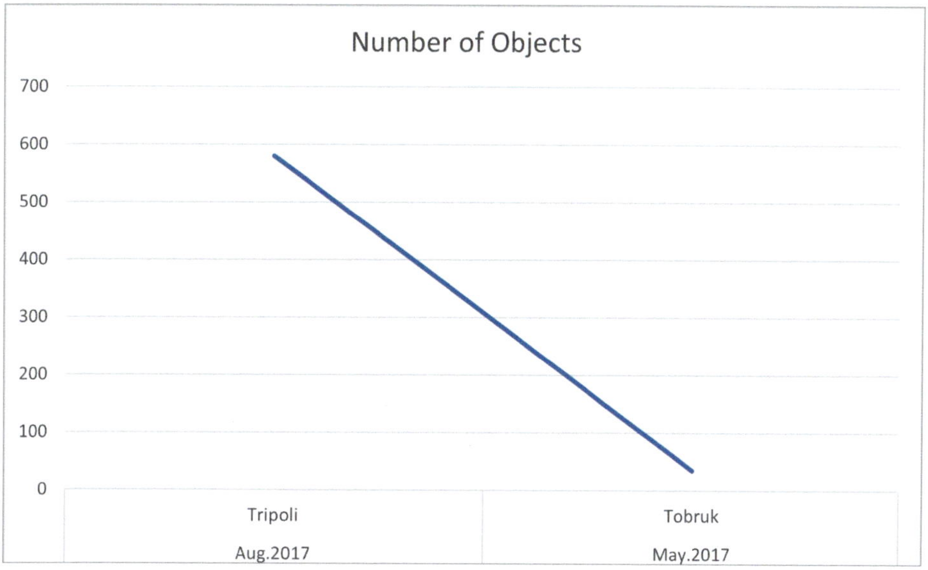

Figure 20. Date and number of seized objects in Libya

8. Mauritania

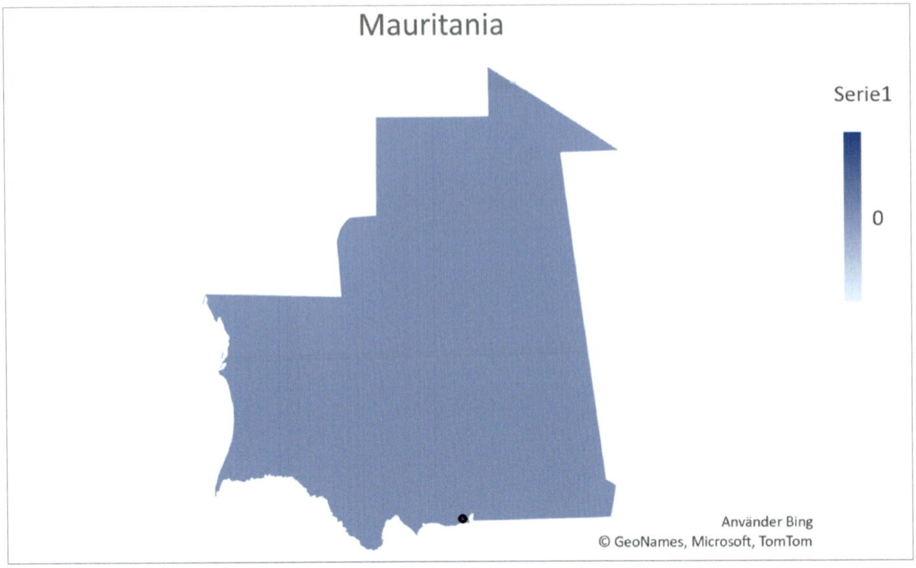

Map 10. Location of cultural properties seizures in Mauritania

9. Morocco

Map 11. Location of cultural properties seizures in Morocco

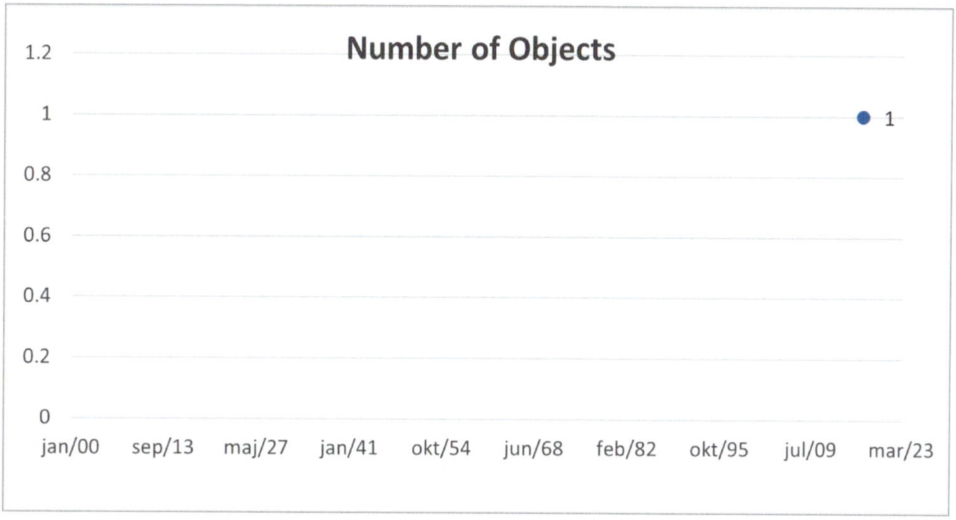

Figure 21. Date and number of seized objects in Morocco

10. Oman

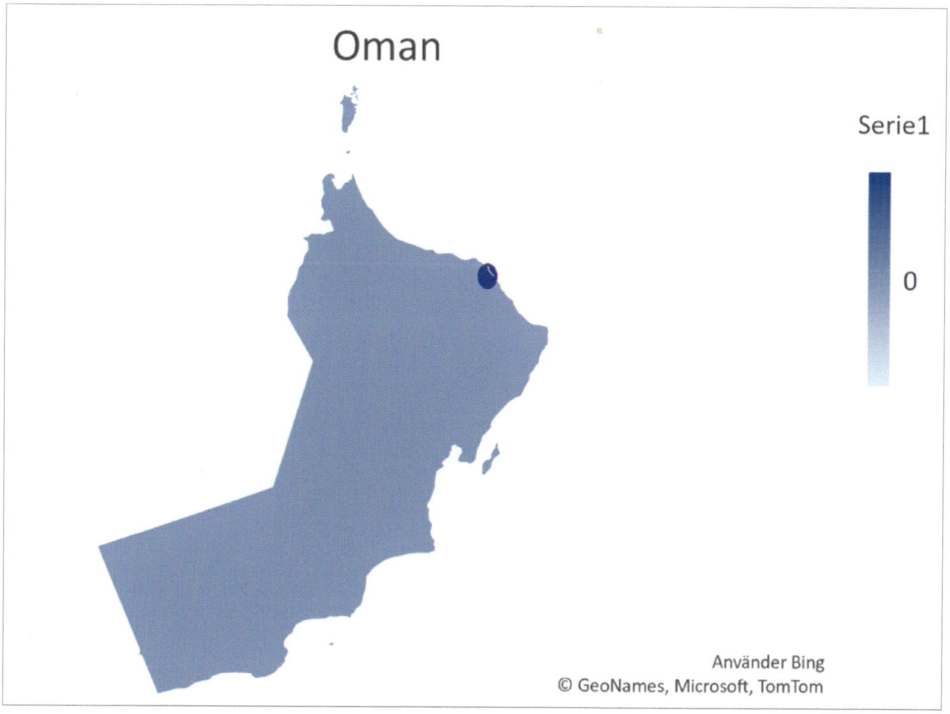

Map 12. Location of cultural properties seizures in Oman

11. Palestine

Map 13. Location of cultural properties seizures in Palestine

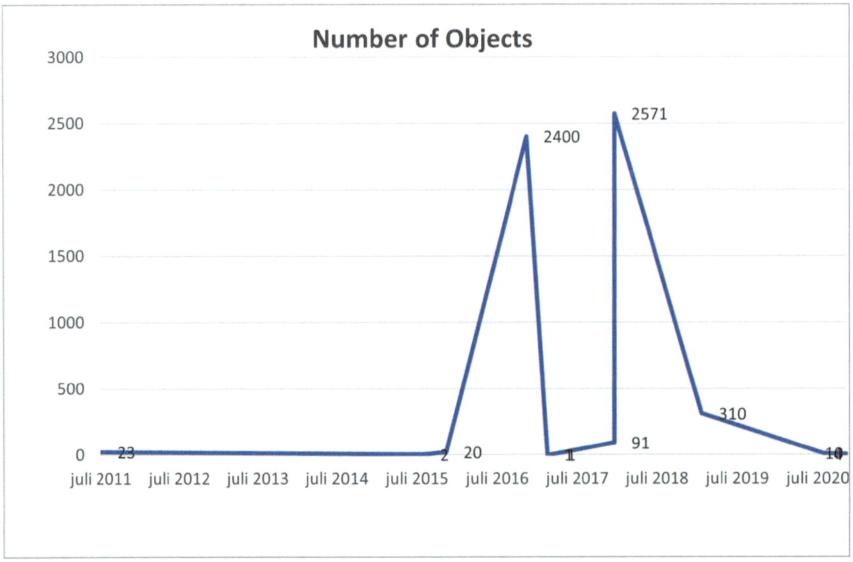

Figure 22. Date and number of seized objects in Palestine

12. Qatar

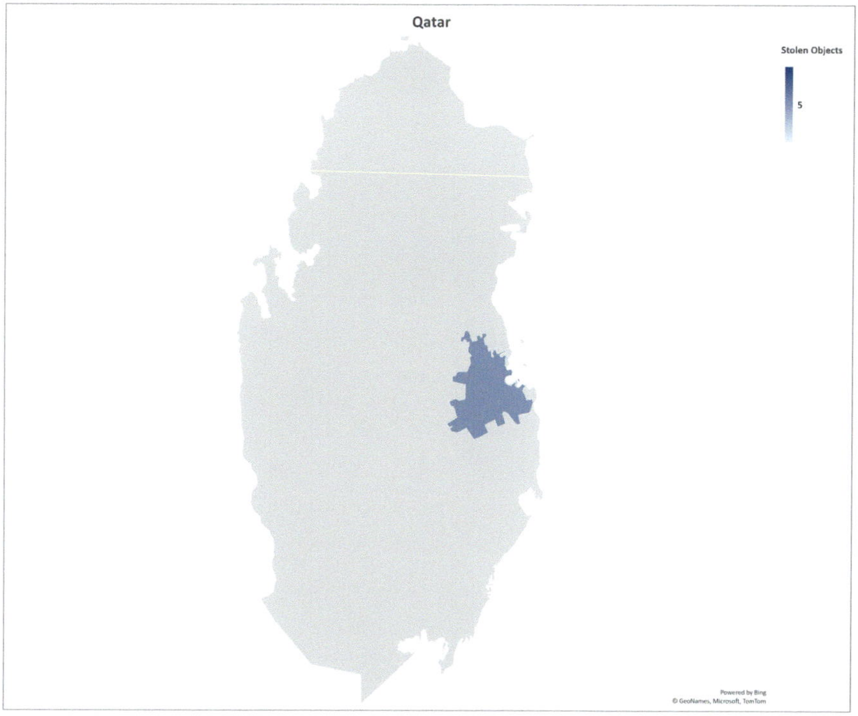

Map 14. Location of cultural properties seizures in Qatar

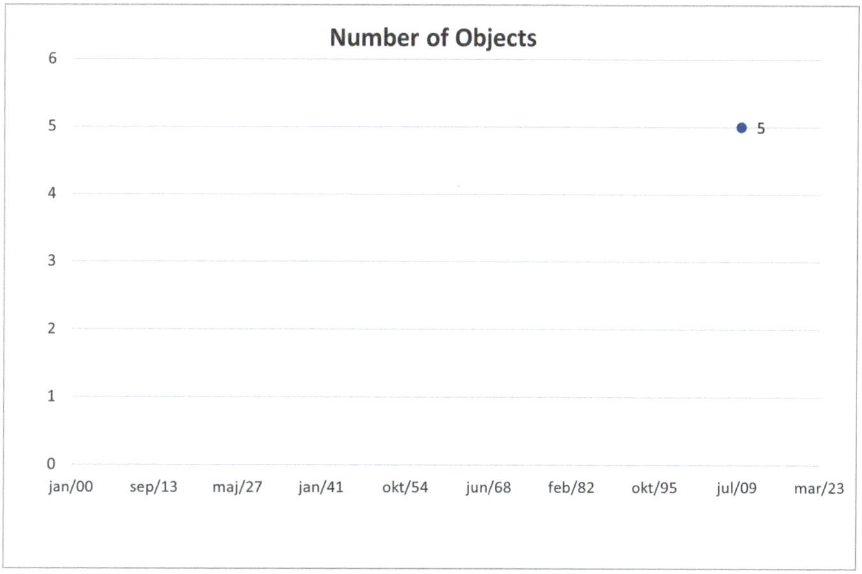

Figure 23. Date and number of seized objects in Qatar

13. Saudi Arabia

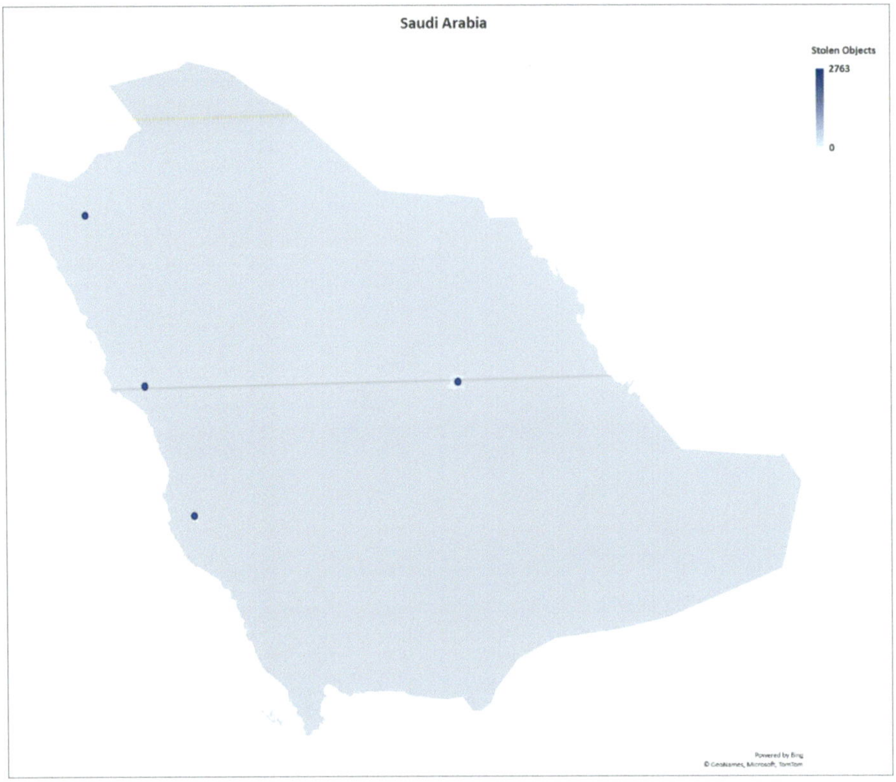

Map 15. Location of cultural properties seizures in Saudi Arabia

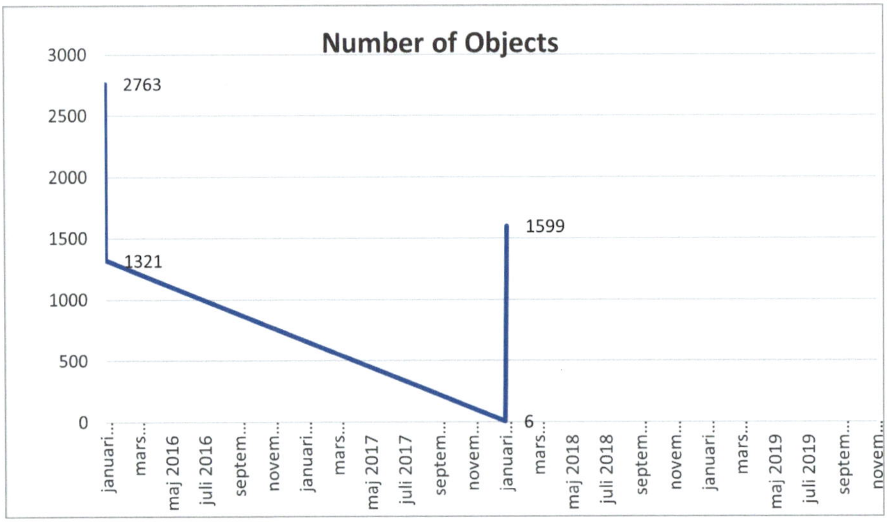

Figure 24. Date and number of seized objects in Saudi Arabia

14. Sudan

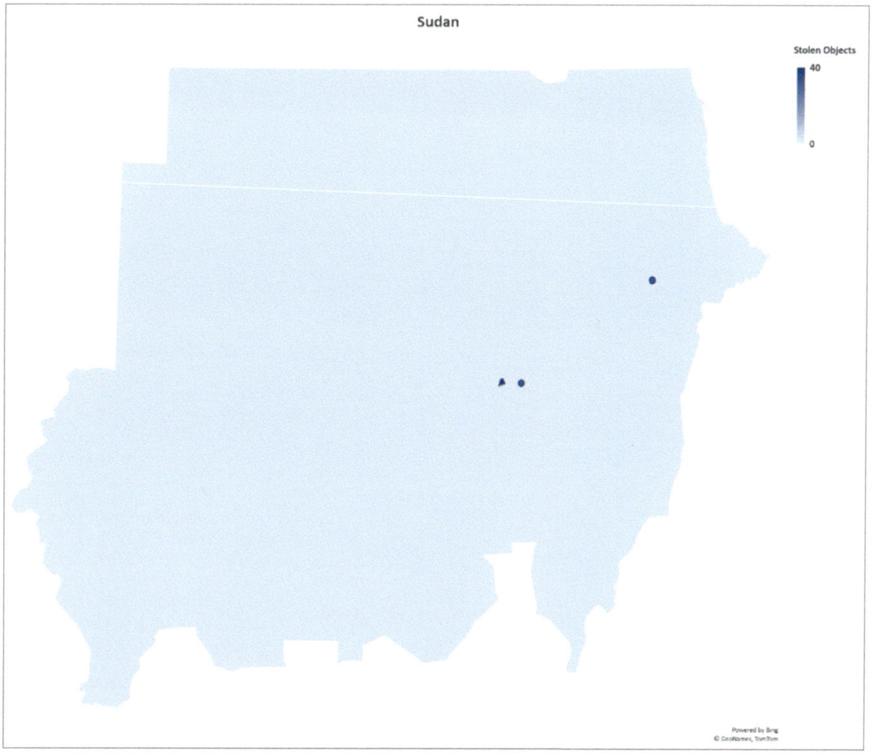

Map 16. Location of cultural properties seizures in Sudan

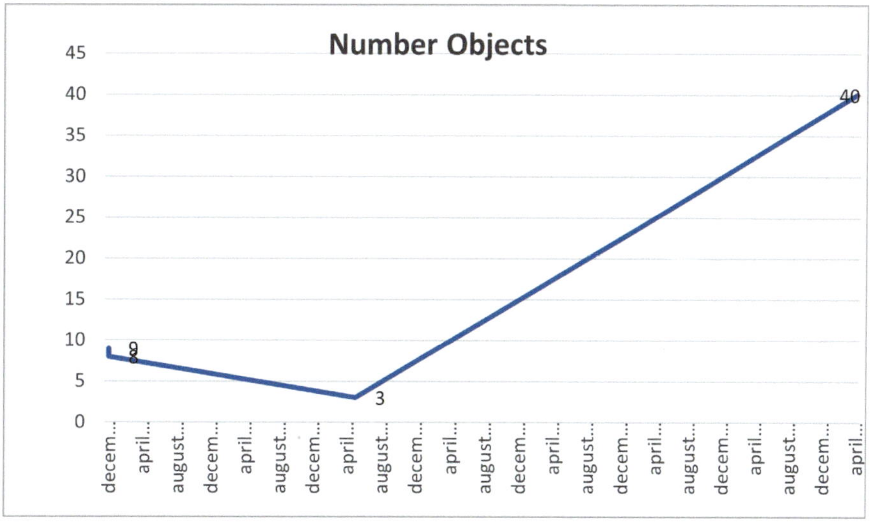

Figure 25. Date and number of seized objects in Sudan

15. Syria

Map 17. Location of cultural properties seizures in Syria

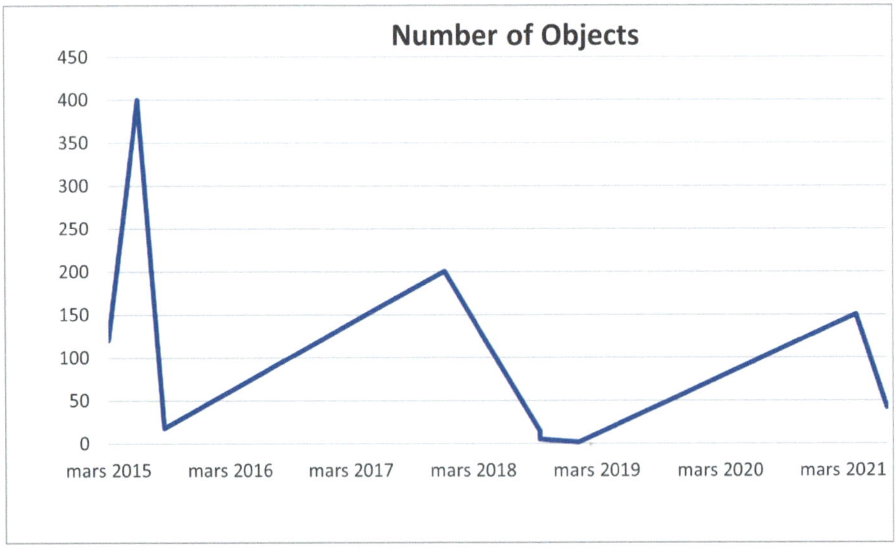

Figure 26. Date and number of seized objects in Syria

16. Tunisia

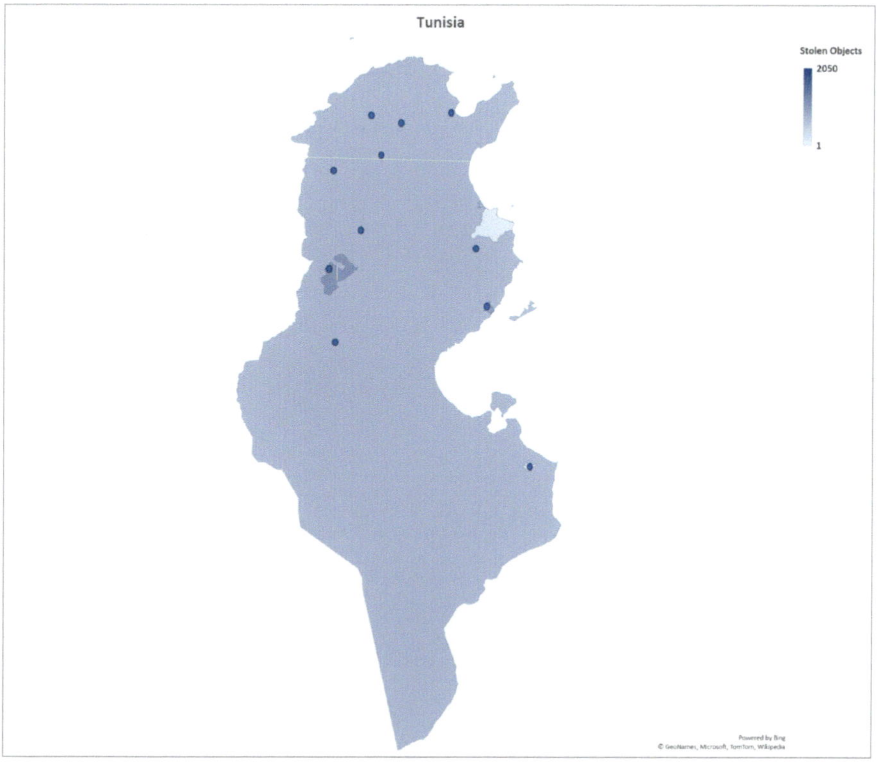

Map 18. Location of cultural properties seizures in Tunisia

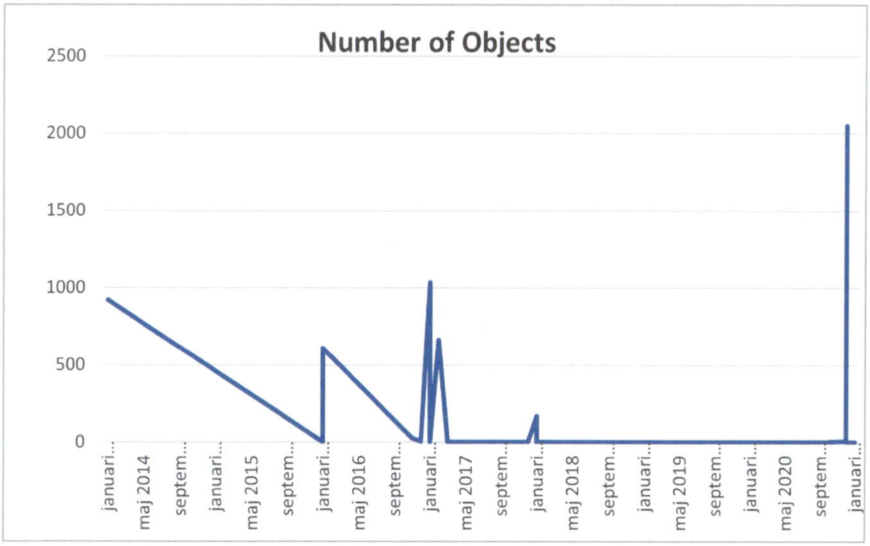

Figure 27. Date and number of seized objects in Tunisia

17. United Arab Emirates

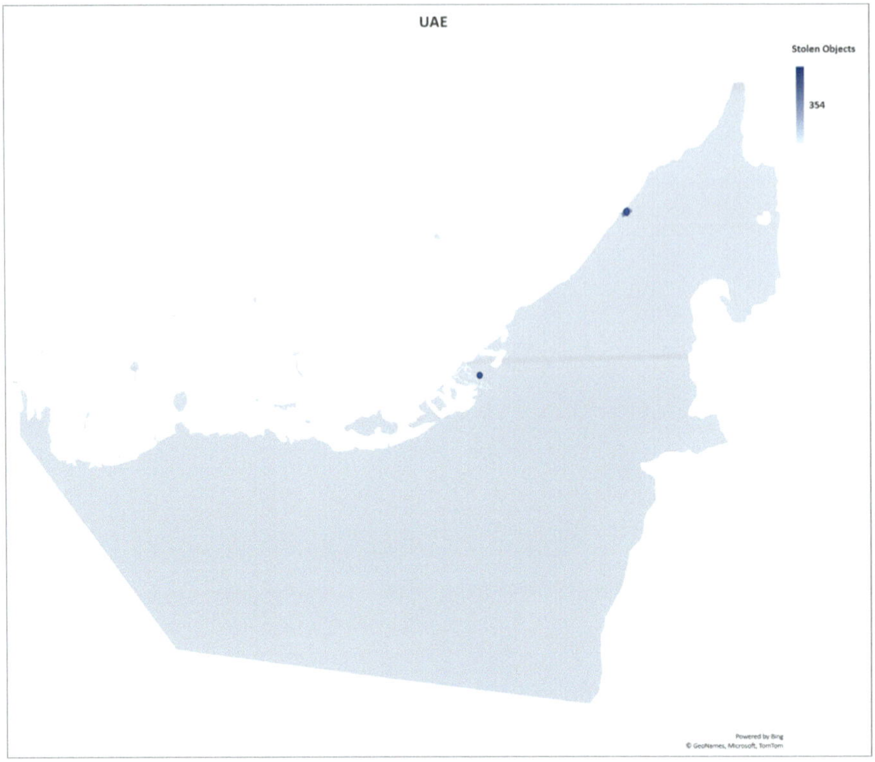

Map 19. Location of cultural properties seizures in United Arab Emirates

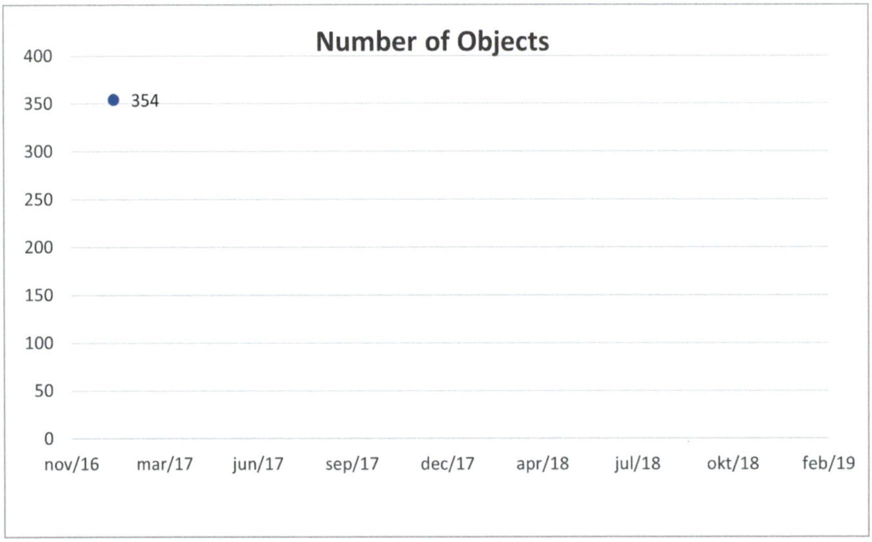

Figure 28. Date and number of seized objects in United Arab Emirates

18. Yemen

Map 20. Location of cultural properties seizures in Yemen

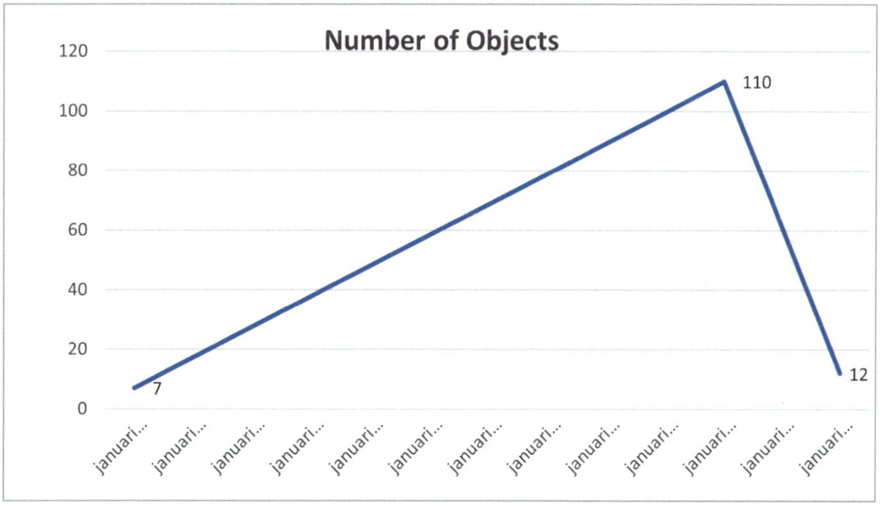

Figure 29. Date and number of seized objects in Yemen

State	Quantity
Mauritania	na
Morocco	na
Oman	na
Qatar	5
Kuwait	15
Sudan	60
Yemen	129
United Arab Emirates	354
Libya	615
Syria	950
Iraq	2883
Jordan	3012
Palestine	5433
Tunisia	5558
Saudi Arabia	5689
Lebanon	6161
Algeria	24030
Egypt	24338

Table 2. Summary of antiquities seizures in Arab States, 2000-2021

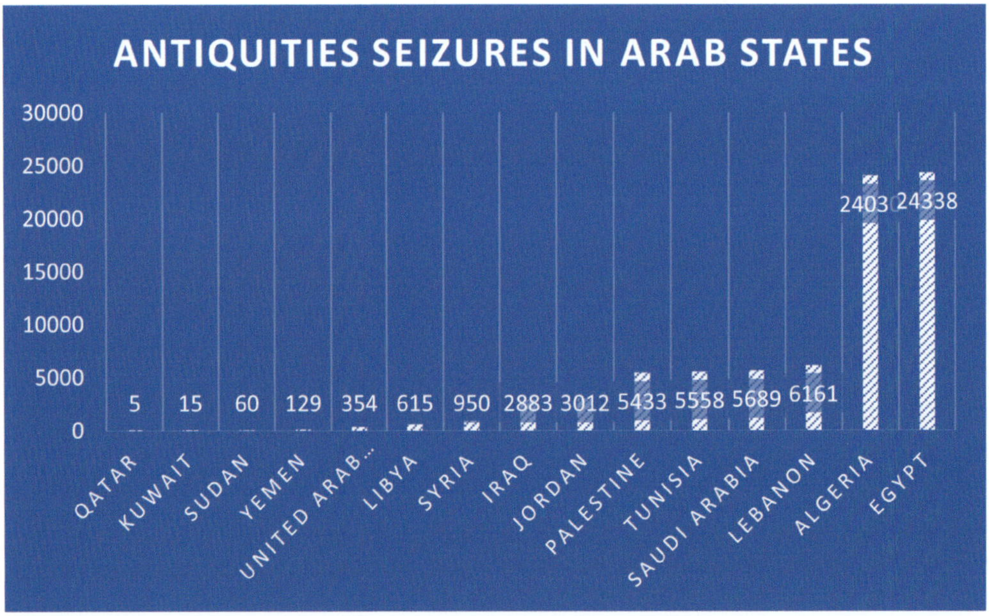

Figure 30. Seizures in Arab States, from least to most

Analysis

Mauritania

According to Professor Ahmed Maouloud Eida El-Hilal, since the gold rush in Sudan in 2012, people in Mauritania started mining gold. When gold was discovered near the mining towns of Tasyasett and Zouerate, thousands of metal detectors were sold. Mauritanian authorities have granted 16,000 licenses for gold-prospecting. However, French radio station RFE confirms that at least twenty thousand Mauritanians are engaged in gold mining, with or without a license. Legally, foreign companies are obliged to hand over archaeological artifacts that they find during their work to the government. And the search for gold ore was accompanied by the search for metal antiquities. Various Facebook pages offered antiquities from Mauritania for sale.[6]

Since antiquities smugglers use the same routes as people smugglers, data on human trafficking may help in tracing out antiquities trafficking. A UNODC (2013) report pointed that Nouakchott city was a key point in migration routes to Western Sahara, Morocco and the Spanish African enclaves. Coastal Nouadhibou city was also used as a route to those destinations, as well as to the Spanish Canary Islands.[7]

Mauritania declared other borders with Algeria and Mali as transit points for terrorists of the Mali-based al-Qaeda in the Islamic Maghreb, as well as other groups in southern Algeria. These areas include Cheggat in the northeast, Ain Ben Tili in the northwest, Dhar Tichitt in the southwest and Lemreyya to the south.[8] In July 2017, the Mauritanian Defense Ministry declared these areas to be restricted military zones and instructed all civilians to avoid the borders and to consider whoever reached them to be a threat.[9]

It is worth mentioning that the destruction of cultural properties in Timbuktu in 2012 was accompanied by the theft of valuable manuscripts.[10] The seizures map may indicate the Gogui border crossing as one of the routes used for smuggling cultural properties from Mali through Mauritania.

---

[6] https://tinyurl.com/36swcdcd

[7] United Nations Office on Drugs and Crime (UNODC). (2013). Transnational Organized Crime in West Africa - Smuggling of Migrants from West Africa to Europe. https://www.unodc.org/toc/es/reports/TOCTAWestAfrica.html

[8] The North Africa Post. Mauritania Declares Borders with Algeria, Mali Military Zones Prohibited to Civilians. https://northafricapost.com/18799-mauritania-declares-borders-algeria-mali-military-zones-prohibited-civilians.html

[9] Africa Times. Mauritania establishes restricted military zone at Mali, Algeria borders. https://africatimes.com/2017/07/18/mauritania-establishes-restricted-military-zone-at-mali-algeria-borders/

[10] Mali and UNESCO receive symbolic reparation on behalf of international community for destruction of Timbuktu's mausoleums. https://whc.unesco.org/en/news/2268

Morocco

Evidence with regard to illicit digging in Morocco points to the eastern region of Erfoud as the main source of prehistoric artefacts and fossils.[11] There has been no border crossing between Morocco and Algeria since 1994, even though travel by air or sea has been allowed since 2000. This suggests that smuggling routes from Morocco to Europe pass through the coastal areas of the country.[12]

The available data do not enable specific routes from Morocco to be traced.

Algeria

Most seizures occurred in the northern part of Algeria. The eastern border crossings with Tunisia – such as Malloula, Babouche and Ouled Moumen – are potential avenues for smuggling activities, considering the political disorder that broke out in Tunisia in 2011 and triggered the Arab Spring.

No seizures were recorded on the nearly 1000-km-long eastern frontiers between Algeria and Libya, probably because the Libyan armed forces declared their side to be a military zone and have prohibited movement there since 2020.[13]

Tunisia

As to the eastern borders between Tunisia and Libya, various seizures documented illicit trafficking of cultural properties from Libya. According to the report of the American Society of Overseas Research (ASOR) on Libyan heritage between 2011-2020,[14] smuggled Libyan cultural properties, including Hebrew manuscripts, were seized in the Tunisian cities of Zaghouan and Tatouine. This flow was reaffirmed by other seizures in frontier towns on the map, which suggest the Dehiba Wazin Border Crossing and Ras Ajdir Border Crossing as potential points in the illicit trafficking of Libyan cultural properties.

Libya

Besides Tunisia, Egypt is a significant place for the trafficking of Libyan antiquities to Egypt (as Libya is a significant place for the trafficking of Egyptian antiquities). The seizures at Mitiga International Airport of Tripoli suggest an air route for illicit trading of Libyan and Egyptian cultural properties.[15] As mentioned elsewhere,

[11] https://tinyurl.com/2u2sju5d

[12] There are various cases confirm the illegal presence of cultural properties smuggled out of the country. One of these is the famous incident of the cancelation of sell an aquatic dinosaur skeleton in 2017 at the auction house at the Drouot Hotel in Paris, the research insured that was unearthed in Morocco, and illegally smuggled out of the country in 2011 according to the Spanish news La Republica. https://tinyurl.com/35dpbpfc

[13] https://www.reuters.com/world/africa/libyas-haftar-closes-border-with-algeria-2021-06-20/

[14] https://www.asor.org/chi/updates/2021/01/illicit-trade-looting-libya

[15] https://tinyurl.com/4rs958zh

in 2017, the Spanish Historical Heritage Brigade detected one of the largest illicit trafficking operations, which delivered goods to the market through Barcelona; one of the suggested routes to Spain was an aerial route through Jordan. Various research indicated that the Egyptian border was a key smuggling point, as it is runs close to the looted ancient city of Cyrenaica.[16] Also in 2017, the seizure of smuggled Libyan antiquities was recorded at the As Sallūm-Musaid Border Crossing.[17]

Egypt

Various seizures of cultural properties were recorded on the northern Egyptian coast. One of these comprised boxes that contained thousands of archaeological items, including Libyan antiquities, which were found at Damietta Port and had been scheduled to be shipped to Thailand. This crime is similar to the case at Port Said in 2011.[18] In 2018 and at the same port, Egyptian authorities seized other cultural properties.[19] Alexandria Port witnessed numerous acts of illicit trafficking, including the case of a diplomat who was involved in the smuggling of Egyptian antiquities to Italy.[20] The Port of Safaga in the east of the country has repeatedly played a role in illicit trafficking to Saudi Arabia.[21]

Cairo Airport reported seizures of goods that were on their way to France,[22] the United Arab Emirates [23] and Israel.[24] Aswan International Airport reported seizures of illicit cultural goods as well.[25]

Sudan

South Sudan is a young nation. Both South Sudan and Sudan are considered Tier 3 countries, which means that the governments of these countries do not meet the minimum standards to address trafficking, nor have they made serious efforts to do so.[26]

Sudan also is a transit country of smuggled people to Yemen and Arab Gulf countries. The Anti-Smuggling Department of the General Administration of Customs has made seizures of antiquities in the cities of Atbara and Khartoum.

---

[16] https://www.asor.org/chi/updates/2021/01/illicit-trade-looting-libya
[17] https://www.elwatannews.com/news/details/2130296
[18] https://www.asor.org/chi/updates/2021/01/illicit-trade-looting-libya
[19] https://tinyurl.com/4y8v4z2k
[20] https://tinyurl.com/2aknrtcc
[21] https://tinyurl.com/7rsxafy8
[22] https://tinyurl.com/yu42mpjb
[23] https://tinyurl.com/53hp9tkb
[24] https://tinyurl.com/59xw99cy
[25] https://tinyurl.com/4j5au7pp
[26] Marchand *et al* 2018.

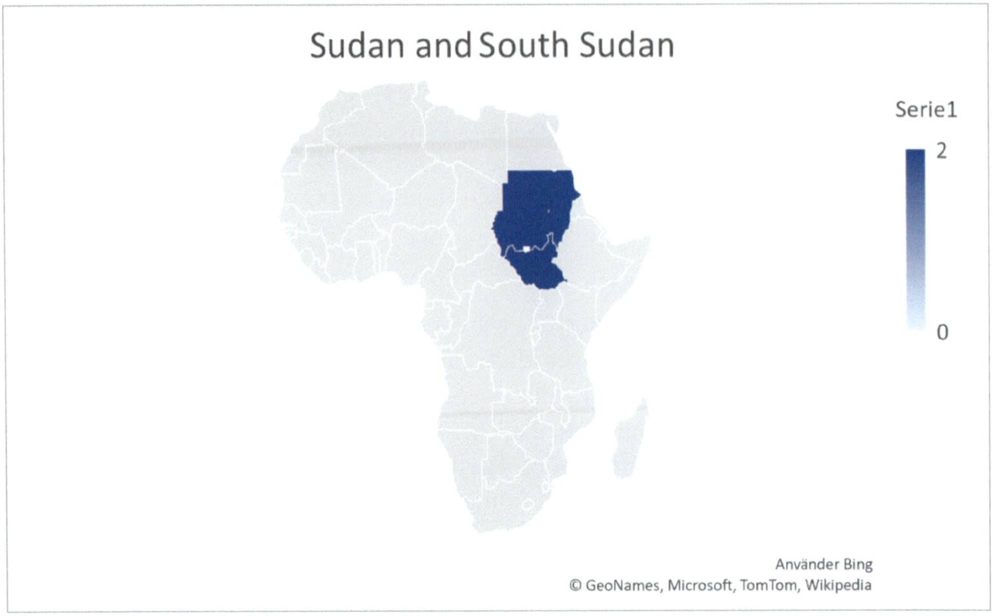

Map 21. Sudan and South Sudan

Based on the limited available data, it is difficult to determine precise routes for illicit trafficking of cultural goods.

Djibouti

Due to its location on the Bab al Mandeb Strait, Djibouti is another transit country of smuggled people (Ethiopians and Somalis) to Yemen and Arab Gulf countries. It is also a Tier 3 country, according to the United States' Department of State.[27]

A coastal country in the Horn of Africa, Djibouti has long witnessed smuggling of people. In recent years, it has witnessed a bi-directional flow. Yemeni authorities have reported that they have detected numerous attempts to smuggle antiquities since the outbreak of the Yemeni conflict. Cultural properties depart from the Port of Aden and take the sea route towards countries in the Horn of Africa, particularly Djibouti.[28]

Somalia

Somalia is yet another Tier 3 country. There, authority is fragmented, as the administrations comprise Puntland and Somaliland as well as Somalia. So, there is a lack of capacity to control borders and combat trafficking. Policies to organize border

[27] Ibid.
[28] https://tinyurl.com/yyfdy9nu

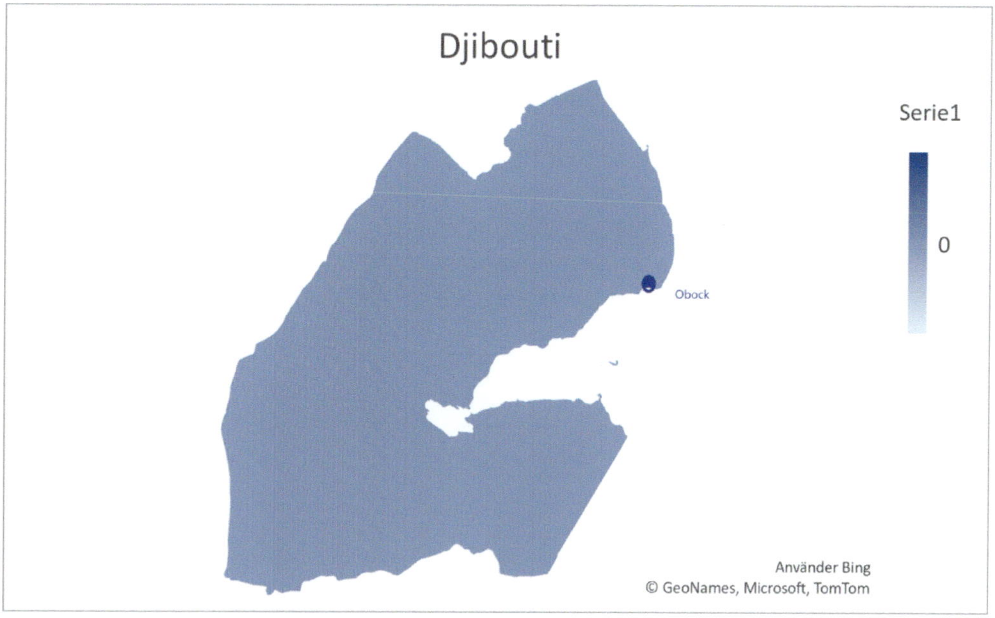

Map 22. Djibouti map

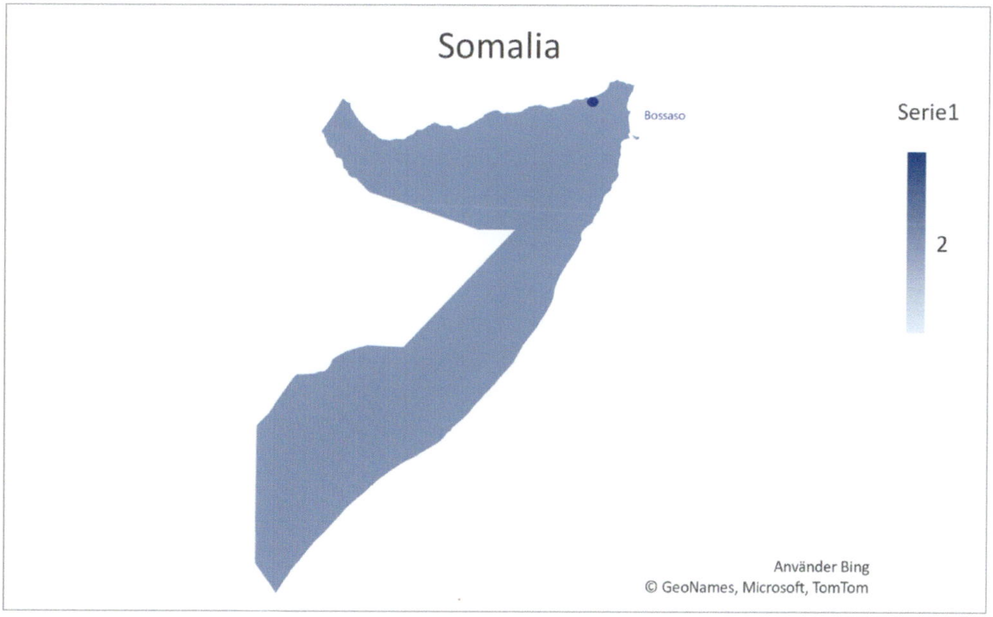

Map 23. Somalia

management are implemented by international organizations – and South Sudan participates in this effort as well. While the Red Sea crossing has witnessed more incidents of abuse and exploitation, the Arabian Sea route is perceived to be more secure; human trafficking routes depart from Bossaso.[29]

In general, the Arab States of the Horn of Africa – Somalia, Djibouti, Sudan and South Sudan – suffer a shortage of resources to combat illicit trafficking of cultural properties. They suffer an almost complete lack of data. Hence, for all of these places, this study has used data on human smuggling to infer potential intelligence on potentially-connected antiquities trafficking. Clearly, there is a great need for further research, in order to be able to begin to address this challenge.

Jordan

Most of the seizures in Jordan occur in the northwest of the country, close to its borders with Syria, Israel and Egypt.

Seizures have been reported at its Jaber Border Crossing with Syria.[30] Seizures have also been reported at its King Hussein Bridge (Allenby Bridge) Border Crossing to Israel,[31] where some of the seized objects had come from Iraq.[32]

Sea routes are also used for illicit trafficking in Jordan. More than 340 Egyptian artifacts were seized by Jordanian customs at the Jordanian Port of Aqaba.[33]

Palestine

Most seizures have occurred close to Area C and the Gaza Strip.[34] Seizures have also been reported at the Rafah Border Crossing between Palestine and Egypt.[35]

Lebanon

Beirut Airport seized antiquities that were headed to Australia on a flight of the Emirates' 'Etihad' airline.[36] Artefacts that had been smuggled from Syria were also seized in the capital, which suggests that Masnaa Border Crossing may be an overland trafficking route. Smuggling cases were also reported in the southern city of Tyre.[37]

[29] Marchand *et al* 2018.
[30] https://tinyurl.com/4m2esefs
[31] https://tinyurl.com/pj8waca4
[32] https://tinyurl.com/yrbjs8r3
[33] https://tinyurl.com/475muv52
[34] https://tinyurl.com/2tvk3apx
[35] https://tinyurl.com/57vswbn6
[36] https://tinyurl.com/532znyen
[37] https://news.culturecrime.org/entry/star2016ancient-artifac.html

In the northern city of Tripoli, antiquities were seized and reported as having been smuggled by ISIS.[38]

Syria

Seizures took place close to Syria's borders with Turkey, Iraq, Lebanon and Jordan. During the occupation of the zone by ISIS, the border between northern Syria and northern Iraq was eliminated; goods, including antiquities, circulated freely within the area under the administration of ISIS. Currently, this area is under the control of Kurdish-led forces. On the border with Turkey, seizures occurred at Bab al-Hawa Border Crossing near Idlib and Bab al-Salama Border Crossing to the north of Aleppo. This area has witnessed intensive smuggling of Syrian antiquities and is still a zone of active conflict between the regime and rebels. On the other side of the border, Turkish authorities frequently seize illicitly-trafficked Syrian antiquities. Recently, on 15th August 2021, Turkish authorities seized 2533 objects from Syria at the Bab al-Hawa Border Crossing. Previously, Turkish authorities detained 93 persons involved in illicit trafficking in 30 provinces across the country. On Syria's border with Lebanon, Masnaa and Aarida Border Crossings are known to have been used for illicit trafficking.[39] On Syria's border with Jordan,[40] control of Daraa and the other border crossing of Nasib long shifted between regime and rebels, until 2018, when it was reopened under firm regime control. These places remain potential crossing points for illicit antiquities.[41] Antiquities from Syria and Iraq have been reaching Europe. It is estimated that 16,000 items from Syria have been seized across the continent.[42]

Iraq

Northeastern Iraq suffered illicit trafficking.[43] Antiquities, which were destined to be dispatched to Syria and Turkey, were seized from the homes of members of ISIS in Mosul. [44,45,46] Kirkuk also witnessed the seizure of antiquities that were destined to be dispatched to Turkey.[47] Numerous seizures occurred in Baghdad as well.[48,49]

Ibrahim Khalil Border Crossing is one of the potential smuggling points from Iraq to Turkey. Antiquities are also taken through Kuwait and Saudi Arabia to the United

[38] https://tinyurl.com/2p8zej3j
[39] https://tinyurl.com/2p9hdtt2
[40] https://tinyurl.com/24zwd7p8
[41] https://tinyurl.com/mrybte3a
[42] https://netcher.eu/project-news/illegal-trafficking-of-cultural-goods-in-countries-in-conflict/
[43] https://tinyurl.com/3jm6yb52
[44] https://tinyurl.com/mpp9skst
[45] https://tinyurl.com/2ehjzfc4
[46] https://tinyurl.com/yphej25m
[47] https://tinyurl.com/3cuekt34
[48] https://tinyurl.com/8bjyevuu
[49] https://tinyurl.com/4see3d4s

Arab Emirates, as well as through Jordan and Iran to trading points and marketplaces elsewhere.

Many artifacts from Syria and Iraq are laundered and moved through Bulgaria or shipped from Turkey to Europe and the United States. The Hobby Lobby Museum case is one of the most emblematic examples.[50]

Saudi Arabia

Seizures in Saudi Arabia indicate that the Egyptian port, Safaga, is a channel to the Saudi capital, Riyadh. In 2018, the Port of Duba (Tabuk) in Saudi Arabia seized a vehicle carrying 1599 cultural objects that were being transported from Turkey to Kuwait.[51] In Badr, there was a seizure of Egyptian artefacts.[52] In Riyadh, there were various seizures of Egyptian objects[53] and Islamic items.[54]

Yemen

The Port of Aden has repeatedly been used to try to smuggle Yemeni antiquities towards countries of the Horn of Africa, especially Djibouti.[55] There, smuggled items are prepared for the next stage – to be smuggled to Europe and the United States.

Kuwait

Kuwait International Airport thwarted an attempt to smuggle Pharaonic antiquities that had been brought from Egypt's Luxor Airport.[56] Egyptian objects, which were being shipped in air freight, were also seized in 2020.[57]

Generally, items that are brought through Kuwait's airport are Egyptian.[58]

Bahrain

There were no reported cases.

[50] https://tinyurl.com/bc4fcjpb
[51] https://theantiquitiescoalition.org/multimedia-resources/interactive-maps/
[52] www.wcoomd.org/-/media/wco/public/global/pdf/topics/enforcement-and-compliance/activities-and-programmes/illicit-trade-report/itr_2016_en.pdf?db=web
[53] www.wcoomd.org/-/media/wco/public/global/pdf/topics/enforcement-and-compliance/activities-and-programmes/illicit-trade-report/itr_2016_en.pdf?db=web
[54] https://tinyurl.com/y7jxpbbr
[55] https://tinyurl.com/yyfdy9nu
[56] https://tinyurl.com/3srxea83
[57] https://tinyurl.com/329crdk8
[58] https://tinyurl.com/59a6c3wx

Oman

It reported seizures of cultural properties in Muscat in 2017, but there is not sufficient data to consider it to be a potentially significant route.[59]

Qatar

There were no reported cases. However, in 2016, the authorities in Switzerland reported finding antiquities from Yemen that had been transferred through Qatar in 2009-2010.[60]

United Arab Emirates

Very few seizure cases have been reported by the United Arab Emirates. Still, those few include Egyptian artefacts that were seized in Sharjah[61] and others that were seized in Abu Dhabi in 2018.[62]

Although the local authorities have reported this low number of seizures, many studies as well as this report indicate that the United Arab Emirates has been a key transit and/or destination country for illicitly-trafficked antiquities.[63]

References

Ahram Gate. 25 December 2016. 344 antiquities were recovered from Jordan smuggled in a shipment of coal at the port of Aqaba. Viewed 30 August 2022. https://tinyurl.com/475muv52

Africa Times. 18 July 2017. Mauritania establishes restricted military zone at Mali, Algeria borders. Viewed 30 August 2022. https://africatimes.com/2017/07/18/mauritania-establishes-restricted-military-zone-at-mali-algeria-borders/

Alanba. 26 September 2019. Seizure of Egyptian antiquities. Viewed 30 August 2022. https://tinyurl.com/3srxea83

Alanba. 25 November 2020. Viewed 30 August 2022. Seizure of Egyptian antiquities in Kuwait. https://tinyurl.com/329crdk8

Al Arabia. 23 February 2021. Intention to smuggling archaeological objects to Australia from Beirut. Viewed 30 August 2022. https://tinyurl.com/532znyen

Al Rai. 1 October 2018. Seizure smuggling antiquities from Syria. Viewed 30 August 2022. https://tinyurl.com/mrybte3a

Al Bawaba. 23 December 2015. Daesh smuggling antiquities. Viewed 30 August 2022. https://tinyurl.com/2p8zej3j

---

[59] www.wcoomd.org/-/media/wco/public/global/pdf/topics/enforcement-and-compliance/activities-and-programmes/illicit-trade-report/itr_2016_en.pdf?db=web

[60] www.wcoomd.org/-/media/wco/public/global/pdf/topics/enforcement-and-compliance/activities-and-programmes/illicit-trade-report/itr_2016_en.pdf?db=web

[61] https://tinyurl.com/bdhu5tbu

[62] https://tinyurl.com/2d73scst

[63] www.wcoomd.org/-/media/wco/public/global/pdf/topics/enforcement-and-compliance/activities-and-programmes/illicit-trade-report/itr_2016_en.pdf?db=web

Al Harf 28 News. 18 April 2021. Smuggling antiquities from Yemen. Viewed 30 August 2022. https://tinyurl.com/yyfdy9nu
Al Monitor. 4 April 2017. Theft of Palestinian antiquities. Viewed 30 August 2022. https://tinyurl.com/2tvk3apx
Al Sharq. 16 October 2020. Morocco recovered 25000 objects from France. Viewed 30 August 2022. https://tinyurl.com/2u2sju5d
Anadolu Agency. 28 March 2013. Objects pertaining to Egypt in Emirates. Viewed 30 August 2022. https://tinyurl.com/53hp9tkb
Anadolu Agency. 22 March 2017. Viewed 30 August 2022. Confiscating objects in Cairo Airport. https://tinyurl.com/59xw99cy
Anadolu Agency. 07 August 2017. Smuggling Libyan antiquities. Viewed 30 August 2022. https://tinyurl.com/4rs958zh
Anadolu Agency. 12 September 2017. Confiscating Ottoman coins in Egypt. Viewed 30 August 2022. https://tinyurl.com/7rsxafy8
Anadolu Agency. 24 December 2017. Viewed 30 August 2022. Seizure of Egyptian coins. https://tinyurl.com/yu42mpjb
Annaharar. 22 June 2021. Smugglers in Baghdad. Viewed 30 August 2022. https://tinyurl.com/4see3d4s
American Society of Overseas Research. 2021. Report: The State of Illicit Trade and Looting Of Libyan Antiquities: 2011–2020. Viewed 30 August 2022. https://www.asor.org/chi/updates/2021/01/illicit-trade-looting-libya
Arab News. 16 July 2018. Saudi heritage. Viewed 30 August 2022. https://tinyurl.com/y7jxpbbr
Arab News. 5 November 2017. Viewed 30 August 2022. Egypt recovers antiquities. https://tinyurl.com/bdhu5tbu
Arabtimesonline. 8 October 2018. Smuggling Egyptian objects in Kuwait. Viewed 30 August 2022. https://tinyurl.com/59a6c3wx
ArThemis. Viewed 30 August 2022. https://tinyurl.com/bc4fcjpb
Campbell, P. 2013. The Illicit Antiquities Trade as a Transnational Criminal Network: Characterizing and Anticipating Trafficking of Cultural Heritage. *International Journal of Cultural Property* 20(2): 113–153.
Culture Crime News. 3 September 2016. Ancient artifact smugglers arrested in south Lebanon. Viewed 30 August 2022. https://news.culturecrime.org/entry/star2016ancient-artifac.html
El Watan News. 25 May 2017. Libyan smuggler. Viewed 30 August 2022. https://www.elwatannews.com/news/details/2130296?t=push
Egyptian Independent. 22 January 2020. Former Italian diplomat receives 15-year sentence for smuggling Egyptian artifacts. Viewed 30 August 2022. https://tinyurl.com/2aknrtcc
Emaratalyoum. 18 October 2018. Smuggling in Abu Dhabi. Viewed 30 August 2022. https://tinyurl.com/2d73scst
France 24. 27 January 2020. Looting antiquities in Mauritania as a result of gold hunting. Viewed 30 August 2022. https://tinyurl.com/36swcdcd
Gulf News. 11 November 2004. Customs officials seize smuggled Iraqi artifacts. Viewed 30 August 2022. https://tinyurl.com/yrbjs8r3
Hardy, S. A. 2016. Illicit trafficking, provenance research and due diligence: The state of the art. Paris: UNESCO. Viewed 30 August 2022. https://archaeologicalethics.org/

blog/illicit-trafficking-provenance-research-and-due-diligence-and-confidence-and-risk-conflict-antiquities/

Khaberni. 11 December 2018. Israel stops smuggling antiquities from Jordan. Viewed 30 August 2022. https://tinyurl.com/pj8waca4

Kurdistan 24. 6 June 2017. Mosul Museum. Viewed 30 August 2022. https://tinyurl.com/mpp9skst

Kurdistan 24. 17 February 2018. Smuggled Iraqi antiquities. Viewed 30 August 2022. https://tinyurl.com/3cuekt34

Marchand, K., J. Reinold, and R. Dias e Silva. 2018. *Study on Migration Routes in the East and Horn of Africa*. Maastricht Graduate School of Governance. Viewed 30 August 2022. https://webcache.googleusercontent.com/search?q=cache:z0M0Zv0TVmcJ:https://www.merit.unu.edu/publications/uploads/1517475164.pdf+&cd=1&hl=es&ct=clnk&gl=se

Masrawy News. 24 April 2019. Smuggling antiquities in Aswan. Viewed 30 August 2022. https://tinyurl.com/4j5au7pp

Mena Monitor. 11 November 2020. Seizure of antiquities in Iraq. Viewed 30 August 2022. https://tinyurl.com/3jm6yb52

Morocco World News. 30 March 2017. Morocco Blocks Sale of Dinosaur Skeleton. Viewed 30 August 2022. https://tinyurl.com/35dpbpfc

Muñoz, P., and C. Morcillo, ABC Spain, 13 May 2018. Las rutas de las 'antigüedades de sangre' de Daesh, al descubierto. Viewed 30 August 2022. https://www.abc.es/espana/abci-rutas-antiguedades-sangre-daesh-descubierto-201805130146_noticia.html

Nahrainnet. 4 August 2018. Smuggling antiquities in Baghdad. Viewed 30 August 2022. https://tinyurl.com/8bjyevuu

NetCher. 7 October 2020. Illegal trafficking of cultural goods in countries in conflict. Viewed 30 August 2022. https://netcher.eu/project-news/illegal-trafficking-of-cultural-goods-in-countries-in-conflict/

North Africa Post. 14 July 2017. Mauritania Declares Borders with Algeria, Mali Military Zones Prohibited to Civilians. Viewed 30 August 2022. https://northafricapost.com/18799-mauritania-declares-borders-algeria-mali-military-zones-prohibited-civilians.html

Paltoday. 25 November 2020. Seizures in Palestine. Viewed 30 August 2022. https://tinyurl.com/57vswbn6

Reuters. 20 June 2021. Libya's Haftar closes border with Algeria. Viewed 30 August 2022. https://www.reuters.com/world/africa/libyas-haftar-closes-border-with-algeria-2021-06-20/

RT News. 13 February 2021. Seizing antiquities from Syria to Jordan. Viewed 30 August 2022. https://tinyurl.com/4m2esefs

Syrianpc. 26 April 2021. Smugglers in Syria. Viewed 30 August 2022. https://tinyurl.com/2p9hdtt2

Taghrib News. 21 May 2018. Smuggling antiquities from Mosul to Syria. Viewed 30 August 2022. https://tinyurl.com/2ehjzfc4

The Antiquities Coalition, Washington, DC. Viewed 30 August 2022. https://theantiquitiescoalition.org/antiquities-coalition-releases-cultural-piracy-mapping-antiquities-seizures-around-the-globe/ https://theantiquitiescoalition.org/multimedia-resources/interactive-maps/ and https://www.prnewswire.

com/news-releases/antiquities-coalition-releases-culture-under-threat-mapping-resource-300251043.html

UNESCO. Mali and UNESCO receive symbolic reparation on behalf of international community for destruction of Timbuktu's mausoleums. 30 March 2021. Viewed 30 August 2022. https://whc.unesco.org/en/news/2268

UNESCO. United Nations Office on Drugs and Crime (UNODC). (2013). Transnational Organized Crime in West Africa- Smuggling of Migrants from West Africa to Europe. Viewed 30 August 2022. https://www.unodc.org/toc/es/reports/TOCTAWestAfrica.html

UNESCO. United Nations Office on Drugs and Crime (UNODC). 2019. Opiate trafficking along the early stages of the Balkan route. Viewed 30 August 2022. https://www.unodc.org/documents/data-and-analysis/Studies/IFF_report_2015_final_web.pdf

UrdoPoint. 2 October 2018. Viewed 30 August 2022. https://tinyurl.com/24zwd7p8

World Customs Organization (WCO), 2016: *Illicit Trade Report*. Viewed 30 August 2022. www.wcoomd.org/-/media/wco/public/global/pdf/topics/enforcement-and-compliance/activities-and-programmes/illicit-trade-report/itr_2016_en.pdf?db=web

Youm 7. 16 July 2018. Seizure of 116 archaeological objects. Viewed 30 August 2022. https://tinyurl.com/4y8v4z2k

Ypagency. 20 February 2018. Detention of smugglers in Iraq. Viewed 30 August 2022. https://tinyurl.com/yphej25m

Chapter Six

Illicit trafficking of cultural properties and financing of terrorism

Illicit trafficking of cultural properties is recognized as a stream of revenue for terrorists and insurgents. It is well-known that some profits from the illicit trade are invested in such illicit activities. There are clear examples of conflicts in Arab States, where participation in political violence has been subsidized by illicit trafficking, such as the case of the Islamic State organization in Syria, Iraq, Yemen, and Libya. In some cases, antiquities are exchanged for weapons. Some of the antiquities that are looted and trafficked in these circumstances end up in the hands of collectors.

In 2018, the Historical Heritage Brigade of the Spanish National Police (*Brigada de Patrimonio Histórico de la Policía Nacional*) arrested two people, Jaume Bagot Peix and Oriol Carreras Palomar, on suspicion of involvement in a trafficking network that was smuggling antiquities from Libya and financing terrorist activity.[1]

Connection to organized crime

The connection between illicit trafficking, organized crime and terrorism was first observed when terrorist groups benefited from the illicit narcotics trade in Latin America, and later in Afghanistan by the Taliban. The term (narco-terrorism) was coined, and terrorist groups alongside transitional criminals have been involved in using new technologies through online sales, using cryptocurrencies which have increased anonymity and reduced risk. The list included many other products such as oil trafficking, used cars, pharmaceuticals, natural resources, cigarettes, gold, human trafficking and antiquities, and the sale of various goods and services. Perpetrators expanded the trade of looted antiquities not only as a revenue generation tool, but also to destroy a past that is not consistent with their interpretation of history.[2]

The United Nations Convention against Transnational Organized Crime, also known as the Palermo Convention, was adopted in 2000 and entered into force in 2003; it has been supplemented by three Protocols.[3] According to the Convention, an organized criminal group involves three or more persons, who collaborate for a period of time and who act with the aim of committing one or more serious crimes or offences, in order directly or indirectly to obtain a financial or other material benefit.

---

1 Temino *et al* 2018.

2 Shelley 2020: 7-8

3 United Nations Convention against Transitional Organized Crime and the Protocols Thereto https://www.unodc.org/unodc/en/organized-crime/intro/UNTOC.html

Organized crimes against cultural properties spread beyond national borders and smuggled items pass through a chain of dealers, through sometimes-rapid transactions.[4] And illicit trafficking of cultural properties has been conducted by organized crime groups – some of whom are dedicated to this activity, some of whom control a sophisticated supply chain from source countries through transit countries to market countries. These organized crime groups and mafias used it as an instrument of money laundering and criminal financing, including terrorism financing. The antiquities market has been considered to be a ready source of stolen artifacts for museums and private collections.[5]

International bodies are aware of the exploitation of globalization and the organization of crimes that are related to illicit trafficking of cultural properties. The United Nations Security Council since 2004 has recognized the connection between illicit trafficking of antiquities and the funding and the spread of terrorism (e. g. Resolutions 2195 and 2199).[6] The last international operation, Pandora V, which took place between 1 June and 31 October 2020, was a successful collaboration among 31 states with INTERPOL and the World Customs Organization. It involved tens of thousands of checks at airports, seaports, border crossing points, auction houses and museums, as well as checks against national and international databases of stolen and missing works of art. At least 67 suspects were arrested and more than 56400 cultural objects were seized.[7]

Illicit trafficking and armed conflict

Since the end of the Second World War, an estimated 250 conflicts have taken place around the world. A large number of people have died during these conflicts. The estimated number is between 70 and 170 million, most of whom were non-combatants.[8]

Compounding that, conflicts have been associated with destruction of heritage and high-scale looting and theft. Cultural property is destroyed or otherwise appropriated and illicit trafficking of cultural property increases. One of the recent examples is from Syria in recent years, where Islamic State (ISIS) fighters reduced the famous ancient city of Palmyra to rubble and looted its antiquities. Besides destruction of heritage and looting of archaeological sites, also theft from museums and collections takes place during conflict.[9] UNESCO sadly concluded that the archaeological site of

[4] Calvani 2008: 34.
[5] Miñana 2017: 58.
[6] Shelley 2020: 7-8.
[7] INTERPOL. More than 56,400 cultural goods seized and 67 arrested. Law enforcement and customs authorities from 31 countries participated in Operation Pandora V. https://www.interpol.int/News-and-Events/News/2021/More-than-56-400-cultural-goods-seized-and-67-arrested
[8] Bassiuoni 2008: 712.
[9] Al Khabour 2015. El conflicto armado en Siria y su repercusión sobre el Patrimonio Cultural: Vol. I Deir Ez-Zor. https://www.academia.edu/14885188/El_conflicto_armado_en_Siria_y_su_repercusi%C3%B3n_sobre_el_Patrimonio_Cultural_Vol_II_Inventario_del_Patrimonio_Cultural_afectado_en_la_provincia_de_Raqqa_marzo_2011_mazro_2015_

Apamea in Syria had 'lost all scientific value' because of the scale of destruction and looting.[10] The same tragedy befell other sites such as Dura-Europos in Syria, which was attacked by 300 people, who dug with bulldozers.

ISIS and illicit trafficking

In Islamic tradition, the word (*al Rikaz*) means buried treasures of the pre-Islamic era (*Jahiliya*). According to the Koran, those who find such treasures should pay a tax or tithe of 20 per cent or one-fifth (*al Khums*) to the state. This standard is echoed in another obligation that affects the regulation of illicit trafficking: *And know that out of all the booty that ye may acquire (in war), a fifth share is assigned to Allah, and to the Messenger, and to near relatives, orphans, the needy, and the wayfarer*. The concept of (*al Rikaz*) still exists in the antiquities law of Sudan (as of 1999, under Article 18).

The organization of the Islamic State in Iraq and Syria or the Islamic State of Iraq and al Sham, ISIS (also known by its Arabic-language acronym, Daesh, and as the Islamic State of Iraq and the Levant, ISIL), proclaimed itself to be the representative of all Muslims and claimed the territories under its control as the land of the Caliphate, where Islamic laws were applied. The concept of *al Khums* was used by the institution that regulated the management of assets that had been extracted from the earth, the *Diwan al Rikaz*. In July 2015, the UNESCO warned that looting under ISIS was taking place on an 'industrial scale'.[11]

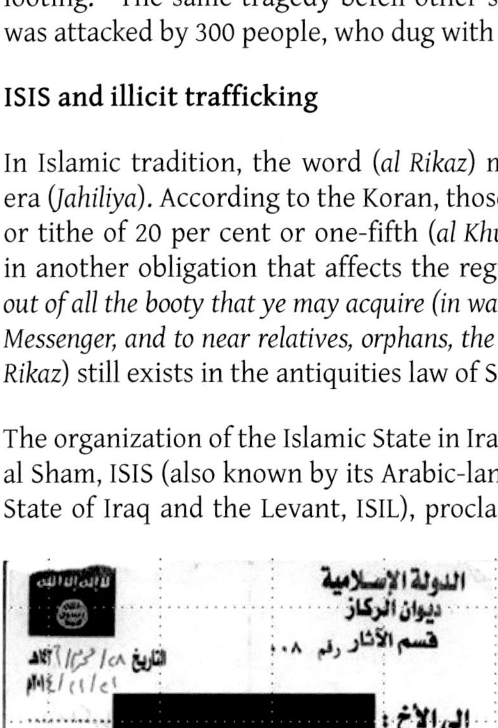
الدولة الإسلامية
ديوان الركاز
قسم الآثار رقم ٠٠٨
التاريخ
إلى الأخ:

Figure 31. Leadership of Abu Sayyaf

Some researchers estimated that ISIS had made several million dollars through looting of archaeological sites in Syria and Iraq since 2014, but the precise amount is unknown. These claims are based on documents belong to Abu Sayyaf, the head of the *Diwan al Rikaz*. In his house, US forces found a large number of stolen artifacts, as well as documents, laptops, flash drives and cell phones that contained

[10] https://www.standard.co.uk/news/world/un-in-plea-to-stop-islamic-state-s-industrial-scale-looting-10360530.html

[11] Artnet 2015. https://news.artnet.com/art-world/unesco-warning-looting-syria-333814

important data on ISIS's activities.[12] Among these documents, there were excavation permits that had been issued by the *Diwan al Rikaz* (Figure 1).[13]

Other researchers criticize this estimation, ascribe it to a shortage of evidence and to the production of propaganda about ISIS, and appeal for skepticism about the authenticity of ISIS documents.[14] It is similarly problematic to estimate the scale and value of illicit trafficking in antiquities during the ongoing conflicts in Syria, Iraq, Libya and Yemen.

Impact on archaeological context and knowledge

In archaeology, once a site has been excavated, its physical manifestation has been 'destroyed'. If the research methodology of the excavation and post-excavation processing are not thorough enough – if it does not preserve the finds and associated deposits, document their nature and the stratigraphic relationships among them – the data is gone forever. Then, without the archaeological context of 'the place where the object was found', it is difficult to understand the history of the artefact and the history of the site, as objects that have been removed from their context cannot say much about the civilizations that produced them – their values, beliefs, traditions, etc.

So, all illicit trafficking has a destructive impact on knowledge (albeit less so in the case of works of art and other objects that are stolen from well-documented collections, which should have been documented in some form, so less knowledge is lost). However, looting of archaeological sites is a catastrophe, because it destroys the context of both the objects that are extracted and the layers from which they are extracted.

It is worth noting that, in Arab States, there are ancient cultures with written records, so objects in context address particularly complicated questions in archaeology, such as apparent contradictions between the texts (in particular, the archives of sites in Mesopotamia or Egypt) and the data from material culture that is obtained from the excavation of settlements and burials. The written sources usually tell us about the ruling class, while the archaeological remains usually document the lives of the lower classes and even non-urban communities, such as shepherds and hunters in rural areas. Consequently, the removal of an item from its context causes irredeemable damage to human knowledge about ancient civilizations.

[12] Terril 2017: 21.
[13] Keller 2015. https://2009-2017.state.gov/e/eb/rls/rm/2015/247610.htm.
[14] Casana 2015: 142–152.

Provenance

The term provenance refers in antiquities to the evidenced ownership history of an object. Due to the fact that there is lack of a universal standard for provenance documentation, dealers trend to create their own provenance documentation. Given the significant number of looted objects that circulate on the market, it becomes difficult to tell if an object has been on the market for many years or has been recently looted. As such, it is common for dealers to have legitimate prior ownership of objects meant to sell. They provide false evidence or documents difficult to trust, such as the signature of a previous owner on the top of an aged label assuming that the object was part of an old collection, or whether the object came from the collection of a 'Belgian gentleman' or from a 'Swiss collection'. To compound the difficulties, in many cases, buyers consider such claims as having a good provenance and purchase these 'provenanced' items even when their suspicious origins as looted or illegally trafficked are expected.[15]

Mackenzie (Mackenzie 2000) describes the antiquities market historically; it was grounded on the vendor's privacy and the purchaser's apathy. Other aspects of the antiquities market in connection to provenance should be mentioned here:

First: prior to the UNESCO Convention 1970, collecting antiquities, whatever their origin, even looted antiquities, was not legally prohibited. Therefore, nobody cared about its provenance.

Second: dealers accept poor documentation of provenance given that authentic documents could be faked or could be easily lost. Based on these findings, documentation does not play a decisive role, and such poor provenance documentation is counted as *de facto* documentation. In this context, poor documentation is often considered better than nothing at all.

Third: dealers are aware of the existence of looted objects, and they prefer transacting with established trusted sources. Occasionally desirable objects to profit from are offered by unknown sources, and such attractive objects encourage dealers to undertake the sale. At that stage, they may ask for documentation, which is generally absent. They will then request the seller to provide a written document that provides legal assurance of legitimacy. Dealers knew that the document was being used fraudulently. Consequently, they are not verifying the seller's title-and therefore investigating the provenance of the object with diligence-rather than protecting themselves against any future inquiry into the transaction. Based on these circumstances, even when the objects in question can be looted or unprovenanced, dealers opt to act with no knowledge or belief that the object has been looted, and to treat all objects as 'innocent until proven guilty'; in Mackenzie's words, neither

[15] Mackenzie 2000:108–109; Mackenzie 2005: 253.

vendor nor purchaser are interested in proving an economically attractive object as guilty.[16]

Fakes and forgeries

Besides the damage to knowledge, forgery of antiquities has been used to support claims (eg. The papyrus of the so-called Gospel of Jesus' Wife) or as an ideological, political and religious weapon especially in the ongoing tensions in the Middle East.[17]

Fakes, forgeries, reproductions and copies have flooded the art market. This can be seen in a documentary film by the German channel *Deutsche Welle* (DW), which presented the research of Stefan Lehmann, who traced one of most talented fraudsters in the art world. The fraudster was called the Spanish Master (*Der Spanische Meister*) and he tricked the world's biggest collections with very sophisticated forgeries.[18]

Based on data that has been collected by INTERPOL, the number of fakes and forgeries has increased greatly and high-level networks of experts are involved in this activity. In the words of the Coordinator of INTERPOL's Works of Art Unit, Corrado Catesi: 'We are witnessing an alarming increase in the traffic of fake cultural objects from conflict zones.'[19]

According to Maamoun Abdulkarim, former director-general of the Directorate-General of Antiquities and Museums (DGAM) in Syria, between 2014 and 2016, the percentage of fakes and forgeries of seized antiquities in Syria and Lebanon increased from 30 per cent to 70 per cent. Those items included fake ancient Bibles, mosaics and medieval coins.[20]

Furthermore, the head of Scientific Departments at the Directorate-General of Antiquities in Lebanon, Asaad Seif, discussed seized items from Syria. He observed that, although authentic objects were seized as well, most of the seized objects were forged antiquities that came from workshops in Syria that already existed before the war.[21]

Recently, the owner of Sadigh Gallery in New York, was charged with grand larceny and other crimes connected to producing fake antiquities that he passed off as ancient artifacts. In the back rooms of the galley, thousands of items were found including: an

[16] Mackenzie 2005: 255–258.
[17] McGrath 2019: 242.
[18] DW. 2016: Der Spanische Meister. https://www.youtube.com/watch?v=sqMmbNVL5SI
[19] https://www.interpol.int/Crimes/Cultural-heritage-crime/The-issues-cultural-property
[20] Philp 2016. ISIS hoodwinks collectors with fake Syrian artefacts. The Times, Friday August 26. 2016. https://www.thetimes.co.uk/article/isis-hoodwinks-collectors-with-fake-syrian-artefacts-fn3lnmmwp
[21] Press 2017. How Antiquities Have Been Weaponized in the Struggle to Preserve Culture. Hyperallergic. December 7, 2017. https://hyperallergic.com/415471/how-antiquities-have-been-weaponized-in-the-struggle-to-preserve-culture/

11th century ceramic sculpture of a Buddha, objects melded after stolen objects from the Iraqi Museum in 2003, sarcophagus valued at 50000 USD, a cylinder seal valued at 40000 USD as well as tools used for modification of antiquities.[22]

References

Al Khabour, A. 2015. El conflicto armado en Siria y su repercusión sobre el Patrimonio Cultural: Vol. I Deir Ez-Zor. Viewed 30 August 2022. https://www.academia.edu/14885188/El_conflicto_armado_en_Siria_y_su_repercusi%C3%B3n_sobre_el_Patrimonio_Cultural_Vol_II_Inventario_del_Patrimonio_Cultural_afectado_en_la_provincia_de_Raqqa_marzo_2011_mazro_2015_

Artnet. 21 September 2015. UNESCO Head Warns of 'Industrial Scale' Looting in Syria. Viewed 30 August 2022. https://news.artnet.com/art-world/unesco-warning-looting-syria-333814

Bassiouni, M.Ch. 2008. The New Wars and the Crisis of Compliance with the Law of Armed Conflict by Non State Actors. *Journal of Criminal Law and Criminology* Spring 2008, 98(3): 711–810. Viewed 30 August 2022. https://www.jstor.org/stable/40042787

Calvani, S. 2008. Frequency and figures of organized crime in art and antiquities, in S. Monacorda (ed.) *Organized crime in art and antiquities.* Milan: International Scientific and Professional Advisory Council. Viewed 30 August 2022. https://www.obs-traffic.museum/organised-crime-art-and-antiquities

Casana, J. 2015. Satellite Imagery-Based Analysis of Archaeological Looting in Syria. *Near Eastern Archaeology, Special Issue: The Cultural Heritage Crisis in the Middle East* 78(3): 142–152.

DW. 2016. Der Spanische Meister. Viewed 30 August 2022. https://www.youtube.com/watch?v=sqMmbNVL5SI

Evening Standard. 2 July 2015. UN in plea to stop Islamic State's 'industrial scale' looting. Viewed 30 August 2022. https://www.standard.co.uk/news/world/un-in-plea-to-stop-islamic-state-s-industrial-scale-looting-10360530.html

INTERPOL. More than 56,400 cultural goods seized and 67 arrested. Law enforcement and customs authorities from 31 countries participated in Operation Pandora V. Viewed 30 August 2022. https://www.interpol.int/News-and-Events/News/2021/More-than-56-400-cultural-goods-seized-and-67-arrested and https://www.interpol.int/Crimes/Cultural-heritage-crime/The-issues-cultural-property

Keller, A. (2015). *Documenting ISIL's antiquities trafficking: The looting and destruction of Iraqi and Syrian cultural heritage: What we know and what can be done.* US Department of State, 29 September. Viewed 30 August 2022. https://2009-2017.state.gov/e/eb/rls/rm/2015/247610.htm.

Mackenzie, S. 2005. Dig a bit deeper. Law, Regulation and the Illicit Antiquities Market. *British Journal of Criminology,* May 2005, 45(3): 249–268.

Mackenzie, S. 2020. Antiquities Trafficking, in S. Mackenzie (ed.) *Transnational Criminology: Trafficking and Global Criminal Markets:* 105–120. Bristol: Bristol University Press.

[22] The New York Times. 2021. *Dealer Made and Sold Fake Antiquities, Investigators Say.* 10 August 2021. https://www.nytimes.com/2021/08/25/arts/design/fake-antiquities-investigation.html

McGrath, J. F. 2019. Learning from Jesus' Wife: What Does Forgery Have to Do with the Digital Humanities? in Hamidović, D., Clivaz, C. and Savant. S. (eds) *Ancient Manuscripts in Digital Culture*. Published by: Brill. Netherland.

Miñana, M.J. 2017. What measures does the UNESCO Secretariat recommend that member states should implement to prevent illicit trade? What can the UNESCO Secretariat offer in the way of facilitation?, in Nordic Council of Ministers *Illicit Trade in Cultural Artefacts*. Nordic Council of Ministers Annual Conference: Copenhagen. Viewed 30 August 2022. http://norden.diva-portal.org/smash/record.jsf?pid=diva2%3A1095129&dswid=-8464

New York Times. 26 August 2021. Dealer Made and Sold Fake Antiquities, Investigators Say. Viewed 30 August 2022. https://www.nytimes.com/2021/08/25/arts/design/fake-antiquities-investigation.html

Philp, C. 2016. ISIS hoodwinks collectors with fake Syrian artefacts. The Times, Friday August 26. 2016. Viewed 30 August 2022. https://www.thetimes.co.uk/article/isis-hoodwinks-collectors-with-fake-syrian-artefacts-fn3lnmmwp

Press, M. 2017. How Antiquities Have Been Weaponized in the Struggle to Preserve Culture. Hyperallergic. Viewed 30 August 2022. https://hyperallergic.com/415471/how-antiquities-have-been-weaponized-in-the-struggle-to-preserve-culture/

Shelley, L., I. 2020. Illicit Trade and Terrorism. *Perspectives on Terrorism* August 2020, 14(4): 7–20.

Temino, I.R., A. Yanez, S.J. Villar, A.R. Mateo, J.R. Rus, J.S. Alvarez and A.L. Berdonces. 2018. Forensic Archaeometry Applied to Antiquities Trafficking: The Beginnings of an Investigation at the Frontiers of Knowledge. *Arts* 7(4): 98. Viewed 30 August 2022. https://www.mdpi.com/2076-0752/7/4/98

Terrill, W.A. 2017. *Antiquities destruction and illicit sales as sources of ISIS funding and propaganda*. Strategic Studies Institute, US Army War College.

Chapter Seven

Measuring illicit trafficking of cultural properties

In order to measure illicit trafficking of cultural properties in Arab States, it is necessary to assess various matters, such as the political and legislative situation within Arab States; how smuggling networks function; what types of objects there are in the market; what states they come from; what market types there are (auction houses, generalist dealers, specialist dealers, online forums, social networks); how accurately objects are described, in terms of provenance and ownership; what trafficking systems there are; how trafficking processes are accomplished; and what trafficking routes there are.

Tracking illicitly-trafficked cultural properties from the country of origin, through transit countries, to destination countries is a monumental challenge. The international community has created several tools that contribute to this effort. According to the Interpol database, at the time of writing, there were 4929 objects that had been stolen in Arab States and reported to Interpol as stolen or missing (Figure 32, though that number is necessarily far less than the total number of cultural objects that have been stolen in those states). To pick out some of the most notable numbers, Comoros, Djibouti, Mauritania, Oman, Palestine, Qatar, Somalia and United Arab Emirates had reported 0 objects (Map 24). Meanwhile, at the other end of the scale, 514 stolen objects had been registered by Egypt, 1118 by Syria and 2786 by Iraq (Figure 33 and Map 24).

Figure 32. 4,929 stolen objects from the Arab States, reported to the INTERPOL

While the Carabinieri's database, at the time of writing, showed that 3381 objects were recovered by the Carabinieri TPC actions and other 312 objects were identified as from Iraq but still unrecovered (Figure 34).

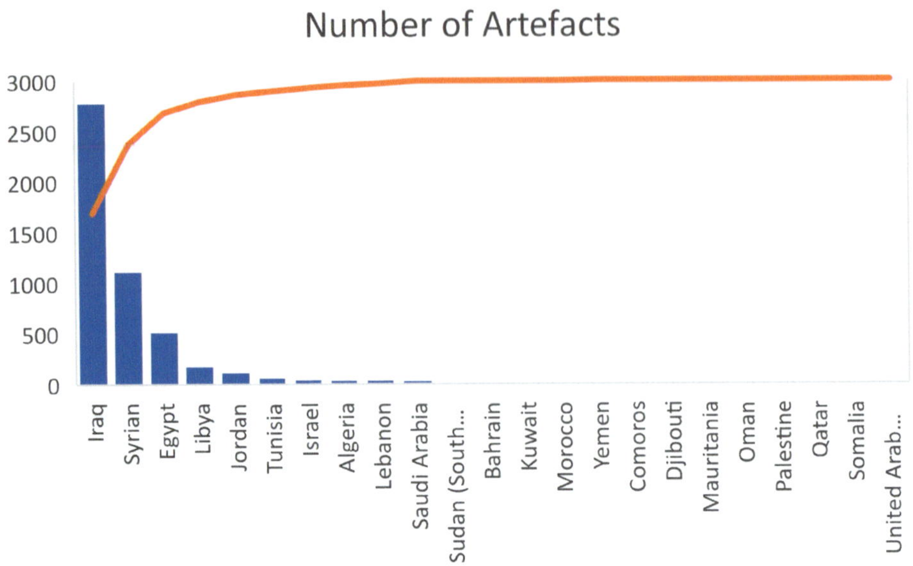

Figure 33. Arab States in accordance with the number of reported stolen objects

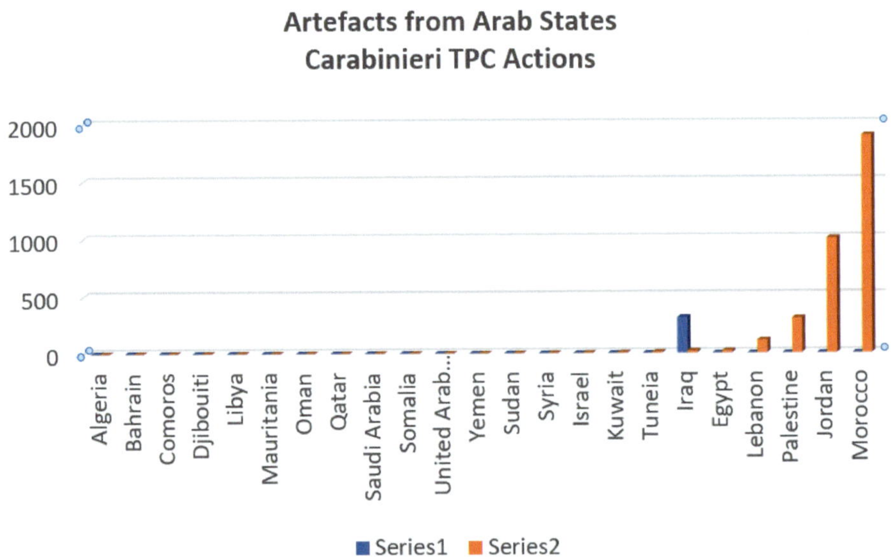

Figure 34. Chart shows artefacts from Arab States: Carabinieri TPC Actions

Objects identified on the market (mostly online) by Carabinieri TPC as of possible illegal origin, and that we signaled to their respective governments. Objects recovered during operations/investigations carried out by Carabinieri TPC.

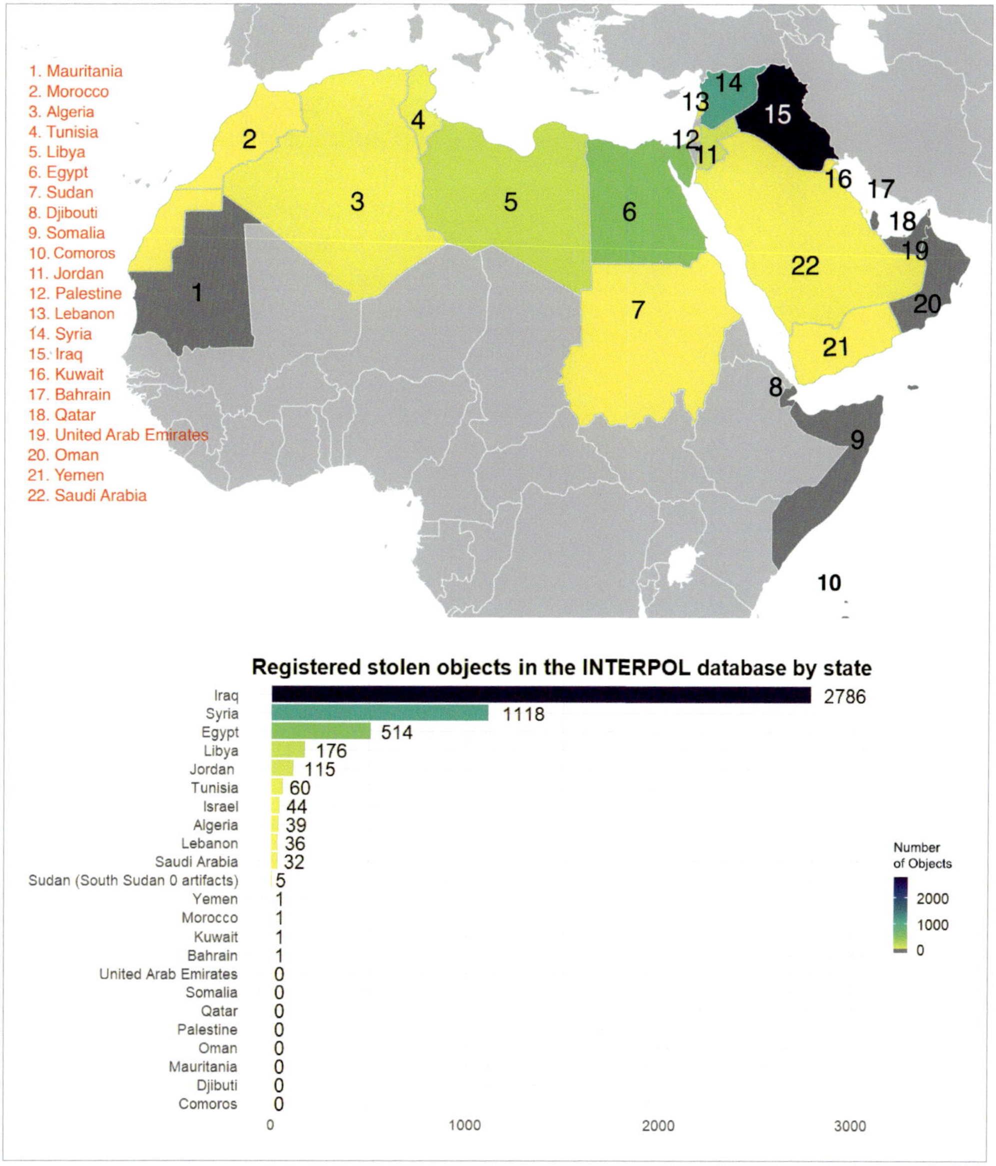

Map 24. States and number of stolen objects

To pick out some of the most notable numbers, Algeria, Bahrain, Comoros, Djibouti, Libya, Mauritania, Oman, Qatar, Saudi Arabia, Somalia, United Arab Emirates and Yemen had reported 0 objects. Meanwhile, 3381 objects had been recovered during the operations carried out by the Carabinieri TPC, from Sudan 1, Syria 1, Israel 2, Kuwait 4, Tunisia 10, Iraq 20, Egypt 21, Lebanon 114, Palestine 305, Jordan 1003 and Morocco 1900 (Table 3).

State	Identified	Recovered
Algeria	0	0
Bahrain	0	0
Comoros	0	0
Djibouiti	0	0
Libya	0	0
Mauritania	0	0
Oman	0	0
Qatar	0	0
Saudi Arabia	0	0
Somalia	0	0
United Arab Emirates	0	0
Yemen	0	0
Sudan	0	1
Syria	0	1
Israel	0	2
Kuwait	0	4
Tunisia	0	10
Iraq	312	20
Egypt	0	21
Lebanon	0	114
Palestine	0	305
Jordan	0	1003
Morocco	0	1900

Table 3. List of artefacts from Arab States: Carabinieri TPC Actions

Both traditional and online art markets can offer a window into the scale of legal and illegal trading in antiquities. For instance, a change in the presence of a category of cultural properties in the market can point to a change in trafficking of cultural properties from its country of origin. In addition, seizures of smuggled antiquities can serve as indicators of smuggling hotspots, trafficking routes and the types of endangered cultural properties that are particularly exposed to looting, theft and forgery.

The Arab Spring and illicit trafficking

During conflicts and other crises, the socio-political context strongly influences the preservation and protection of cultural heritage. For instance, as a result of political unrest in, and the loss of governmental control over, territories in Arab States – such as Tunisia, Libya, Egypt, Syria and Yemen – as well as longer-running conflicts – such as Palestine since 1948, Lebanon between 1975 and 1990 and Iraq since 1990 – members of local communities have been approached by already-existing illicit trafficking networks. These networks tempt the villagers, who lack economic opportunities, to participate in cultural property crime. For this reason, even at times of peace and before Arab Spring, it was common for archaeological and heritage authorities to report the use of (or intention to use) earth-penetrating devices by treasure hunters at many sites within Arab States.

Typology of looted and stolen antiquities

In general terms, paintings and other artworks are not the typical target of theft in Arab States. Smugglers follow the traditional advice on choosing an item for smuggling: it should be '*a portable, concealable and valuable item*'. These items have the advantage of being portable or easy to transport, sometimes in the pocket, and it is difficult to trace them back to the archaeological site where they were extracted. Among the most popular items are small items such as (fake as well as genuine) ancient religious manuscripts and books (like Bibles and Korans), coins and figurines. Antiquities that have been seized in Damascus have included these items, as well as mosaics.

Regionally, there are particular targets in particular zones. For example, in the territory of Mesopotamia that spans both Syria and Iraq, cylinder seals, stamp seals, cuneiform tablets, envelopes, imprints, funerary portraits and small statues are often targeted. In Egypt, papyri, small statues and stamp seals are often targeted. In Morocco, prehistoric objects, lithic artefacts and fossils are the most commonly sought items.

Smugglers typically avoid heavy and large objects. They may even cut statues apart, sell the head and other parts of the body separately or indeed only extract the most portable and most characteristic and so the most valuable parts, such as the head, hands and feet. ICOM has published Red Lists on the most vulnerable objects from the most vulnerable regions.

Smuggling networks

Illicit trafficking may involve tangible objects (humans, narcotics, and antiquities), intangible objects (digital ids and services) and/or money (money laundering, illicit financial flows, tax avoidance informal economies). Each type of crime has its own methods, stages and networks. Between source and market, there are often complex trafficking networks – and smuggling often involves professional networks or organized criminals. So, in order to measure illicit trafficking of cultural properties, we need to understand its networks, stages and routes.

Although these distinctions reflect net flows and some objects move against the dominant flow, there is an international tendency to divide countries in the context of illicit trafficking into three basic groups: source countries, transit countries and market countries.

Source countries, are the start point of the chain. They are characterized by rich heritage and poor or corrupt authorities that struggle to combat looting and theft. Some suffer additional and exacerbating challenges, such as war, conflict and political unrest. Looters are typically opportunists and 'subsistence diggers'.

Transit countries have little robust or corrupt border control, free trade agreements and/or flexible antiquities laws (e.g. the United Arab Emirates and Bulgaria). In these places, items are laundered onto the legal market or transported to market countries. Various countries have been identified as typical transit countries, including Turkey for material from Arab States, Pakistan and post-Soviet states for Central and South Asian antiquities and Belgium for material from West Africa.[1]

Market countries are usually wealthy countries, where the smuggled cultural properties end up in galleries, museums or private collections (e.g. the United States, the United Kingdom and Japan).

Tracing the entire process, from looting until purchase of stolen cultural properties, suggests two additional categories of countries:

Source-market countries: in many cases, source countries are also market countries. For example, in the United States, there is market demand for cultural properties from its indigenous communities. Numerous antiquities laws, in Arab States and other source countries around the world, recognize the right to own and collect antiquities, usually on condition that records are maintained and shared with the state, often on condition that antiquities are not (re)sold.

Source-transit countries: in these countries, looted objects can pass through the hands of local dealers. They constitute grey markets, which legitimize such objects, so that they are ready to be transferred to market countries. Hardy pointed out that looted coins from Bulgaria pass from looters to local collectors and regional market before they end up in market countries.[2] The best example is Israel. According to Israeli antiquities law, dealers are allowed to buy and sell antiquities that were collected before 1978; objects that have been found since then are state property. The Israeli Antiquities Authority (IAA) gives each object an ID number. Yet, often, when the object is sold, the dealers simply transfer the number to a new piece. Burleigh cited the chief of the Theft Prevention Unit of the IAA: '*If they sell an oil lamp, they take the ID number from the one they sold and glue it to another oil lamp that came out of the field last night*'.[3]

Trafficking stages

Campbell studied smuggling networks of cultural properties,[4] applying a criminal network approach and assessing the involvement of fluidly-structured networks and formally-hierarchical groups. In this assessment, the smuggling process is divided into various stages alongside source, transit and destination or market countries. Campbell presents a four-stage structure:

[1] Hardy 2016. http://www.unesco.org/new/fileadmin/MULTIMEDIA/HQ/CLT/pdf/Hardy_2016_UNESCO_antiquities_trafficking_review_materia.pdf.
[2] Ibid.
[3] Burleigh 2008: 20, 60-64
[4] Campbell 2013: 113-153

In the first stage, looting and theft

The first stage comprises the illegal removal of objects, through theft from a museum, collection, religious place or secular place, or through looting in the form of illegal extraction of archaeological deposits. Generally, the acts are undertaken by individuals, although they may be undertaken by groups as well, even, in some cases, by armed groups such as militias. Looters' knowledge is limited to the location of archaeological sites and landscapes. For transport of looted items across national borders, they need early-stage intermediaries.

Networks function through short-term contacts between replaceable individuals, who are linked to each other through mutually beneficial connections with a non-centralised organization. Participants vary from farmers to university-trained antiquities experts. Typically, they are not professional criminals, but rather criminal opportunists, who participate to increase their income. Some of them participate in these networks only once, while others do so repeatedly.[5]

The second stage, transport

Looters sell stolen artifacts to early-stage intermediaries who visit villages or archaeological sites and choose valuable items to transport and sell to higher-level dealers. Low-quality or less marketable items, which are not worth the time of professional middlemen, may be sold in online forums.[6]

Early-stage intermediaries are connected to smuggling networks and border checkpoints that enable access to neighboring countries. Networks in this stage are often more organized and sometimes include criminals who are involved in the smuggling of other goods, such as drugs and arms.

Once objects have crossed the borders of their country of origin, smuggling chains dispatch them to other countries, whose regulations are more flexible, such as Switzerland and the United Arab Emirates, where they can be laundered.

The Third Stage, laundering

Narcotics do not need to be laundered – they can continue the journey to market countries or be consumed where they are. In contrast, cultural objects must be laundered to appear legitimate, in order to be sold in market countries.

The late-stage intermediaries form larger chains of middlemen, antiquities professionals and laundering specialists. They re-evaluate items and facilitate their entry into the gray market through improper transactions. Items get forged

[5] Ibid.
[6] Terrill 2017: 19

provenance documents or fake import-export certificates.[7] In the case of antiquities from conflict zones such as Syria and Iraq, fake papers are issued that indicate different countries of origin.[8] Thus, they get introduced into the licit market and sold to collectors in market countries. It can take years before objects reappear on the licit market at a more opportune time.[9]

The fourth stage, purchasing

Collectors in market countries purchase laundered antiquities, typically knowing that the objects have a dubious provenance, sometimes knowing that the objects have been laundered.[10]

It is worth mentioning that the profits from looted antiquities vary from the first stage to last stage. Brodie assessed the share of the final market price that flowed back to the original looter and found that up to 98 per cent of the money in the trade stayed at the market end. So, typically, looters receive very little, while large sums end up in the pockets of middlemen.[11]

It is worth mentioning the key role of the free ports in the illicit trafficking of cultural properties. Free ports are warehouses located in free zones. Customs' presence is not mandatory in free zones. Any non-EU goods can be introduced there without presentation and declaration to customs, free of import/ export duties and taxes (Articles 158 and 245 of the European Union Customs Code). The cultural goods became common for the storage in free zones including antiquities, art, precious stones...etc. They can be stored, moved, used or exported to their final destination as well as become subject of economic transactions in a high degree of secrecy.[12] However, these artworks may be provided with export papers without inquiring into the circumstances of their import into the country. Given the proximity of Hong Kong to China, looted antiquities from China have been smuggled easily into Hong Kong for many years. International purchasers can buy looted antiquities and the dealers will arrange to transport the objects to where they will be entered with documents showing their authorized export from Hong Kong, covering up their looted origins[13]. Brodie stated that the Swiss police seized 10000 antiquities from four warehouses in Geneva Free port that belonged to an Italian antiquities dealer.[14]

[7] Hardy 2016
[8] Terrill 2017: 20
[9] Campbell 2013
[10] Ibid.
[11] Brodie 1998: 7–9. https://traffickingculture.org/publications/brodie-n-1998-pity-the-poor-middlemen-culture-without-context-3-7-9/
[12] https://www.lexology.com/library/detail.aspx?g=e5e21b63-1e68-4d24-a30e-550045c3574d
[13] Mackenzie 2020: 111
[14] Brodie and Renfrew 2005. https://www.researchgate.net/publication/234147856_Looting_and_the_world's_archaeological_heritage_The_inadequate_response

Trafficking stages			
Stealing	Transporting	Laundering	Purchasing
Looters	Early-Stage Middleman	Late-Stage Middleman	Collectors

Table 4. The four stages of antiquities trafficking (inspired by Campbell 2013)

Museums and stolen antiquities

Over the course of decades, several museums in Arab States have been plundered and otherwise damaged. The National Museum of Beirut became a battlefield during the Lebanese Civil War (1975-1990). Due to the tactical benefit of its high vantage point, militias fought to occupy it.[15] Although the situation of museums in **Lebanon** has improved, there are still incidents. In 2013, the Museum of Byblos was burgled.[16]

Following the Iraqi occupation of **Kuwait** in 1990-1991, the Kuwaiti National Museum was plundered, and around 40000 objects were transferred to Baghdad, while 200 were damaged and 60 went missing. UNESCO asked Iraq to return the stolen objects, in accordance with the Hague Convention of 1954, then United Nations Resolution 687 of 1991 obliged it to do so.[17]

In April 1991, after the fall of Baghdad, the **Iraq** Museum was tragically looted and many artifacts remain missing.[18] Such activity increased in recent years, especially after ISIS looted various museums, including Mosul Museum in 2015.[19]

Museums have not only been targeted at times of armed conflict. Various assaults on museums in Arab States have been recorded.

Following the outbreak of the Arab Spring in 2011, museums suffered attacks on their collections. In **Egypt**, during the uprising of 2011, more than 50 objects were stolen from the Egyptian Museum on Tahrir Square.[20] As UNESCO confirmed, during unrest in 2013, the Mallawi National Museum in Minya, Egypt was looted and almost the entire collection disappeared.[21] As observed by the Minister of Antiquities, in 2014,

[15] Yan 2018. https://deeply.thenewhumanitarian.org/peacebuilding/articles/2018/07/18/saga-of-beit-beirut-a-museum-struggles-to-remember-civil-war

[16] https://al-akhbar.com/Community/47984

[17] Bloom and Gould 2000. https://archive.aramcoworld.com/issue/200005/patient.restoration-the.kuwait.national.museum.htm

[18] Cordoba 2000. https://www.obs-traffic.museum/iraq-museum-and-other-assaults-brief-news-about-plundering-iraqi-museums-and-systematic-looting

[19] UN 2015. https://news.un.org/en/story/2015/02/492082-iraq-unesco-outraged-over-terrorist-attack-against-mosul-museum

[20] https://tinyurl.com/epaw8tpj

[21] https://en.unesco.org/news/unesco-mission-confirms-plunder-mallawi-museum

the Islamic Art Museum in Cairo was 'completely destroyed' (practically wrecked) by a car bomb.[22]

In **Syria**, already in the early years of the war, various museums and warehouses were pillaged, such as Heraqla Warehouse, Raqqa Museum, the Citadel of Jaabar, the Museum of Hama, the Museum of Folklore in Aleppo and Maarrat Museum.[23] These included Palmyra Museum, which was pillaged by ISIS.[24] Besides theft, museums have also fallen victim to bombing and destruction by all of the parties to the conflict, like Raqqa Museum, which was bombarded by the Syrian Arab Air Force.[25]

Libya also suffered thefts from its collections, such as the Benghazi Treasure, from which 364 gold coins, 2433 silver pieces and 4,484 bronze pieces were stolen; the Bani Walid Museum, from which 113 artifacts were stolen; and the Sousse Museum, from which five pieces of pottery were stolen. Other plundered institutions included Tocra Museum, Shahat Museum, the Red Saraya Museum, Misurata Museum, Tolmitha Museum[26] and Sbratha Classical Museum.[27]

In **Tunisia**, in 2013, a statue dating back to the fifth century was stolen from the Museum of Early Christian Art in Carthage.[28]

In **Yemen**, many artifacts were stolen from Mukalla Museum in the city of Mukalla and the Archeology Museum in Aden. Numerous other museums have been victims of theft, including the Museum of Archeology in Zanzibar[29] and the Museum of Taez.[30]

Museums have been targeted in **Algeria** as well. In 2019, the Ministry of Culture confirmed that the National Museum of Antiquities and Islamic Arts had been vandalized and looted during protests against presidential candidate Abdelaziz Bouteflika.[31]

In **Morocco**, among others, the Al-Abriz Museum in Rabat was burgled.[32] In **Sudan**, the Museum of Gebel Bargal was plundered at least 10 times.[33]

In **Saudi Arabia**, in 2015, a private museum of archaeological and historical artifacts, in the city of Rijal Alma was burgled and 1000 artefacts were estimated to have been

[22] https://egyptianstreets.com/2014/01/24/historic-islamic-art-museum-completely-destroyed/
[23] UNESCO. http://www.unesco.org/new/en/safeguarding-syrian-cultural-heritage/situation-in-syria/movable-heritage/museums/
[24] Unesco. https://en.unesco.org/courier/october-december-2017/curbing-spoils-war
[25] Al Khabour 2019
[26] https://tinyurl.com/2du8yj2b
[27] https://tinyurl.com/57p9v4af
[28] https://tinyurl.com/2pwznrbh
[29] https://tinyurl.com/365czvuu
[30] https://www.france24.com/en/20200724-bombed-and-looted-yemen-battles-to-save-its-heritage
[31] https://tinyurl.com/2ju7e7dc
[32] https://assahraa.ma/journal/2009/96918
[33] https://tinyurl.com/5esze4cy

stolen. Similarly, in 2019, a Turkish citizen tried to steal antiques from a museum near the Two Holy Mosques in Mecca.[34]

In **Palestine**, in 2016, the Palestinian Heritage Museum in Nazareth was burgled and various artefacts were stolen.[35] Naturally, such thefts were committed long before the Arab Spring. For instance, in **Israel**, in 1983, the L.A. Mayer Museum of Islamic Art in Jerusalem was burgled and 100 historic clocks and watches were stolen from its 200-piece collection.[36]

The response of Arab States to protect their museums has been insufficient. Generally, national museums in the capitals have better security than regional museums in other cities, towns and villages. There is a shortage of academic staff, guards and warehouses; and the staff are not qualified in accordance with international standards that have been established by ICOM.

Some States have tried to safeguard their museums. For example, according to the Director-General of the Directorate-General of Antiquities and Museums, in 2014, Syria emptied 29 of the 34 archaeological museums and transferred their contents to Damascus; approximately 30000 items were transferred by military planes from Deir ez-Zor to Damascus; and 24000 items were transferred from Aleppo Museum to Damascus. The DGAM hid provincial museums' items in secret locations.[37]

In most of the Arab States, in general, museums suffer shortages of human and financial resources, which affect their productivity and effectiveness as educational institutions. They lack good documentation, inventory lists, and effective systems to control humidity and light in vitrines and warehouses. Furthermore, conflicts and other crises make museums more vulnerable to theft and vandalism.

Tools and databases of stolen and missing cultural properties

Several international organizations have created databases of stolen and missing cultural properties and other tools to assist in the fight against illicit trafficking. Some of them are open to the public, while others require any user to have an account or other authorization. There are several prominent examples.

INTERPOL database

The International Criminal Police Organization (INTERPOL) has a database of stolen and missing works of art. It contains descriptions and images of more than 52000 items.

[34] https://tinyurl.com/ms48huae
[35] https://www.bokra.net/Article-1357627
[36] https://www.reuters.com/article/uk-israel-clocks-idUKL1260470920071112
[37] https://tinyurl.com/49fh9ape

Only authorized entities such as national police agencies, UNESCO, ICOM and ICCROM can provide data for Interpol to add to the database. Objects are only added to the database if they are fully identifiable.[38]

INTERPOL has also launched an app called ID-Art to provide access to the database. Using this app, Italy's Carabinieri Headquarters for the Protection of Cultural Heritage has identified two stolen statues and the Netherlands has identified two stolen paintings.[39]

ICOM Red Lists

The International Council of Museums (ICOM) publishes Red Lists of Cultural Objects at Risk and maintains a publicly-accessible database online. These Red Lists identify various categories of particularly vulnerable archaeological objects and works of art, to assist in the prevention of illegal trading and illegal export. These Red Lists include

INTERPOL

ID-ART EXTRACTO DE LA BASE DE DATOS DE INTERPOL SOBRE OBRAS DE ARTE ROBADAS

CARACTERÍSTICAS:

Título	GOD OF HATRA
Artista	-
Tipo de objeto	Escultura/estatua > Un personaje > Torso
Periodo	-
Medio	Escultura/estatua > Relieve/bajo relieve
Material	Marmol Piedra
Forma	Irregular
Descripción	Aureola

Figure 35. ID-ART, INTERPOL

[38] https://www.interpol.int/Crimes/Cultural-heritage-crime/Stolen-Works-of-Art-Database

[39] https://www.interpol.int/News-and-Events/News/2021/INTERPOL-launches-app-to-better-protect-cultural-heritage

Arab States that have suffered exceptional political unrest and armed conflict: Yemen, Egypt, Syria, Iraq and Libya.[40] Similarly, ICOM has published other tools to combat illicit trafficking, such as the series of publications of '100 Missing Objects', as well as the Code of Ethics for Museums.

Object ID

It was developed by the UNESCO, INTERPOL and the Paul Getty Trust. It is an international standard that facilitates the recovery of cultural objects in case of loss, theft and illicit export. It consists of the main characteristics of an object – measurements, material and distinguishing features – and images for identification. Object ID is used by specialists and non-specialists, such as agents of police authorities and custom services. It has been translated into 17 languages (Figure 34).[41]

UNESCO-WCO Model Export Certificate

The Model Export Certificate for Cultural Objects was jointly prepared by UNESCO and the World Customs Organization (WCO), with the aim of fighting illicit trafficking of cultural properties and identifying and tracing cultural objects. It is a recommended standard and facilitates the work of customs officials.[42]

UNESCO List of National Cultural Heritage Laws

UNESCO records a wide range of national heritage laws from different regions. These laws are divided into various categories: Armed Conflict, Cultural Diversity, Immovable Cultural Heritage, Intangible Cultural Heritage, Movable Cultural Heritage-Cultural Property, Natural Heritage and Underwater Cultural Heritage.[43]

WCO ARCHEO

Archeo is an electronic information exchange platform, which was designed by the World Customs Organization to bring law enforcement agents and cultural heritage professionals together, in order to facilitate the identification of suspect items.[44]

Carabinieri database

The Carabinieri Headquarters for the Protection of Cultural Heritage (*Comando Carabinieri Tutela Patrimonio Culturale - TPC*) was instituted in 1969. Since the 1980s, the

[40] https://icom.museum/en/our-actions/heritage-protection/red-lists/
[41] https://www.interpol.int/Crimes/Cultural-heritage-crime/Object-ID
[42] http://www.unesco.org/new/en/culture/themes/illicit-traffic-of-cultural-property/legal-and-practical-instruments/unesco-wco-model-export-certificate/
[43] https://en.unesco.org/cultnatlaws/list
[44] http://www.wcoomd.org/en/topics/enforcement-and-compliance/activities-and-programmes/cultural-heritage-programme.aspx

TPC has been using a sophisticated 'database of illegally removed cultural artefacts' to facilitate its work.[45]

References

Al Akhbar. 19 March 2013. Jubail Museum. Viewed 30 August 2022. https://al-akhbar.com/Community/47984

Al Arab. 11 November 2013. Theft from a Tunisian museum. Viewed 30 August 2022. https://tinyurl.com/2pwznrbh

Al Jamal. 13 June 2013. Museums in Yemen. Viewed 30 August 2022. https://tinyurl.com/365czvuu

Al Khaleej online Net. 9 March 2019. Theft in Museums in Algeria. Viewed 30 August 2022. https://tinyurl.com/2ju7e7dc

Al Jazeera Net. 24 July 2019. Libyan antiquities in conflict. Viewed 30 August 2022. https://tinyurl.com/2du8yj2b

Al Khabour, A. 2019. El patrimonio cultural en Siria e Iraq: Desafíos y esperanzas. *Isimu,* Vol. 22. Viewed 30 August 2022. *https://www.academia.edu/41350973/EL_PATRIMONIO_CULTURAL_EN_SIRIA_E_IRAQ_DESAF%C3%8DOS_Y_ESPERANZAS*

Assahraa. 20 November 2009. Theft in Morocco. Viewed 30 August 2022. https://assahraa.ma/journal/2009/96918

Bloom, J., and L.E. Gould. 2000. The Kuwait National Museum. *Saudi Aramco World*, 51(5): 10–21. Viewed 30 August 2022. https://archive.aramcoworld.com/issue/200005/patient.restoration-the.kuwait.national.museum.htm

Bokra Net. 23 December 2016. Theft in Palestinian museum. Viewed 30 August 2022. https://www.bokra.net/Article-1357627

Brodie, N. 1998. Pity the poor middlemen. *Culture Without Context* 3: 7-9. Viewed 30 August 2022. *https://traffickingculture.org/publications/brodie-n-1998-pity-the-poor-middlemen-culture-without-context-3-7-9/*

Brodie, N. and C. Renfrew. 2005. Looting and the world's archaeological heritage: The inadequate response. *Annual Review of Anthropology* 34(1): 343–361. Viewed 30 August 2022. https://www.researchgate.net/publication/234147856_Looting_and_the_world's_archaeological_heritage_The_inadequate_response

Burleigh, N. 2008. Collecting Pieces of God. *Archaeology*, November/December 2008, 61(6): 20, 60–64. Viewed 30 August 2022. https://tinyurl.com/5h2ddu4a

Calvani, S. 2008. Frequency and figures of organized crime in art and antiquities, in S. Monacorda (ed.) *Organized crime in art and antiquities.* Milan: International Scientific and Professional Advisory Council. Viewed 30 August 2022. https://www.obs-traffic.museum/organised-crime-art-and-antiquities

Campbell, P. 2013. The Illicit Antiquities Trade as a Transnational Criminal Network: Characterizing and Anticipating Trafficking of Cultural Heritage. *International Journal of Cultural Property* 20(2): 113-153.

Cordoba, J.M. 2000. On the Iraq Museum and Other Assaults Brief News about the Plundering of Iraqi Museums and the Systematic Looting of Iraqi Archaeological Heritage. *Isimu* III: 15–46. Viewed 30 August 2022. https://www.obs-traffic.

[45] http://www.carabinieri.it/multilingua/en/the-carabinieri-tpc

museum/iraq-museum-and-other-assaults-brief-news-about-plundering-iraqi-museums-and-systematic-looting

Egyptian Streets. 24 January 2014. Historic Islamic Art Museum 'Completely Destroyed'. Viewed 30 August 2022. https://egyptianstreets.com/2014/01/24/historic-islamic-art-museum-completely-destroyed/

France 24. 24 July 2020. Bombed and looted: Yemen battles to save its heritage. Viewed 30 August 2022. https://www.france24.com/en/20200724-bombed-and-looted-yemen-battles-to-save-its-heritage

Hafryat. 5 March 2018. ISIS in Syria. Viewed 30 August 2022. https://tinyurl.com/49fh9ape

Hardy, S.A. 2016. Illicit trafficking, provenance research and due diligence: The state of the art. Paris: UNESCO. Viewed 30 August 2022. https://archaeologicalethics.org/blog/illicit-trafficking-provenance-research-and-due-diligence-and-confidence-and-risk-conflict-antiquities/

ICOM. The ICOM Red Lists of Cultural Objects at Risk are practical tools to curb the illegal traffic of cultural objects. Viewed 30 August 2022. https://icom.museum/en/our-actions/heritage-protection/red-lists

INTERPOL. Stolen Works of Art Database. Viewed 30 August 2022. https://www.interpol.int/Crimes/Cultural-heritage-crime/Stolen-Works-of-Art-Database

INTERPOL. INTERPOL launches app to better protect cultural heritage. Viewed 30 August 2022. https://www.interpol.int/News-and-Events/News/2021/INTERPOL-launches-app-to-better-protect-cultural-heritage

INTERPOL. Object ID. Viewed 30 August 2022. https://www.interpol.int/Crimes/Cultural-heritage-crime/Object-ID

Mackenzie, S: 2020: Antiquities Trafficking. *Transnational Criminology: Trafficking and Global Criminal Markets*: 105-120. Published by: Bristol University Press. (2020).

Resalnews. 20 May 2021. Looting antiquities in Sudan. Viewed 30 August 2022. https://tinyurl.com/5esze4cy

Reuters. 12 November 2007. Israeli museum recovers stolen antique clocks. Viewed 30 August 2022. https://www.reuters.com/article/uk-israel-clocks-idUKL1260470920071112

RT Arabic. 18 July 2019. Looted objects from Cairo. Viewed 30 August 2022. https://tinyurl.com/epaw8tpj

RT Arabic. 11 November 2019. Turkish thief. Viewed 30 August 2022. https://tinyurl.com/ms48huae

Shorouk News. 27 February 2013. Theft of Libyan objects. Viewed 30 August 2022. https://tinyurl.com/57p9v4af

Terrill, W.A. 2017. *Antiquities destruction and illicit sales as sources of ISIS funding and propaganda.* Strategic Studies Institute, US Army War College.

The Carabinieri. Viewed 30 August 2022. www.carabinieri.it

UNESCO. UNESCO mission confirms plunder of Mallawi Museum. Viewed 30 August 2022. https://en.unesco.org/news/unesco-mission-confirms-plunder-mallawi-museum

UNESCO. Looting of museums and warehouses in Syria. Viewed 30 August 2022. https://www.unesco.org/en/node/66281

UNESCO. Curbing the spoils of war. Viewed 30 August 2022. https://en.unesco.org/courier/october-december-2017/curbing-spoils-war

UNESCO. UNESCO - WCO Model Export Certificate. Viewed 30 August 2022. http://www.wcoomd.org/-/media/wco/public/global/pdf/topics/enforcement-and-compliance/activities-and-programmes/cultural-heritage/model-export-certificate_-unseco_wco.pdf?la=en

UNESCO. List of National Cultural Heritage Laws. Viewed 30 August 2022. https://en.unesco.org/cultnatlaws/list

United Nations. 26 February 2015. Iraq: UNESCO outraged over terrorist attack against Mosul Museum. Viewed 30 August 2022. https://news.un.org/en/story/2015/02/492082-iraq-unesco-outraged-over-terrorist-attack-against-mosul-museum

World Customs Organization (WCO). Cultural Heritage Programme. Viewed 30 August 2022. http://www.wcoomd.org/en/topics/enforcement-and-compliance/activities-and-programmes/cultural-heritage-programme.aspx

Yan, V. 2018. Saga of Beit Beirut, A museum struggles to remember civil war. Published by: The New Humanitarian. Peacebuilding Deeply. Viewed 30 August 2022. https://deeply.thenewhumanitarian.org/peacebuilding/articles/2018/07/18/saga-of-beit-beirut-a-museum-struggles-to-remember-civil-war

Chapter Eight

Arab States and the international conventions on combating illicit trafficking of cultural properties

Legislative Context

After the Second World War, cultural properties suffered various types of destruction, appropriation and looting. The international community's response to the removal and illegal export of cultural properties, its effort to combat trafficking of cultural properties, was structured through two important treaties:

First, the **1954 Hague Convention** for the Protection of Cultural Property in the Event of Armed Conflict – with its First Protocol in 1954 and its Second Protocol in 1999 – was completely dedicated to cultural properties displaced by war, revolution and rebellion and became a successful instrument of humanitarian law. Safeguarding cultural properties and avoiding the exposure of heritage to destruction or damage was prioritized.[1] Second, the **1970 UNESCO Convention** on the Means of Prohibiting and Preventing the Illicit Import, Export and Transfer of Ownership of Cultural Property addressed cultural properties that were stolen from museums, religious or secular public monuments or institutions during peacetime as well as during armed conflict.

The 1970 Convention focused on three needs:

1. **Prevention:** To fight against illicit trafficking of cultural properties by creating accurate inventories; establishing export certification; controlling trade; applying sanctions; and educating the local population about the importance of their heritage.
2. **Restitution**: To secure the return of objects that have been stolen from a museum, public monument, religious monument or similar institution, by guiding States Parties to undertake appropriate measures to seize and return any cultural property that has been stolen and/or illegally exported from another State Party.
3. **International cooperation**: To strengthen international cooperation between States Parties such as by negotiating bilateral treaties and by controlling the export, import and international trade of cultural property, in order to be more effective in the fight against the illicit trafficking of cultural property.

[1] http://www.unesco.org/new/en/culture/themes/armed-conflict-and-heritage/convention-and-protocols/1954-hague-convention/

Through this Convention, items that had been documented before they were stolen were meaningfully protected, but ones that had been stolen through illegal excavation and therefore lacked documentation to prove their origins were still exceptionally vulnerable.[2] For such cases of return or restitution of objects that had been stolen from private property or coming from illicit excavations, Article 9 encouraged bilateral negotiations between States.

Other organizations, conventions, regulations and resolutions have been established to address the issue of illicit trafficking of cultural properties. These include:

The **Intergovernmental Committee for the Promotion of the Return of Cultural Property to their Country of Origin or its Restitution in the Event of Illegal Appropriation (ICPRCP)** 'was established by Resolution 20 C4 / 7.6 / 5 of the 20th session of the Conference General of UNESCO in 1978 as a permanent intergovernmental body'.[3] It addressed the return or restitution of pillaged or lost cultural property, in particular for those cases that had occurred before the entry into force of the 1970 Convention.

World natural and cultural heritage is protected under the **1972 UNESCO Convention.**[4]

The United Nations aimed to strengthen cooperation in combating illicit trafficking of movable cultural properties through the **1990 Model Treaty for the Prevention of Crimes that Infringe on the Cultural Heritage of Peoples in the Form of Movable Property.**[5]

Since UNESCO asked the International Institute for the Unification of Private Law (UNIDROIT) to study private law questions that are not directly dealt with by the 1970 Convention, that Convention has been supplemented by the **1995 UNIDROIT Convention on Stolen or Illegally Exported Cultural Objects.** The concepts of *Due Diligence* and *Bona Fide (Good Faith)* were the foundations of its efforts to achieve the restitution of stolen or illegally exported items.[6]

It is worth mentioning UNESCO and UNIDROIT's **Model Provisions on State Ownership of Undiscovered Cultural Objects** of 2011. They aim to assist domestic legislative bodies to recognize the State's ownership of undiscovered cultural objects, thereby also to facilitate restitution.[7]

2 https://en.unesco.org/fighttrafficking/1970
3 https://en.unesco.org/fighttrafficking/icprcp
4 https://whc.unesco.org/en/conventiontext/
5 https://www.unodc.org/documents/treaties/organized_crime/Model_Treaty.pdf
6 https://www.unidroit.org/about-unidroit/overview/
7 https://unidroit.org/english/documents/2012/study70a/s-70a-intro-ef.pdf

The United Nations' **2000 Palermo Convention against Transnational Organized Crime**, adopted by General Assembly Resolution 55/25 on 15 November 2000,[8] addressed organized crime and money laundering and their connection to illicit trafficking of cultural properties,[9] while the **2001 UNESCO Convention on the Protection of the Underwater Cultural Heritage** was established to enable States to better protect their submerged cultural heritage.[10] The **Council of Europe Convention on Offences relating to Cultural Property** was adopted on 3 May 2017 (Council of Europe Treaty Series No. 221) and addressed the destruction and illicit trafficking of cultural properties.[11]

Not only UNESCO, but also the United Nations General Assembly, is concerned with the issue of return or restitution of cultural property to the country of origin. Since 1972, many resolutions on the **Protection and the Return of Cultural Property** have been adopted, as part of the Preservation and Further Development of Cultural Values.[12]

In cooperation with UNESCO, the United Nations' Department of Economic and Social Affairs drove relevant recommendations on protection against trafficking in cultural property, such as **ECOSOC Resolution 2008/23 on Protection against Trafficking in Cultural Property** on 24 July 2008, which emphasized the significance of cultural property to the heritage of humankind.[13]

The UN Security Council has targeted the destruction and illicit trafficking of cultural property with numerous resolutions.[14] UNESCO has developed initiatives to safeguard cultural heritage, based on United Nations Security Council **Resolutions 2199 (2015), 2214 (2015), 2253 (2015) and 2266 (2016)**,[15] with a particular focus on conflict zones in the Arab Region: Yemen, Libya, Syria and Iraq. In 2017, the United Nations Security Council adopted **Resolution 2347**, which established the protection of cultural heritage as a major security issue.[16]

Notably, as Canada did in 1985 with regard to **import into Canada** of cultural property that has been illegally exported from foreign states,[17] Germany recently adopted new legislation, the **2016 revision of the Act to Protect Cultural Property**, which

---

8 https://www.unodc.org/unodc/en/organized-crime/intro/UNTOC.html
9 https://www.unodc.org/unodc/en/organized-crime/intro/UNTOC.html
10 https://en.unesco.org/underwater-heritage/2001
11 https://www.coe.int/en/web/culture-and-heritage/convention-on-offences-relating-to-cultural-property
12 https://en.unesco.org/fighttrafficking/icprcp
13 https://www.un.org/development/desa/dspd/un-resolutions-on-ecosoc-2008.html
14 Resolutions 1267 (1999), 1373 (2001), 1483 (2003), 1546 (2004), 2056 (2012), 2071 (2012), 2085 (2012), 2100 (2013), 2139 (2014), 2170 (2014), 2195 (2014), 2199 (2015), 2249 (2015), 2253 (2015) and 2322 (2016), 2347 (2017) and 2462 (2019) as well as its Presidential Statement S/PRST/2012/26.
15 https://unesdoc.unesco.org/ark:/48223/pf0000244857
16 https://en.unesco.org/news/unesco-and-european-union-join-forces-lawyers-police-and-customs-officers-curb-illicit
17 *https://laws-lois.justice.gc.ca/eng/acts/C-51/page-1.html#h-138693*

consists of four major pillars: (1) import and export provisions; (2) provisions for the return of cultural property; (3) due diligence provisions in dealing with cultural property; and (4) penal sanctions.[18]

Recently, too, **EU Import Regulation (EU) 2019/880**, on the introduction and import of cultural goods, was developed by the EU Commission, the EU Council, and the European Parliament; was passed by the European Parliament of the Council on 17 April 2019; and entered into force on 28 June 2019. The Regulation is binding on all EU countries and unifies and strengthens the protection of cultural property from non-EU States against being trafficked into the EU.[19]

National-level antiquities laws in the Arab Region

Historical context: Most states in the Arab Region were territories of the Ottoman Empire for four centuries (1516-1918) and were regulated by Islamic law until 1869. The Antiquities **Law of 1869** (*Asar-I Antika Nizamnamesi* 1869) permitted trade in antiquities within Ottoman territory and prohibited export of antiquities. The **Law of 1874** prohibited excavations for antiquities without permission from the Ministry of Education and regulated the partition of antiquities: it gave one-third to the State, one-third to the landowner and one-third to the finder; illegally-excavated antiquities were seized by the state. The **Law of 1884** declared the Ottoman State to be the sole owner of antiquities and prohibited sale or transfer of antiquities that were found anywhere within the Ottoman Empire. Furthermore, the division of finds changed to give half to the State and half to the landowner. According to the **Law of 1906**, all antiquities that were found on public or private lands were state property and their removal from the country was prohibited.[20]

After the dissolution of the Ottoman Empire, most Arab States were subject to a transitional period of colonial rule before they gained their independence. In terms of antiquities regulations, the region's states have predictably taken different paths.

Arab States and the 1970 UNESCO Convention

There have been few efforts to standardize legislations in Arab States with the aim of protecting cultural properties. Primarily, there was the Standardized Law on Antiquities, which was itself only a proposal, never a law. It was presented by the Arab League Educational, Cultural and Scientific Organization (ALECSO). There was also the Model Law for the Protection of Writings of the Islamic Arab tradition, which was only a draft.[21]

---

[18] Peters 2019

[19] *https://eur-lex.europa.eu/legal-content/EN/TXT/PDF/?uri=CELEX:32019R0880&from=EN*

[20] Al Khabour 2018: 2–4. https://www.uco.es/ucopress/ojs/index.php/astarte/article/view/11480

[21] Irsheid 1997

This report builds on research that was published in 2012 by Ridha Fraoua, a Doctor of Law and expert in cultural heritage legislation (named the 2012 research in advance within this text).[22] He examined 17 Arab States in the framework of illicit trafficking of cultural properties and the implementation of the 1970 UNESCO Convention to combat illicit trafficking of cultural properties. Data on the legislation of Arab States has been collected from international bodies and national institutions – among other sources, the websites of ministries of culture, ministries of the interior and ministries of justice.

Due to discrepancies in laws on the protection of cultural heritage from one federation to the other in the United Arab Emirates, the 2012 study examined the legislation of the Emirate of Sharjah. In order to supplement the previous detailed study, this report has followed the same structure and further covered 3 of the 5 other Arab States – Kuwait, Libya, and Qatar. Somalia[23] and Djibouti do not have antiquities laws. Furthermore, a review of the latest changes and updates to the laws of the examined Arab States was conducted, in order to synthesize information on the situation of heritage sites and objects in relation to national laws, the 1970 Convention and the 1995 UNIDROIT Convention. The consulted antiquities laws of the examined Arab States are enclosed in Appendix 2. The 20 States in question have been examined with an eye to the twelve points that were addressed by the 2012 study. Some points are mentioned only briefly, as there have been no significant changes since 2012 and the 3 added States did not differ in responding to these points. Other points have been discussed in more detail, as there have been more significant changes in that time.

Implementation of and accession to international conventions

Arab States have varied in their responses to international efforts to strengthen the international framework of treaties and conventions on the return of stolen or illegally-exported cultural properties. These different responses are reflected in implementation and accession to the three international conventions dedicated to the fight against illicit trafficking of cultural properties. For example, Kuwait ratified the 1970 UNESCO Convention as early as 1972, while Yemen ratified it in 2019 (Table 5).[24] Only three Arab States have acceded to the 1995 UNIDROIT Convention (Table 6)[25] and recently, on 3 August 2022, Morocco has ratified the 1995 Convention, it will

[22] Fraoua 2012. http://www.unesco.org/new/fileadmin/MULTIMEDIA/HQ/CLT/pdf/Fraoua_en.pdf

[23] Dr. Sada Mire, former Head of Somaliland Archaeology, confirmed me in personal communication that Somalia faces the challenges of lacks a legislative framework and legal measures. A preliminary Somaliland Archaeological Policy has been drafted by Somaliland Archaeology and the Ministry of Tourism and Culture and agreed with the Somaliland Parliament and the President. Currently, they are working on the recognition of international legislation for world heritage by the Somaliland government as well as national antiquities laws.

[24] They Are: Algeria, Djibouti, Egypt, Iraq, Jordan, Kuwait, Lebanon, Libya, Morocco, Oman, Palestine, Qatar, Saudi Arabia, Syria, Tunisia, United Arab Emirates and Yemen. https://treaties.un.org/pages/showDetails.aspx?objid=08000002801170ec

[25] Three Arab States are parties to the Convention, namely: Algeria 2015, Tunisia 2017 and Syria 2018. https://www.unidroit.org/about-unidroit/membership-old/

Participant	Action	Date of Notification/Deposit	Date of Effect
Algeria	Ratification	24/06/1974	24/09/1974
Djibouti	Ratification	09/04/2018	09/07/2018
Egypt	Acceptance	05/04/1973	05/07/1973
Iraq	Acceptance	12/02/1973	12/05/1973
Jordan	Ratification	15/03/1974	15/06/1974
Kuwait	Acceptance	22/06/1972	22/09/1972
Lebanon	Ratification	25/08/1992	25/11/1992
Libya	Ratification	09/01/1973	09/04/1973
Morocco	Ratification	Ratification	03/05/2003
Oman	Acceptance	02/06/1978	02/09/1978
Palestine	Ratification	22/03/2012	22/06/2012
Qatar	Acceptance	20/04/1977	20/07/1977
Saudi Arabia	Acceptance	08/09/1976	08/12/1976
Syria	Acceptance	21/02/1975	21/05/1975
Tunisia	Ratification	10/03/1975	10/06/1975
United Arab Emirates	Ratification	09/10/2017	09/01/2018
Yemen	Ratification	03/06/2019	03/09/2019

Table 5. The UNESCO Convention on the means of prohibiting and preventing the illicit import, export and transfer of ownership of cultural property[28]

STATE	SIGNATURE	ENTRY INTO FORCE
Algeria	09-04-2015	01-10-2015
Syria	27-04-2018	01-10-2018
Tunisia	02-03-2017	01-09-2017

Table 6. UNIDROIT Convention on stolen or illegally exported cultural objects[29]

enter into force for Morocco on 1 February 2023.[26] Ratification of the 1954 Hague Convention for the Protection of Cultural Property in the Event of Armed Conflict and its two Protocols (1954 and 1999) has varied likewise (Table 7).[27]

Bilateral and multilateral conventions among Arab States are still limited and the role of the Arab League and the Arab League Educational, Cultural and Scientific

[26] https://www.unidroit.org/morocco-accedes-to-the-1995-unidroit-convention-on-stolen-or-illegally-exported-cultural-objects/

[27] **Member States are 19:** Algeria, Bahrain, Egypt, Iraq, Jordan, Kuwait, Lebanon, Libya, Mauritania, Morocco, Oman, Palestine, Qatar, Saudi Arabia, Sudan, Syria, Tunisia, United Arab Emirates and Yemen. https://en.unesco.org/protecting-heritage/convention-and-protocols/1954-convention

1954 Protocol are 16: Bahrain, Egypt, Iraq, Jordan, Kuwait, Lebanon, Libya, Morocco, Palestine, Saudi Arabia, Syria, Tunisia and Yemen.

Second Protocol are 10: Bahrain, Egypt, Jordan, Lebanon, Libya, Morocco, Oman, Palestine, Qatar and Saudi Arabia.

[28] https://treaties.un.org/pages/showDetails.aspx?objid=08000002801170ec

[29] https://www.unidroit.org/instruments/factoring/status/

State	1954 Convention	1954 Protocol	Second Protocol
Algeria			
Bahrain	26-08-2008	28-08-2008	26-08-32008
Egypt	17/08/1955	17/08/1955	03/08/2005
Iraq	21/12/1967	21/12/1967	
Jordan	02/10/1957	02/10/1957	05-05-2009
Kuwait	06/06/1969	17/02/1970	
Lebanon	01/06/1960	01/06/1960	08-10-2020
Libya	19/11/1957	19/11/1957	20-07-2001
Mauritania			
Morocco	30/08/1968	30/08/1968	05-12-2013
Oman	26/10/1977		16-05-2011
Palestine	22/03/2012	22/03/2012	22/03/2012
Qatar	31/07/1973		04-09-2000
Saudi Arabia	20/01/1971	06/11/2007	06/11/2007
Sudan	23-07-1970		
Syria	06/03/1958	06/03/1958	
Tunisia	28/01/1981	28/01/1981	
United Arab Emirates			
Yemen	06/02/1970	06/02/1970	

Table 7. 1954 Hague Convention for the Protection of Cultural Property in the Event of Armed Conflict and its two (1954 and 1999) Protocols, Status of Ratification[30]

Organization (ALECSO)[31] is not significant in terms of legislative reform. Some Arab States have made amendments to national antiquities laws such as Article 42 of Egyptian Law No. 91 of 2018, where potential penalties for antiquities smuggling now include life imprisonment. But the real legislative gaps on a national level have not been addressed.

The **1995 UNIDROIT Convention** is worthy of consideration within the Arab legislative frameworks. To understand why Arab States do not accept the UNIDROIT Convention, it helps to reflect on the origin of the Convention as simplified by Dr. Lyndel Prott,[32] when she was Chief of the International Standards Section of UNESCO. In general terms, each state has its own import and export laws – and it rarely accepts the legislative framework of other states, especially when that differs greatly from its own. International organizations such as UNESCO and ICOM are entrusted to harmonize different States' laws, so that they may be applied to promote the common good. The 1995 UNIDROIT Convention was established to fill some gaps in the 1970 UNESCO Convention, to combat illicit trafficking and to be used by both

[30] https://en.unesco.org/protecting-heritage/convention-and-protocols/1954-convention
[31] ALIESCO. http://www.alecso.org/nsite/en/
[32] Prott 1997. https://www.theartnewspaper.com/1997/01/01/the-arguments-for-and-against-unidroit

states that requested and states that hosted cultural properties. One of the challenges when restitution claims are conducted is the varying span of time for a *bona fide* (good faith) purchaser to be accepted as the owner of the item in question. Some authorities require no period of possession to gain ownership, others require a short period, still others require a long period; meanwhile, yet others do not recognize it.

The UNIDROIT Convention offers a wide range of possibilities to facilitate restitution matters. Surprisingly, however, it has been misunderstood by the majority of States. The **first** misunderstanding is that UNIDROIT Convention is, in Prott's words: '*a blank cheque' for the enforcement of source countries' export laws abroad*', which is incorrect. Under the Convention, cultural properties that have been exported illegally can be restituted if the demanding State can attest to specific points, such as the significance of an item in the religious life of the community. The decision on the proof of validity is in hands of the judge in the country where the item is located – they decide whether the argument justifies the application of this Convention. The **second** misunderstanding is that the Convention will open the door for many restitution requests. The contrary has happened, as the costs of proving the significance of an object, as well as the elevated costs of judicial action in market countries, has prompted the question of whether the object is worth the cost. The **third** is the ease of compensation for purchasers. The **fourth** is the applicability of the Convention: like other legal instruments, it is not retroactive; it does not legalise prior illegal transactions; it simply explicitly recognizes that it cannot be used to police prior illegal transactions. The **fifth** and final misunderstanding is that the Convention will alter the market's relationship between dealer and purchaser in terms of secrecy.[33]

UNESCO encourages the adoption of the UNIDROIT Convention to fight the transfer of illegally-trafficked objects into the licit trade.

Similarly, the research of Fraoua[34] focused on two key matters: Arab States' position with regard to the 1995 UNIDROIT Convention; and their position with regard to the Intergovernmental Committee for Promoting the Return of Cultural Property to its Countries of Origin or its Restitution in case of Illicit Appropriation (ICPRCP).

The abstention of Arab States from adopting the 1995 UNIDROIT Convention is motivated by three arguments: the Convention is not retroactive; there is a time limit on action; and there is compensation for *bona fide* purchasers.[35] These points were also discussed in Prott's review.[36] Thus, Arab States also misinterpreted the UNIDROIT Convention as a renunciation of the right to claim cultural properties that had been removed illegally before the Convention would enter into force.

33 Ibid.
34 Fraoua 2012
35 Ibid.
36 Prott 1997

The 2012 research criticized Arab States' position based on the fact that most Western laws require claims against *bona fide* acquisitions to be made within five years of finding the object. Likewise, compensation for *bona fide* acquisitions is already established in numerous antiquities laws in Arab States, such as those of Lebanon (Art.18),[37] Qatar (Art. 29b)[38] and Saudi Arabia (Art.79).[39] Therefore, the UNIDROIT Convention is helpful for States Parties since it, in Fraoua's words: it '*pays fair compensation [only] to the good-faith purchaser or legitimate owner*' and '*allows for derogation from the bona fide purchaser's right of ownership without violating the constitutional guarantee of ownership*'.[40] Where legislation permits restitution without compensation, states can apply Article 9, Paragraph 1 of the Convention:

'Nothing in this Convention shall prevent a Contracting State from applying any rules more favorable to the restitution or the return of stolen or illegally exported cultural objects than provided for by this Convention.'[41]

The second interesting point in the abovementioned research is about the Intergovernmental Committee for the Promotion of the Return of Cultural Property to their Country of Origin or its Restitution in the Event of Illegal Appropriation (ICPRCP), which was established by UNESCO in 1978. It deals with return or restitution of pillaged or lost cultural property for cases that occurred before the entry into force of the 1970 Convention. Fraoua[42] described the region's states' cooperation with the ICPRCP as insufficient, as only two States were on the Committee: Iraq and Libya. This report supports that opinion, since the region's representation is still limited to two States: Egypt and Iraq[43] and the Arab States do not benefit from the ICPRCP's role, intervention and procedures in relation to the restitution of cultural properties.[44]

This research picks out other gaps in Arab States' laws as well. For example, Egyptian Law specifies deterrent penalties, yet the fines are insufficient to serve as a deterrent. Similarly, there is a paradox of judicial principle with regard to illegal excavation of antiquities, as it is not a crime as long as it occurs on land that is not owned by the State or in an area that is not classified as archaeological. Logically, laws should prohibit unlicensed excavation of antiquities even on private property and on State land that is not classified as an archaeological area.

---

[37] https://en.unesco.org/sites/default/files/lebanon_law37_2008_araorof.pdf

[38] https://sherloc.unodc.org/cld/uploads/res/document/qat/law-no-2-of-1980_html/qatar_aw_2_1980_arabe_orof.pdf

[39] https://en.unesco.org/sites/default/files/saudi_herlaw14_entof

[40] Fraoua 2012.

[41] https://www.unidroit.org/instruments/cultural-property/1995-convention

[42] Fraoua 2012

[43] https://en.unesco.org/fighttrafficking/icprcp

[44] Fraoua 2012: 3–4

Definition of the concept of cultural objects

The definition of cultural objects varies from one state to another across the region. Following Fraoua[45] and adding Kuwait, Libya and Qatar, the classification is as follows:

- States that apply the internationally-established concept of cultural properties: Algeria and Lebanon.
- States that apply the concept of cultural objects as antiquities in the form of movable and immovable property: Bahrain, Egypt, Jordan, Palestine, the Emirate of Sharjah, Saudi Arabi, Sudan, Syria, Yemen, Qatar, Libya and Kuwait.
- States that apply the concept of cultural objects as objects of a cultural or historical nature: Morocco and Comoros.
- States that apply the concept of cultural objects as cultural heritage: Algeria.
- States that apply the concept of cultural objects as objects of archaeological, historical or traditional heritage: Tunisia.
- States that apply the concept of cultural objects as antiquities and cultural heritage as well as cultural objects: Oman and Iraq.
- States that apply the concept of cultural objects as tangible cultural heritage: Mauritania.

The legal definition is based on one of two criteria: **value or chronology.** North African countries, except for Libya and the Comoros, use value-based definitions; meanwhile, Middle Eastern countries use chronology-based definitions (e.g. 40 years in Qatar, 40 years in Kuwait, 50 years for documents and 100 years for other objects in Libya) and also enable cultural authorities to protect more-recently-produced properties if they have importance to the country. For example, since 2013, Syria's Directorate of Antiquities and Museums (DGAM) has included traditional objects less than 200 years old, due to the emergence of a significant trend to export traditional swords, textiles and carpets to Gulf States.[46]

Nonetheless, most of these definitions do not match the terminology of the international conventions. Thereby, they make international cooperation difficult.

Legal rules on the ownership and transfer of ownership of cultural objects

Trafficking of cultural properties is prohibited and all 20 countries' laws contain provisions on the ownership and transfer of ownership of cultural objects. Authorization from the State is required to transfer ownership of inventoried movable cultural property and the State has the right of first refusal in relation to purchases of newly-identified objects.

The 2012 study pointed out that cultural objects are under public ownership, except if they are under *waqf* ownership or the possessor can provide documentation of

[45] Ibid.
[46] Maamoun Abdul Karim, former General Director of DGAM, Syria. Personal communication.

legal private ownership.[47] According to Article 5 of Kuwait's law, all antiquities found underground in Kuwaiti territory are state property. Antiquities found on the surface remain under the control of the land's proprietor unless the State decides that they need to be acquired.[48] According to Article 11 of Libya's law, if it does not need to be acquired by the State, an object that has been discovered may be given to the person who discovered it, with a certificate of ownership to document the legality of its private ownership.[49] According to Article 5 of Qatar's law, all movable and immovable antiquities existing above ground or underground are deemed to be state property.[50]

In most Arab States, private ownership of a land does not mean ownership of objects located on land or belowground, and objects found fortuitously, are State property.

It is not permitted the transport of movable antiquities without authorization in Lebanon,[51] Syria,[52] Libya (Art. 20) and Kuwait (Art. 23).

The 2012 study noticed that the legal system of ownership and transfer of ownership does not ensure the validity of ownership of the stolen or illegally exported property. Inventories and solid documentation are highly recommended.[53]

Inventory of cultural objects

The 20 analysed Arab States' regulations emphasize the maintenance of inventories of cultural objects (e.g. Libyan Antiquities Law Article 4, Qatari Antiquities Law Article 4 and Kuwaiti Antiquities Law Article 2). Nonetheless, none of these states has a complete and reliable inventory. Lebanese museums partly adhere to international standards, for instance, by using Object ID.[54] Raqqa Museum exemplifies the importance of inventories for efforts to recover stolen cultural properties. After the fall of Raqqa in 2013, the museum's staff transferred the most valuable objects to the Central Bank of Raqqa. But rebels robbed the bank and stole a range of goods, including the museum's objects. The Focus Raqqa project has built a database of the 513 stolen items, which is based on a simple inventory and is to be submitted to INTERPOL through Syria's DGAM. Focus Raqqa 2.0 has been launched, to piece together an inventory of the artefacts that have been stolen from the museum's premises.[55]

[47] Fraoua 2012
[48] https://en.unesco.org/sites/default/files/kuw_decree_11_law_antiquities_engtof.pdf
[49] https://sherloc.unodc.org/cld/uploads/res/document/lby/law-no-3-of-1994-on-cultural-property-protection_html/libya_cltherlaw_94_arorof.pdf
[50] qatar_aw_2_1980_arabe_orof.pdf (unodc.org)
[51] *https://en.unesco.org/sites/default/files/lebanon_law37_2008_araorof.pdf*
[52] https://en.unesco.org/sites/default/files/sy_antiquitieslaw1963_engtof.pdf
[53] Fraoua 2012
[54] Ibid.
[55] https://www.globalheritage.nl/news/focus-raqqa-20-receives-funding

Archaeological excavations

Article 5d of the 1970 UNESCO Convention encourages regulation of archaeological excavations. Legislation in all of the 20 analysed Arab States regulated archaeological excavations (e.g. Libyan Antiquities Law Article 25,[56] Qatari Antiquities Law Article 31[57] and Kuwait Antiquities Law Article 25[58]).

There are four basic types of archaeological excavations:

- National excavations: conducted by the local staff of the State, composed of qualified archaeologists and specialists from other disciplines from departments of archaeology or other units of universities.
- International excavations: conducted by foreign universities or museums, after obtaining permission from the State through bilateral agreements.
- Joint excavations: composed of experts from both countries; research, conservation, restoration and publication are arranged according to prior agreements.
- Emergency excavations: usually conducted by the local staff of the State, in response to construction of public infrastructure – such as roads, buildings, and other public works – and private structures.

Archaeological objects that are revealed through excavation are owned by the State. In special cases, the rules can change, for example when UNESCO launched the international call to rescue archaeological sites in the Euphrates Valley in Syria, as those sites were going to be submerged through the construction of Tabqa Dam between 1968-1973. According to an exception that Syria established under Article 1 of Legislative Decree 295 of 1969, the law permitted the donation of 50% of the finds to the international expeditions that participated in archaeological work.[59]

Trade in cultural objects

Article 10a of the 1970 UNESCO Convention[60] asks States to regulate the trade in cultural objects. Arab States' responses varied. In Egypt, Jordan, Iraq, Syria and Yemen, trade in antiquities is prohibited. In Libya, trade *without permission of the competent authorities* is prohibited. In Algeria, Saudi Arabia, the Emirate of Sharjah, Tunisia, Sudan, Kuwait and Qatar, it is permitted. The relevant laws in Bahrain, Comoros and Morocco do not say anything about it.[61]

[56] https://sherloc.unodc.org/cld/uploads/res/document/lby/law-no-3-of-1994-on-cultural-property-protection_html/libya_cltherlaw_94_arorof.pdf
[57] https://sherloc.unodc.org/cld/uploads/res/document/qat/law-no-2-of-1980_html/qatar_aw_2_1980_arabe_orof.pdf
[58] https://en.unesco.org/sites/default/files/kuw_decree_11_law_antiquities_engtof.pdf
[59] https://en.unesco.org/sites/default/files/sy_antiquitieslaw1963_engtof.pdf
[60] https://en.unesco.org/fighttrafficking/1970
[61] See Appendix 2, Antiquities laws of Arab States

Penalties are established to prevent illicit trade. For example, under Article 41 of Iraq's Law 55 of 2002, anyone who knowingly takes an article of antiquities out of Iraq, or who attempts to do so, shall be punished by death.[62]

Controls on the export and import of cultural objects

Article 6 of the 1970 UNESCO Convention asks States to regulate export and import of cultural objects and Article 7bi prohibits the import of objects that have been stolen from museums or similar institutions.

Export:

Export standards exist in Algeria, Saudi Arabia, Bahrain, Comoros, Egypt, Iraq, Jordan, Morocco, Mauritania, Oman, the Emirate of Sharjah, Sudan, Tunisia, Yemen,[63] Qatar, Kuwait and Libya.[64]

Export is subject to a tax in some States. For example, in Saudi Arabia, antiquities are subject to an export tax of 15-25% of their financial value. Meanwhile, in Syria, such exports are exempted from customs duties.[65]

Import:

Legislation varies across the region in relation to the regulation of the import of cultural objects. In Algeria, Comoros, Egypt, Tunisia, Oman, Sudan and Libya, the relevant laws do not include provisions on import. Saudi Arabia and Yemen emphasize the condition of reciprocity, while Jordan focuses on proof of legal possession. Bahrain, the Emirate of Sharjah, Iraq, Lebanon, Mauritania, Palestine and Syria are more specific in their rules on import.[66] Article 44 of the Kuwaiti antiquity's legislation punishes anyone who has imported antiquities from outside Kuwait and has not informed the competent authorities within three days. Article 29 of the Qatari antiquities' legislation[67] states that cultural property that is imported into Qatar without an export license from the country of origin should be seized and delivered to the Museums Authority, to enable the investigation of its source. If the investigation proves that this cultural property has been smuggled, or that it was taken out of the exporting country in violation of the laws in force, and that the importer was aware of this, it shall be confiscated and considered to be state property. The state may return it to the country of origin on condition of reciprocity. If the investigation proves that the importer acted in good faith, the Museums Authority may decide to seize it in return for fair compensation, if the State has an interest in its acquisition.

62 https://en.unesco.org/sites/default/files/ir_law55200_engtno.pdf
63 Fraoua 2012
64 See Appendix 2, Antiquities laws of Arab States
65 Fraoua 2012
66 Ibid.
67 See Appendix 2, Antiquities laws of Arab States

Institutional aspects

States under Articles 5 and 14 of the 1970 Convention are encouraged to set up one or more national services for the protection of cultural heritage, with qualified staff and an adequate budget.

All 20 analysed States have established an authority to preserve and protect cultural heritage. However, most of those States have not established a special authority or 'squad' dedicated completely to combating illicit trafficking of cultural properties. This body has been created in Algeria, Egypt, Lebanon, Jordan, Morocco, Palestine, Tunisia[68] and, most recently, Libya (in 2019). In the rest of the States, the administrative body collaborates with security agencies and customs authorities.

In some Arab States, more specialized divisions have set up to fight illicit trade and smuggling. For example, Egypt has two departments to combat antiquities smuggling – the Department of Archaeological Seizures, which controls everything that is smuggled inside Egypt, and the Department to Control Borders, which monitors air, sea and land ports to combat smuggling out of Egypt. If they are illegally exported, the Antiquities Repatriation Department works to recover them.[69]

Bilateral agreements

Article 9 of the 1970 UNESCO Convention encourages the use of bilateral agreements to combat illicit trafficking.

Market countries such as the United States of America and Switzerland have concluded several bilateral agreements with source countries. Of the Arab States, Algeria and Egypt have concluded bilateral agreements with each other to fight against illicit trafficking of their cultural properties.[70] Recently, Libya has made the 2018 Cultural Property Protection Agreement with the USA.[71] Since the war in Iraq, foreign legislation – such as the United States' Emergency Protection for Iraqi Cultural Heritage Act of 2004 – has provided additional protection of antiquities from Iraq.[72]

International cooperation in police and customs matters

Arab States collaborate with INTERPOL. In case of theft or illegal export, heritage authorities inform the national police, which in turn informs the national central bureau of INTERPOL. Apparently, the collaboration with INTERPOL is much closer than with the WCO.[73] Based on the examination of the quantity of stolen cultural objects in

[68] Fraoua 2012
[69] https://gate.ahram.org.eg/News/2881223.aspx
[70] Fraoua 2012
[71] https://2017-2021.state.gov/united-states-and-libya-sign-cultural-property-protection-agreement/index.html
[72] Anderson 2017: 81
[73] Fraoua 2012

the INTERPOL database (as presented in Chapter 7), the level of collaboration should increase.

The 2012 study confirmed that the UNESCO-WCO export certificate for cultural objects is not commonly used by the Arab States. Adopting that model would standardize export certificates and thus facilitate the rapid identification of illicit movement of cultural property.

General information and public awareness

Article 10 of the 1970 Convention requires States Parties to use education to reduce the illegal removal of cultural properties from any State Party to the Convention, by '*develop[ing] in the public mind a realization of the value of cultural property and the threat to the cultural heritage created by theft, clandestine excavations and illicit exports*'.[74]

The 2012 study noticed that Arab States do not have a specific information policy with regard to illicit trafficking, though campaigns to raise awareness of the importance of the cultural heritage are held frequently.[75]

Ethical standards

Heritage authorities and heritage professionals are aware of the ethical standards of ICOM's Code of Ethics and UNESCO's International Code of Ethics for Dealers in Cultural Property. However, the implementation of these ethical standards at a local level is still limited in Arab States.

In sum, Arab States are affected by the cross-border phenomenon of illicit trafficking of cultural properties and have made adjustments at different levels of national legislation to implement the 1970 UNESCO Convention. Resources and efforts are needed in terms of scientific research, data collection, implementation of international standards and coordination with international bodies in order to make progress in combating illicit trafficking.

Discussion

The cross-border phenomenon of illicit trafficking of cultural properties has been targeted by international organizations, regional authorities, and local law enforcement and has now been documented around the world. The international conventions could be used to develop significant measures and tools to clamp down on theft of documented and recorded antiquities from museums and collections. The most successful convention has been the 1970 UNESCO Convention, which has widely been accepted by Arab States. Yet, the illicit trade of illegally-excavated and/or

[74] https://en.unesco.org/fighttrafficking/1970
[75] Fraoua 2012

illegally-exported cultural properties has required further legislative response. The 1995 UNIDROIT Convention has supplemented the 1970 UNESCO Convention and has established legal rules to facilitate the recovery of stolen properties, but has not been accepted by many Arab States, because it has been interpreted as a legitimization of past looting and an acceptance of the loss of cultural properties that were stolen or illegally exported before the joining of the UNIDROIT Convention. On the other hand, comparing the domestic laws in Arab States, there have been varying degrees of advancement in terms of protecting heritage and combating illicit trafficking of cultural properties. These discrepancies in laws and policies have resulted in discrepancies in the treatment of cultural property. The 1970 UNESCO Convention could, to a certain degree, bring Arab States' legislation into closer alignment and make them attune their national policies to fight against illicit trade.

The questionable legal framework of Israel should be addressed alongside the Arab States. Israel has not signed the 1970 UNESCO Convention, but has implemented its own antiquities laws in 1979, nationalizing ownership of Israeli antiquities, and in 1989, establishing the Israel Antiquities Authority (IAA). The effectiveness of Israel's legislation on the trade of antiquities has been questioned. Since 1967, more than 11000 of the 14000 registered archaeological sites have been looted – and there has also been intensive looting of unregistered sites.[76] Likewise, the legality of sale, purchase and export of antiquities in Israel has encouraged the free movement of illegally-obtained antiquities. Israeli antiquities law has generated confusion between prohibited excavation of antiquities and permitted trading of antiquities that were obtained before the entry into force of the 1978 law. The result has been the conversion of Israel into a 'collector's paradise'.[77] Greater collaboration of Israel with Arab States is strongly required to combat illicit trafficking in Arab States.

Gaps in the domestic laws of Arab States could be addressed through the adoption of more multilateral and bilateral agreements; the use of the tools that are provided by international organizations such as ICOM, the WCO and UNESCO, including Object ID, the Model Export Certificate and Red Lists. Success in preventing illicit trafficking is dependent upon production and maintenance of inventories of archaeological sites and museum collections; revision of legal frameworks, education and awareness-raising; adherence to codes of ethics; and strengthening of collaboration with the WCO, INTERPOL and other competent authorities.

[76] Anderson 2017
[77] Kersel and Bouchenaki 2020

References

Ahram. 31 July 2021. Director of recovered antiquities. Viewed 30 August 2022. https://gate.ahram.org.eg/News/2881223.aspx

ALESCO. Arab League Educational, Cultural and Scientific Organization (ALECSO). Viewed 30 August 2022. http://www.alecso.org/nsite/en/

Al Khabour, A. 2018. Il ruolo della Legge sulle Antichità Siriane per la protezione del patrimonio culturale fino allo scoppio della guerra civile in Siria nel 2011. *Astarté: Estudios del Oriente Próximo y el Mediterráneo. Vol. 1,* pp.1-13. UCO Press, Editorial Universidad de Córdoba, Spain. Viewed 30 August 2022. https://www.uco.es/ucopress/ojs/index.php/astarte/article/view/11480

Anderson, M. 2017. *Antiquities: What Everyone Needs to Know.* Oxford: Oxford University Press.

Council of Europe. Council of Europe Convention on Offences relating to Cultural Property. Viewed 30 August 2022. https://www.coe.int/en/web/culture-and-heritage/convention-on-offences-relating-to-cultural-property

European Union. REGULATION (EU) 2019/880 OF THE EUROPEAN PARLIAMENT AND OF THE COUNCIL of 17 April 2019 on the introduction and the import of cultural goods. Viewed 30 August 2022. https://eur-lex.europa.eu/legal-content/EN/TXT/PDF/?uri=CELEX:32019R0880&from=EN

Fraoua, R. 2012. Legislative and institutional measures to combat trafficking in cultural property in Arab States. Paris. Viewed 30 August 2022. https://en.unesco.org/sites/default/files/fraoua_en.pdf

Irsheid, C. 1997. The Protection of Cultural Property in the Arab World. *International Journal of Cultural Property* 6(1): 11- 46.

Justice Law Website. Cultural Property Export and Import Act. R.S.C., 1985, c. C-51. Viewed 30 August 2022. https://laws-lois.justice.gc.ca/eng/acts/C-51/page-1.html#h-138693

Kersel, M. and Bouchenaki, M. 2020. Middle East and North Africa, in F. Francioni and A.F. Vrdoljak (eds) *The Oxford Handbook of International Cultural Heritage Law.* Oxford: Oxford University Press.

Leiden University. Focus Raqqa 2.0 receives funding! Viewed 30 August 2022. https://www.globalheritage.nl/news/focus-raqqa-20-receives-funding

Peters, R. 2019. Preventing Trafficking in Cultural Property: Import and Export Provisions as Two Sides of the Same Coin. *Santander Art and Culture Law Review,* 2019. 2/2019 (5), 00-95-108. Viewed 30 August 2022. https://www.ejournals.eu/SAACLR/2019/2-2019/art/16195/

Prott, L. 1997. The arguments for and against UNIDROIT. The Art Newspaper. 15 January 1997. Viewed 30 August 2022. https://www.theartnewspaper.com/1997/01/01/the-arguments-for-and-against-unidroit

UNESCO. The UNESCO 1970 Convention. Viewed 30 August 2022. https://en.unesco.org/fighttrafficking/1970

UNESCO. 1954 Hague Convention for the Protection of Cultural Property in the Event of Armed Conflict. https://unesdoc.unesco.org/ark:/48223/pf0000379633

UNESCO. 1954 Hague Convention for the Protection of Cultural Property in the Event of Armed Conflict and its two (1954 and 1999) Protocols Status of Ratification. Viewed

30 August 2022. https://en.unesco.org/protecting-heritage/convention-and-protocols/1954-convention

UNESCO and the European Union join forces with lawyers, police and customs officers to curb illicit trafficking in cultural property. Viewed 30 August 2022. https://en.unesco.org/news/unesco-and-european-union-join-forces-lawyers-police-and-customs-officers-curb-illicit

UNESCO. About the Convention on the Protection of the Underwater Cultural Heritage. Viewed 30 August 2022. https://en.unesco.org/underwater-heritage/2001

UNESCO. Convention Concerning the Protection of the World Cultural and Natural Heritage. Viewed 30 August 2022. https://whc.unesco.org/en/conventiontext/

UNESCO. Iraq Antiquities Law. Viewed 30 August 2022. https://en.unesco.org/sites/default/files/ir_law55200_engtno.pdf

UNESCO. Kuwait Antiquities Law. Viewed 30 August 2022. https://en.unesco.org/sites/default/files/kuw_decree_11_law_antiquities_engtof.pdf

UNESCO. Lebanese Antiquities Law. Viewed 30 August 2022. https://en.unesco.org/sites/default/files/lebanon_law37_2008_araorof.pdf

UNESCO. Return and Restitution Intergovernmental Committee. Viewed 30 August 2022. https://en.unesco.org/fighttrafficking/icprcp

UNESCO. Saudi Antiquities Law. Viewed 30 August 2022. https://en.unesco.org/sites/default/files/saudi_herlaw14_entof

UNESCO. Syria Antiquities Law. Viewed 30 August 2022. https://en.unesco.org/sites/default/files/sy_antiquitieslaw1963_engtof.pdf

UNIDROIT. Morocco has ratified the 1995 UNIDROIT Convention will enter into force for Morocco on 1 February 2023. Viewed 28 August 2022. https://www.unidroit.org/morocco-accedes-to-the-1995-unidroit-convention-on-stolen-or-illegally-exported-cultural-objects/

UNIDROIT. Status. Viewed 30 August 2022. https://www.unidroit.org/instruments/factoring/status/

UNIDROIT. The International Institute for the Unification of Private Law (UNIDROIT). Viewed 30 August 2022. https://www.unidroit.org/about-unidroit/overview/

UNIDROIT. Model Provisions on State Ownership of Undiscovered Cultural Objects. Viewed 30 August 2022. https://unidroit.org/english/documents/2012/study70a/s-70a-intro-ef.pdf

UNIDROIT. Membership. Viewed 30 August 2022. https://www.unidroit.org/about-unidroit/membership-old/

UNIDROIT. 1995 CONVENTION. UNIDROIT CONVENTION ON STOLEN OR ILLEGALLY EXPORTED CULTURAL OBJECTS. Viewed 30 August 2022. https://www.unidroit.org/instruments/cultural-property/1995-convention/

United Nations. United Nations Convention against Transnational Organized Crime and the Protocols Thereto. Viewed 30 August 2022. https://www.unodc.org/unodc/en/organized-crime/intro/UNTOC.html

United Nations. Treaty Collection. Viewed 30 August 2022. https://treaties.un.org/pages/showDetails.aspx?objid=08000002801170ec

United Nations. UN Resolutions on ECOSOC 2008. Viewed 30 August 2022. https://www.un.org/development/desa/dspd/un-resolutions-on-ecosoc-2008.html

United Nations Office on Drugs and Crime (UNODC). Libya Antiquities Law. Viewed 30 August 2022. https://sherloc.unodc.org/cld/uploads/res/document/lby/law-no-3-of-1994-on-cultural-property-protection_html/libya_cltherlaw_94_arorof.pdf

United Nations Office on Drugs and Crime (UNODC). Model treaty for the prevention of crimes that infringe on the cultural heritage of peoples in the form of movable property. Viewed 30 August 2022. https://www.unodc.org/documents/treaties/organized_crime/Model_Treaty.pdf

United Nations Office on Drugs and Crime (UNODC). Qatar Antiquities Law. Viewed 30 August 2022. https://sherloc.unodc.org/cld/uploads/res/document/qat/law-no-2-of-1980_html/qatar_aw_2_1980_arabe_orof.pdf

U.S. Embassy in Libya. United States and Libya Sign Cultural Property Protection Agreement – February 23, 2018. Viewed 30 August 2022. https://2017-2021.state.gov/united-states-and-libya-sign-cultural-property-protection-agreement/index.html

Chapter Nine

Conclusion

The phenomenon of illicit trafficking of cultural properties in Arab States is complex and multifaceted. Numerous factors contributed to its growth and made it a lucrative activity in and outside the Arab Region, until looting and theft became an industrial-scale illicit trade, then became a more institutionally-targeted crime, besides being a loss of human heritage and historical memory. The socio-political context, the legal framework, the limited understanding of the dimensions of the challenges and the lack of resources are some of the major influences on the profiles of Arab States with regard to combating illicit trafficking.

This report provides a bird's-eye view of the reality of illicit trafficking of cultural properties within the studied area, the 22 Arab States that are recognized by the Arab League, namely: Algeria, Bahrain, Comoros, Djibouti, Egypt, Iraq, Jordan, Kuwait, Lebanon, Libya, Mauritania, Morocco, Oman, Palestine, Qatar, Saudi Arabia, Somalia, Syria, Sudan, Tunisia, United Arab Emirates, Yemen and Israel.

This report has gathered and synthesized the currently available evidence and information on the illicit trade, from threats to heritage sites and objects, to potential routes for illicit trafficking, in order to determine gaps and diagnose weaknesses in Arab States' policies towards heritage, then to identify their needs and the challenges to combatting illicit trafficking.

The report has been limited by its dependence on desk-based research, as the accessible data, documents, reports and databases are themselves limited and fragmentary – and much is not available at all. Over and above this difficulty, there is a lack of sharing between competent authorities, which creates additional difficulty in comparing evidence and analyses, often on specific questions and sensitive issues that are related to security and confidence. Therefore, many questions remain unanswered. More coordination, new modalities of wider dissemination of data and greater network capacity are recommended for interventions in the issue of illicit trafficking in the Arab States.

Based on the findings of this report, the scale of damage to archaeological sites across the Arab States is remarkable. New technologies, including GIS and satellite imagery, have recorded changes in pre- and post-conflict archaeological landscapes. These have generated evidence of intensive looting and other damage to the archaeological landscape, especially in states that suffer political instability, power shifts and conflict such as Egypt, Iraq, Libya, Syria and Yemen. This evidence also suggests the involvement of radical groups and other belligerents, as well as members of the army, in the looting of archaeological sites, as in Syria. Similarly, the spread of looting and theft of cultural properties demonstrates that governments do not have complete control over archaeological sites, owing to the lack of financial and human resources. This is a serious challenge, which must be addressed at both the regional and the international level. Obviously, looted objects flow out to potential purchasers through traditional channels and online marketplaces. It must be assumed that a considerable number of looted objects are circulating on the black market, waiting for their moment to be laundered and integrated in the licit market. However, this process may take several years.

The online market for looted and stolen cultural properties has grown in recent years. Developments in technology and the spread of access to the web and social media have facilitated the formation of connections between buyers and sellers and the creation of wide networks. Based on observation of cultural properties that have been offered for sale on specialist online platforms, low-value items are the main constituent of the market. Contrary to widespread assumptions, the Surface Web is the preferred place to trade in antiquities; the Dark Web does not appear to be widely used, due to the limited number of sellers, the rarity of informative classification of cultural objects that would enable those objects to be found easily and the anonymity that impedes the development of relationships of trust between sellers and buyers. On the other hand, Facebook, Telegram, eBay, WhatsApp, Viber and similar applications are widely used to create contacts and exhibit looted objects. Transactions appear to be made the usual way in Arab States, through direct payments to established regional contacts. Social media and mobile applications are valuable tools in these activities.

Looking at looted archaeological objects (risk objects) from Arab States in the trafficking chain, a brief study of the Swedish market demonstrated that less than 6% of those objects had been checked against a stolen art database. This report's probe indicated that more than half of the risk objects had no recorded collecting history in Europe prior to 1995 and that over 72% of them had no named provenance. This is worrying and requires further research on the European and North American markets. The creation of catalogues, basic databases and customized search engines would help to evaluate the looting, theft and laundering of objects from Arab States. It would also help to produce a guide to international, national and transnational law, to assist efforts to restitute stolen objects to their rightful homes.

The mapping of illicit trafficking routes is a challenging task, since traffickers of antiquities use the same routes as traffickers of humans, weapons, drugs and other illicit commodities; vary their routes; and try to preserve the secrecy of their routes. Arab States are affected by illicit trafficking in various ways, as source countries, transit countries or both. This report has examined 18 Arab States that have reported seizures of cultural properties and identifies some potential routes. The main countries where cultural properties arrive and are prepared for transit and delivery to markets are the United Arab Emirates and Israel. Antiquities from Libya move through Tunisia and Egypt – three countries that have suffered political instability and remarkable looting and theft of cultural properties. Other notable routes include from Egypt to or through Saudi Arabia; between Iraq and Syria, then through the typical transit country, Turkey, which has played an essential role in the movement of cultural objects from their countries of origin; from Yemen through Djibouti, as has been confirmed through numerous seizures of smuggled cultural properties and repeated attempts to smuggle cultural properties; from Jordan through the 'trafficker's paradise' of Israel. This report has also identified exit points and vulnerable border crossings within Arab States. Combating this traffic will require rigorous border management in countries that remain hampered by corruption and inefficiency among officials.

The findings emphasize the connection of illicit trafficking of cultural properties to organized crime through destruction of internationally-protected sites, looting, theft and fraudulent appropriation of cultural properties. These offences are directly connected to more serious crimes, including terrorist financing. Terrorist groups such as ISIS have acted destructively towards heritage, national identity, science and human knowledge. It has not been possible to determine the scale of profits from illicit trafficking of antiquities in ISIS territory, due to the lack of reliable sources with material evidence. The report also highlights the dissemination of fakes, forgeries, reproductions and copies in the art market of cultural objects from Arab States.

This report offers a broad view of illicitly-trafficked cultural properties, their types and countries of origin, according to the INTERPOL database. There are 4,929 stolen objects that have been reported and recorded as stolen or missing from the region. Some Arab States have not reported any thefts to the INTERPOL database, including Comoros, Djibouti, Mauritania, Oman, Palestine, Qatar, Somalia and the United Arab Emirates. Meanwhile, others did – the countries with the highest recorded numbers of stolen cultural goods are Iraq with 2,786, Syria with 1,118 and Egypt with 514. With regard to the types of illicitly-trafficked objects, small, portable objects, which are difficult to trace and easy to sell, are the most popular for trafficking – for example, coins, figurines and manuscripts. Besides these generalities, certain objects are particularly targeted in certain regions, such as cylinder seals, cuneiform tablets and small statues in Iraq and Syria; statues in Egypt; and prehistoric objects, lithic artefacts and fossils in Morocco. The report has investigated smuggling networks and smuggling processes and within source, transit and destination or market countries. It recommends a range of tools that are offered by international organizations, such as ICOM's Red Lists and Object ID and UNESCO and the WCO's Model Export Certificate, as well as relevant databases and applications, such as INTERPOL's database and the Carabinieri's database.

Finally, the report has reviewed international conventions and treaties that are dedicated to combatting illicit trafficking and the legislative framework of Arab States. It has found a notable lack of cooperation, discrepancies between laws and very limited use of bilateral agreements. The report analysed the implications and implementations of the 1970 UNESCO Convention and the 1995 UNIDROIT Convention, thereby identifying gaps in the national antiquities laws of 20 Arab States. (The other two, Somalia and Djibouti, do not have legislative frameworks that are tailored to heritage issues.) The report has also considered the situation in relation to Israel and other states that permit the sale, purchase and transfer of ownership of cultural properties and the consequent challenges to the fight against illicit trafficking.

Finally, Arab States have the potential to benefit from their various areas of expertise and to enhance information-sharing, cross-border collaboration, dissemination of good practices on national and regional level, harmonization of national antiquities laws and lesson-learning procedures.

Recommendations

Building on the analysis of the evidence, documents and data that have been consulted during the research, the report has identified a number of recommendations to advance the fight against illicit trafficking of cultural properties in Arab States.

Recommendation one

Create national **inventories of museums' existing collections.** Digitize the inventory and make it accessible and easily consultable. Adopt international inventory standards, such as Object ID.

Inventories of museum collections are essential to proving ownership if an object is stolen.

Recommendation two

Create **inventories of all heritage sites**, religious places and archaeological sites.

A complete map of heritage sites, which has been augmented with satellite imagery, is essential to the monitoring of heritage sites and to the protection of those sites from illegal excavations, damages from construction work and urban expansion.

Recommendation three

Create national **databases of stolen artefacts** using museum registers, excavation reports, academic publications, images and drawings, in order to provide the maximum available data about the lost object, thereby to facilitate its identification and recovery when it surfaces on the market. For religious manuscripts and books, cooperation with churches and *awqaf* (endowments) as well as archives are essential for the provision of high-quality data for the database.

These national databases should be shared through the competent authorities with international databases, such as INTERPOL's database of stolen works of art.

Recommendation four

Create national committees under the auspices of the Arab League, which are dedicated to achieving agreement among warring parties on the **neutrality of heritage sites** and the avoidance of their use by any party under any circumstances.

Recommendation five

Establish specialized '**heritage squads**' to identify stolen and otherwise illegally-removed cultural objects, to deal with crimes related to antiquities smuggling and to enhance international cooperation with other States in the Arab region and beyond.

Recommendation six

Adopt new regulations in Arab States that are dedicated to shutting down online markets for cultural properties, preventing the use of metal detectors, and publishing a 'toolkit' in Arabic on good practices, due diligence and codes of ethics.

Recommendation seven

Enhance bilateral collaboration between Arab States to control **border crossing points**, in order to ensure their capacity to combat smuggling. A cultural object without proper paperwork should be seized before leaving the territory of its country of origin. Once a smuggled object reaches Europe, it is in a zone of free movement and consequently difficult to seize.

Recommendation eight

Harmonize antiquities **legislation in the Arab States**, as well as regulate export, import, ownership and provenance documentation in accordance with international standards.

Recommendation nine

Utilize the UNESCO-WCO ***export certificate.*** This standard facilitates both legal circulation of exported items and detection of illegal movement of such items.

Recommendation ten

Create a representative committee of Arab States to tackle **restitution** matters.

It should consist of experts with juridical backgrounds, who have been trained to make optimal use of the international conventions.

Recommendation eleven

Target demand in the market countries, to shrink the **chain of supply and demand.** The connection between demand in market countries and supply in source countries has been extensively discussed and is widely accepted by academics.

Recommendation twelve

Criminalize illicit trafficking of cultural properties at an international level, based on international conventions like the 2000 Palermo Convention, United Nations Security Council Resolutions 2199 (2015) and 2347 (2017), since antiquities trafficking often fits the criteria of organized crime and is sometimes perpetrated by an organized criminal group and/or connected to money laundering, corruption, tax evasion and terrorism.

The prosecution of Ahmad al-Faqi al-Mahdi for the war crime of the destruction of cultural heritage in Timbuktu in 2012 is an inspiring case for the criminalization of illicit trafficking of cultural properties.

Recommendation thirteen

Encourage Arab States to ratify international conventions like the 1970 UNESCO Convention and the 1995 UNIDROIT Convention.

Recommendation fourteen

As a special measure for Arab States at times of armed conflict, consider the possibility of **transferring museums' collections**, or their most symbolic objects, from locations in conflict zones to other safe Arab States, with the guarantee of their return at the end of the conflict.

The Spanish experience during the civil war of 1936-1939 is a good example, when art was evacuated from Spain and deposited in France, then returned after the war. Applying the insights from this experience in Arab States would safeguard their museums and guarantee the security of cultural properties at risk of theft and illicit trafficking.

Recommendation fifteen

Strengthen law enforcement collaboration in Arab States in the monitoring of **auction houses, galleries and free ports**, and the sharing of data with organizations such as the UNODC, the WCO and INTERPOL.

Recommendation sixteen

Raise awareness, including by disseminating animated films and public information campaigns that highlight the importance of heritage and the penalties for illicit trafficking of cultural properties.

In Sweden for example, in collaboration with #United4Heritage, a large campaign was launched at airports, at border crossings and on television, as well as in museum exhibitions.

Recommendation seventeen

Increase **employment and social protection** of professionals. The employment of more guards on heritage sites is essential to the protection of archaeological sites from looting.

Recommendation eighteen

Enhance **education**, training and digitization, in order to engage younger generations in the protection and preservation of cultural heritage and to emphasize the mission of museums to preserve cultural heritage for future generations in a digital age.

Recommendation nineteen

Adopt the '**Guiding Law for the Preservation and Protection of Arab Antiquities**' that was proposed by the Arab Parliament in 2020.

Annex 1

References

Africa Times. 18 July 2017. Mauritania establishes restricted military zone at Mali, Algeria borders. Viewed 30 August 2022. https://africatimes.com/2017/07/18/mauritania-establishes-restricted-military-zone-at-mali-algeria-borders/

Ahram. 31 July 2021. Director of recovered antiquities. Viewed 30 August 2022. https://gate.ahram.org.eg/News/2881223.aspx

Ahram Gate. 25 December 2016. 344 antiquities were recovered from Jordan smuggled in a shipment of coal at the port of Aqaba. Viewed 30 August 2022. https://tinyurl.com/475muv52

Al Akhbar. 19 March 2013. Jubail Museum. Viewed 30 August 2022. https://al-akhbar.com/Community/47984

Alanba. 26 September 2019. Seizure of Egyptian antiquities. Viewed 30 August 2022. https://tinyurl.com/3srxea83

Alanba. 25 November 2020. Viewed 30 August 2022. Seizure of Egyptian antiquities in Kuwait. https://tinyurl.com/329crdk8

Al Arab. 11 November 2013. Theft from a Tunisian museum. Viewed 30 August 2022. https://tinyurl.com/2pwznrbh

Al Arabia. 23 February 2021. Intention to smuggling archaeological objects to Australia from Beirut. Viewed 30 August 2022. https://tinyurl.com/532znyen

Al Bawaba. 23 December 2015. Daesh smuggling antiquities. Viewed 30 August 2022. https://tinyurl.com/2p8zej3j

Al Harf 28 News. 18 April 2021. Smuggling antiquities from Yemen. Viewed 30 August 2022. https://tinyurl.com/yyfdy9nu

ALESCO. Arab League Educational, Cultural and Scientific Organization (ALECSO). Viewed 30 August 2022. http://www.alecso.org/nsite/en/

Al Jamal. 13 June 2013. Museums in Yemen. Viewed 30 August 2022. https://tinyurl.com/365czvuu

Al Jazeera Net. 24 July 2019. Libyan antiquities in conflict. Viewed 30 August 2022. https://tinyurl.com/2du8yj2b

Al Khabour, A. 2015. El conflicto armado en Siria y su repercusión sobre el Patrimonio Cultural: Vol. I Deir Ez-Zor. Viewed 30 August 2022. https://www.academia.edu/14885188/El_conflicto_armado_en_Siria_y_su_repercusi%C3%B3n_sobre_el_Patrimonio_Cultural_Vol_II_Inventario_del_Patrimonio_Cultural_afectado_en_la_provincia_de_Raqqa_marzo_2011_mazro_2015_

Al Khabour, A. (2015): *El conflicto armado en Siria y su repercusión sobre el Patrimonio Cultural: Vol. III: Inventario del Patrimonio Cultural afectado en la provincia de Hasakeh (marzo 2011-marzo 2015)*. Viewed 30 August 2022. https://www.academia.edu/15115500/El_conflicto_armado_en_Siria_y_su_repercusi%C3%B3n_sobre_el_Patrimonio_Cultural_Vol_III_Inventario_del_Patrimonio_Cultural_afectado_en_la_provincia_de_Hasakeh_marzo_2011_mazro_2015_

Al Khabour, A. 2018. Il ruolo della Legge sulle Antichità Siriane per la protezione del patrimonio culturale fino allo scoppio della guerra civile in Siria nel 2011. *Astarté:*

Estudios del Oriente Próximo y el Mediterráneo. Vol. 1, pp.1-13. UCO Press, Editorial Universidad de Córdoba, Spain. Viewed 30 August 2022. https://www.uco.es/ucopress/ojs/index.php/astarte/article/view/11480

Al Khabour, A. 2019. El patrimonio cultural en Siria e Iraq: Desafíos y esperanzas. *Isimu,* Vol. 22. Viewed 30 August 2022. https://www.academia.edu/41350973/EL_PATRIMONIO_CULTURAL_EN_SIRIA_E_IRAQ_DESAF%C3%8DOS_Y_ESPERANZAS

Al Khaleej online Net. 9 March 2019. Theft in Museums in Algeria. Viewed 30 August 2022. https://tinyurl.com/2ju7e7dc

Al Monitor. 4 April 2017. Theft of Palestinian antiquities. Viewed 30 August 2022. https://tinyurl.com/2tvk3apx

Al Rai. 1 October 2018. Seizure smuggling antiquities from Syria. Viewed 30 August 2022. https://tinyurl.com/mrybte3a

Al Sharq. 16 October 2020. Morocco recovered 25000 objects from France. Viewed 30 August 2022. https://tinyurl.com/2u2sju5d

Anadolu Agency. 28 March 2013. Objects pertaining to Egypt in Emirates. Viewed 30 August 2022. https://tinyurl.com/53hp9tkb

Anadolu Agency. 22 March 2017. Viewed 30 August 2022. Confiscating objects in Cairo Airport. https://tinyurl.com/59xw99cy

Anadolu Agency. 07 August 2017. Smuggling Libyan antiquities. Viewed 30 August 2022. https://tinyurl.com/4rs958zh

Anadolu Agency. 12 September 2017. Confiscating Ottoman coins in Egypt. Viewed 30 August 2022. https://tinyurl.com/7rsxafy8

Anadolu Agency. 24 December 2017. Viewed 30 August 2022. Seizure of Egyptian coins. https://tinyurl.com/yu42mpjb

Annaharar. 22 June 2021. Smugglers in Baghdad. Viewed 30 August 2022. https://tinyurl.com/4see3d4s

American Society of Overseas Research. 2021. Report: The State of Illicit Trade and Looting Of Libyan Antiquities: 2011–2020. Viewed 30 August 2022. https://www.asor.org/chi/updates/2021/01/illicit-trade-looting-libya

Anderson, M. 2017. *Antiquities: What Everyone Needs to Know.* Oxford: Oxford University Press.

Arab News. 16 July 2018. Saudi heritage. Viewed 30 August 2022. https://tinyurl.com/y7jxpbbr

Arab News. 5 November 2017. Viewed 30 August 2022. Egypt recovers antiquities. https://tinyurl.com/bdhu5tbu

Arabtimesonline. 8 October 2018. Smuggling Egyptian objects in Kuwait. Viewed 30 August 2022. https://tinyurl.com/59a6c3wx

ArThemis. Viewed 30 August 2022. https://tinyurl.com/bc4fcjpb

Artnet. 21 September 2015. UNESCO Head Warns of 'Industrial Scale' Looting in Syria. Viewed 30 August 2022. https://news.artnet.com/art-world/unesco-warning-looting-syria-333814

Assahraa. 20 November 2009. Theft in Morocco. Viewed 30 August 2022. https://assahraa.ma/journal/2009/96918

Art Loss Register (ALR) database. Viewed 30 August 2022. https://www.artloss.com/

Athar Project. Viewed 30 August 2022. https://atharproject.org/

Athar Sale. Coins online. Commissions online Market. Viewed 30 August 2022. https://tinyurl.com/2zn5nwrt https://tinyurl.com/y5ndxj59

Bassiouni, M.Ch. 2008. The New Wars and the Crisis of Compliance with the Law of Armed Conflict by Non State Actors. *Journal of Criminal Law and Criminology* Spring 2008, 98(3): 711–810. Viewed 30 August 2022. https://www.jstor.org/stable/40042787

Bloom, J., and L.E. Gould. 2000. The Kuwait National Museum. *Saudi Aramco World*, 51(5): 10–21. Viewed 30 August 2022. https://archive.aramcoworld.com/issue/200005/patient.restoration-the.kuwait.national.museum.htm

Bokra Net. 23 December 2016. Theft in Palestinian museum. Viewed 30 August 2022. https://www.bokra.net/Article-1357627

Brodie, N. 1998. Pity the poor middlemen. *Culture Without Context* 3: 7–9. Viewed 30 August 2022. https://traffickingculture.org/publications/brodie-n-1998-pity-the-poor-middlemen-culture-without-context-3-7-9/

Brodie, N. and C. Renfrew. 2005. Looting and the world's archaeological heritage: The inadequate response. *Annual Review of Anthropology* 34(1): 343–361. Viewed 30 August 2022. https://www.researchgate.net/publication/234147856_Looting_and_the_world's_archaeological_heritage_The_inadequate_response

Brodie, N. 2015. The Internet Market in Antiquities, in F. Desmarais (ed.) *Countering Illicit Traffic in Cultural Goods: The Global Challenge of Protecting the World's Heritage.* Paris: ICOM. Viewed 30 August 2022. https://traffickingculture.org/app/uploads/2016/01/2015-Brodie-ICOM-Internet.pdf

Burleigh, N. 2008. Collecting Pieces of God. *Archaeology*, November/December 2008, 61(6): 20, 60–64. Viewed 30 August 2022. https://tinyurl.com/5h2ddu4a

Calvani, S. 2008. Frequency and figures of organized crime in art and antiquities, in S. Monacorda (ed.) *Organized crime in art and antiquities.* Milan: International Scientific and Professional Advisory Council. Viewed 30 August 2022. https://www.obs-traffic.museum/organised-crime-art-and-antiquities

Campbell, P. 2013. The Illicit Antiquities Trade as a Transnational Criminal Network: Characterizing and Anticipating Trafficking of Cultural Heritage. *International Journal of Cultural Property* 20(2): 113-153.

Casana, J. 2015. Satellite Imagery-Based Analysis of Archaeological Looting in Syria. *Near Eastern Archaeology, Special Issue: The Cultural Heritage Crisis in the Middle East* 78(3): 142–152.

Cordoba, J.M. 2000. On the Iraq Museum and Other Assaults Brief News about the Plundering of Iraqi Museums and the Systematic Looting of Iraqi Archaeological Heritage. *Isimu* III: 15–46. Viewed 30 August 2022. https://www.obs-traffic.museum/iraq-museum-and-other-assaults-brief-news-about-plundering-iraqi-museums-and-systematic-looting

Culture Crime News. 3 September 2016. Ancient artifact smugglers arrested in south Lebanon. Viewed 30 August 2022. https://news.culturecrime.org/entry/star2016ancient-artifac.html

Council of Europe. Council of Europe Convention on Offences relating to Cultural Property. Viewed 30 August 2022. https://www.coe.int/en/web/culture-and-heritage/convention-on-offences-relating-to-cultural-property

Council of Europe. European Landscape Convention (Florence, 2000). Viewed 30 August 2022. https://www.coe.int/en/web/landscape/the-european-landscape-convention

Council of Europe. Convention for the Protection of the Archaeological Heritage of Europe (revised) (Valletta, 1992). Viewed 30 August 2022. https://www.coe.int/en/web/culture-and-heritage/valletta-convention

DW. 2016: Der Spanische Meister. Viewed 30 August 2022. https://www.youtube.com/watch?v=sqMmbNVL5SI

eBay. Antiquities Buying Guide. Viewed 30 August 2022. https://pages.ebay.co.uk/buy/guides/antiquities/

Egyptian Independent. 22 January 2020. Former Italian diplomat receives 15-year sentence for smuggling Egyptian artifacts. Viewed 30 August 2022. https://tinyurl.com/2aknrtcc

Egyptian Streets. 24 January 2014. Historic Islamic Art Museum 'Completely Destroyed'. Viewed 30 August 2022. Viewed 30 August 2022. https://egyptianstreets.com/2014/01/24/historic-islamic-art-museum-completely-destroyed/

El Watan News. 25 May 2017. Libyan smuggler. Viewed 30 August 2022. https://www.elwatannews.com/news/details/2130296?t=push

Emaratalyoum. 18 October 2018. Smuggling in Abu Dhabi. Viewed 30 August 2022. https://tinyurl.com/2d73scst

European Commission. Copernicus Support Office for European Commission - DG GROW. 2017. Copernicus For Cultural Heritage Workshop. Viewed 30 August 2022. https://workshop.copernicus.eu/sites/default/files/content/attachments/ajax/copernicus_cultural_heritage_workshop_report.pdf

European Union. REGULATION (EU) 2019/880 OF THE EUROPEAN PARLIAMENT AND OF THE COUNCIL of 17 April 2019 on the introduction and the import of cultural goods. Viewed 30 August 2022. https://eur-lex.europa.eu/legal-content/EN/TXT/PDF/?uri=CELEX:32019R0880&from=EN

European Commission, CECOJI-CNRS — UMR 6224. 2011. *Study on preventing and fighting illicit trafficking in cultural goods in the European Union*. Brussels: European Commission. Final report October 2011. Viewed 30 August 2022. https://op.europa.eu/en/publication-detail/-/publication/ca56cfac-ad6b-45ab-b940-e1a7fa4458db

EUROPAPARLAMENTETS OCH RÅDETS FÖRORDNING (EU) 2019/880 av den 17 april 2019 om införsel och import av kulturföremål. Viewed 30 August 2022. https://eur-lex.europa.eu/legal-content/SV/TXT/PDF/?uri=CELEX:32019R0880&from=PL

Evening Standard. 2 July 2015. UN in plea to stop Islamic State's 'industrial scale' looting. Viewed 30 August 2022. https://www.standard.co.uk/news/world/un-in-plea-to-stop-islamic-state-s-industrial-scale-looting-10360530.html

France 24. 27 January 2020. Looting antiquities in Mauritania as a result of gold hunting. Viewed 30 August 2022. https://tinyurl.com/36swcdcd

France 24. 24 July 2020. Bombed and looted: Yemen battles to save its heritage. Viewed 30 August 2022. https://www.france24.com/en/20200724-bombed-and-looted-yemen-battles-to-save-its-heritage

Fraoua, R. 2012. Legislative and institutional measures to combat trafficking in cultural property in Arab States. Paris. Viewed 30 August 2022. https://en.unesco.org/sites/default/files/fraoua_en.pdf

Gulf News. 11 November 2004. Customs officials seize smuggled Iraqi artifacts. Viewed 30 August 2022. https://tinyurl.com/yrbjs8r3

Hadjimitsis, D.G., K. Themistocleous, B. Cuca, A. Agapiou, V. Lysandrou, R. Lasaponara, N. Masini, and G. Schreier. 2020. *Remote Sensing for Archaeology and Cultural Landscapes Best Practices and Perspectives Across Europe and the Middle East*. Springer International. Viewed 30 August 2022. https://doi.org/10.1007/978-3-030-10979-0

Hafryat. 5 March 2018. ISIS in Syria. Viewed 30 August 2022. https://tinyurl.com/49fh9ape

Hardy, S.A. 2016. Illicit trafficking, provenance research and due diligence: The state of the art. Paris: UNESCO. Viewed 30 August 2022. https://archaeologicalethics.org/blog/illicit-trafficking-provenance-research-and-due-diligence-and-confidence-and-risk-conflict-antiquities/

ICOM. The ICOM Red Lists of Cultural Objects at Risk are practical tools to curb the illegal traffic of cultural objects. Viewed 30 August 2022. https://icom.museum/en/our-actions/heritage-protection/red-lists

ICOM. Red Lists Database. Viewed 30 August 2022. https://icom.museum/en/resources/red-lists/

International Foundation for Art Research. Viewed 30 August 2022. https://www.ifar.org/

INTERPOL. 6 May 2020. 101 arrested and 19,000 stolen artefacts recovered in international crackdown on art trafficking. Viewed 30 August 2022. https://www.interpol.int/News-and-Events/News/2020/101-arrested-and-19-000-stolen-artefacts-recovered-in-international-crackdown-on-art-trafficking

INTERPOL. More than 56,400 cultural goods seized and 67 arrested. Law enforcement and customs authorities from 31 countries participated in Operation Pandora V. Viewed 30 August 2022. https://www.interpol.int/News-and-Events/News/2021/More-than-56-400-cultural-goods-seized-and-67-arrested https://www.interpol.int/Crimes/Cultural-heritage-crime/The-issues-cultural-property

INTERPOL. Stolen Works of Art Database. Viewed 30 August 2022. https://www.interpol.int/Crimes/Cultural-heritage-crime/Stolen-Works-of-Art-Database

INTERPOL. INTERPOL launches app to better protect cultural heritage. Viewed 30 August 2022. https://www.interpol.int/News-and-Events/News/2021/INTERPOL-launches-app-to-better-protect-cultural-heritage

INTERPOL. Object ID. Viewed 30 August 2022. https://www.interpol.int/Crimes/Cultural-heritage-crime/Object-ID

INSPIRE Directive. Viewed 30 August 2022. https://inspire.ec.europa.eu/inspire-directive/2

Irsheid, C. 1997. The Protection of Cultural Property in the Arab World. *International Journal of Cultural Property* 6(1): 11–46. Cambridge: Cambridge University Press.

Janssen, D. 2021. The Dark Web: What is it Exactly and What can you Find There? Vpnoverview. Viewed 30 August 2022. https://vpnoverview.com/privacy/anonymous-browsing/the-dark-web/

Justice Law Website. Cultural Property Export and Import Act. R.S.C., 1985, c. C-51. Viewed 30 August 2022. https://laws-lois.justice.gc.ca/eng/acts/C-51/page-1.html#h-138693

Khaberni. 11 December 2018. Israel stops smuggling antiquities from Jordan. Viewed 30 August 2022. https://tinyurl.com/pj8waca4

Keller, A. 2015. *Documenting ISIL's antiquities trafficking: The looting and destruction of Iraqi and Syrian cultural heritage: What we know and what can be done*. US Department of

State, 29 September. Viewed 30 August 2022._https://2009-2017.state.gov/e/eb/rls/rm/2015/247610.htm.

Kersel, M. and Bouchenaki, M. 2020. Middle East and North Africa, in F. Francioni and A.F. Vrdoljak (eds) *The Oxford Handbook of International Cultural Heritage Law*. Oxford: Oxford University Press.

Kurdistan 24. 6 June 2017. Mosul Museum. Viewed 30 August 2022. https://tinyurl.com/mpp9skst

Kurdistan 24. 17 February 2018. Smuggled Iraqi antiquities. Viewed 30 August 2022. https://tinyurl.com/3cuekt34

Leiden University. Focus Raqqa 2.0 receives funding! Viewed 30 August 2022. https://www.globalheritage.nl/news/focus-raqqa-20-receives-funding

League of Arab States. Viewed 30 August 2022. https://arab.org/directory/league-of-arab-states/

Lugan, J. 2002. Identifying Archaeological Metal. Canadian Conservation Institute (CCI) Notes 4/1. Originally published 2002, revised 2007. Minister of Public Works and Government Services Canada, 2007 Cat. Viewed 30 August 2022. https://www.canada.ca/en/conservation-institute/services/conservation-preservation-publications/canadian-conservation-institute-notes/identifying-archaeological-metal.html

Lundgren, F. 2020. Utredningsåtgärder För Museipersonal Vid Krav På Återlämnande Av Kulturföremål i Museets Ägo, (English title: '*Procedures of Investigation for Museum Staff at the Reception of a Claim of Repatriation of an Object in the Museum's Possession*') Swedish National Museum of World Cultures. Sweden.

Mackenzie, S. 2002. Organised Crime and Common Transit Networks. *Trends and Issues in Crime and Criminal Justice* 233 (July 2002). Australian Institute of Criminology.

Mackenzie, S. 2005. Dig a bit deeper. Law, Regulation and the Illicit Antiquities Market. *British Journal of Criminology*, May 2005, 45(3): 249–268.

Mackenzie, S. 2020. Antiquities Trafficking, in S. Mackenzie (ed.) *Transnational Criminology: Trafficking and Global Criminal Markets*: 105–120. Bristol: Bristol University Press.

Marchand, K., J. Reinold, and R. Dias e Silva. 2018. *Study on Migration Routes in the East and Horn of Africa*. Maastricht Graduate School of Governance. Viewed 30 August 2022. https://webcache.googleusercontent.com/search?q=cache:z0M0Zv0TVmcJ:https://www.merit.unu.edu/publications/uploads/1517475164.pdf+&cd=1&hl=es&ct=clnk&gl=se

Masrawy News. 24 April 2019. Smuggling antiquities in Aswan. Viewed 30 August 2022. https://tinyurl.com/4j5au7pp

Mazad Qatar. Viewed 30 August 2022. https://mzadqatar.com/products/14181927 https://en.mzadqatar.com/products/14558063

McGrath, J.F. 2019. Learning from Jesus' Wife: What Does Forgery Have to Do with the Digital Humanities?, in D. Hamidović, C. Clivaz, and S. Savant (eds) *Ancient Manuscripts in Digital Culture*. Brill: Leiden.

Mena Monitor. 11 November 2020. Seizure of antiquities in Iraq. Viewed 30 August 2022. https://tinyurl.com/3jm6yb52

Miñana, M.J. 2017. What measures does the UNESCO Secretariat recommend that member states should implement to prevent illicit trade? What can the UNESCO Secretariat offer in the way of facilitation?, in Nordic Council of Ministers *Illicit Trade in Cultural Artefacts*. Nordic Council of Ministers Annual Conference:

Copenhagen. Viewed 30 August 2022. http://norden.diva-portal.org/smash/record.jsf?pid=diva2%3A1095129&dswid=-8464

Morocco World News. 30 March 2017. Morocco Blocks Sale of Dinosaur Skeleton. Viewed 30 August 2022. https://tinyurl.com/35dpbpfc

Muñoz, P., and Morcillo, C., ABC Spain, 13 May 2018. Las rutas de las 'antigüedades de sangre' de Daesh, al descubierto. Viewed 30 August 2022. https://www.abc.es/espana/abci-rutas-antiguedades-sangre-daesh-descubierto-201805130146_noticia.html

Nahrainnet. 4 August 2018. Smuggling antiquities in Baghdad. Viewed 30 August 2022. https://tinyurl.com/8bjyevuu

New York Times. 26 August 2021. Dealer Made and Sold Fake Antiquities, Investigators Say. Viewed 30 August 2022. https://www.nytimes.com/2021/08/25/arts/design/fake-antiquities-investigation.html

NetCher. 7 October 2020. Illegal trafficking of cultural goods in countries in conflict. Viewed 30 August 2022. https://netcher.eu/project-news/illegal-trafficking-of-cultural-goods-in-countries-in-conflict/

North Africa Post. 14 July 2017. Mauritania Declares Borders with Algeria, Mali Military Zones Prohibited to Civilians. Viewed 30 August 2022. https://northafricapost.com/18799-mauritania-declares-borders-algeria-mali-military-zones-prohibited-civilians.html

Paltoday. 25 November 2020. Seizures in Palestine. Viewed 30 August 2022. https://tinyurl.com/57vswbn6

Parcak, S. 2015. Archaeological Looting in Egypt: A Geospatial View (Case Studies from Saqqara, Lisht, and el Hibeh). *Near Eastern Archaeology, Special Issue: The Cultural Heritage Crisis in the Middle East* 78(3): 196–203.

Peters, R. 2019. Preventing Trafficking in Cultural Property: Import and Export Provisions as Two Sides of the Same Coin. *Santander Art and Culture Law Review*, 2019. 2/2019 (5), 00-95-108. Viewed 30 August 2022. https://www.ejournals.eu/SAACLR/2019/2-2019/art/16195/

Philp, C. 2016. ISIS hoodwinks collectors with fake Syrian artefacts. The Times, Friday 26 August 2016. Viewed 30 August 2022. https://www.thetimes.co.uk/article/isis-hoodwinks-collectors-with-fake-syrian-artefacts-fn3lnmmwp

Press, M. 2017. How Antiquities Have Been Weaponized in the Struggle to Preserve Culture. Hyperallergic. Viewed 30 August 2022. https://hyperallergic.com/415471/how-antiquities-have-been-weaponized-in-the-struggle-to-preserve-culture/

Prott, L. 1997. The arguments for and against UNIDROIT. The Art Newspaper. January 15. 1997. Viewed 30 August 2022. https://www.theartnewspaper.com/1997/01/01/the-arguments-for-and-against-unidroit

Red Arch Cultural Heritage Law and Policy Research. Viewed 30 August 2022. https://www.redarchresearch.org/K-9-Artifact-Finders.html

Resalnews. 20 May 2021. Looting antiquities in Sudan. Viewed 30 August 2022. https://tinyurl.com/5esze4cy

RT Arabic. 18 July 2019. Looted objects from Cairo. Viewed 30 August 2022. https://tinyurl.com/epaw8tpj

RT Arabic. 11 November 2019. Turkish thief. Viewed 30 August 2022. https://tinyurl.com/ms48huae

RT News. 13 February 2021. Seizing antiquities from Syria to Jordan. Viewed 30 August 2022. https://tinyurl.com/4m2esefs

Reuters. 12 November 2007. Israeli museum recovers stolen antique clocks. Viewed 30 August 2022. https://www.reuters.com/article/uk-israel-clocks-idUKL1260470920071112

Reuters. 20 June 2021. Libya's Haftar closes border with Algeria. Viewed 30 August 2022. https://www.reuters.com/world/africa/libyas-haftar-closes-border-with-algeria-2021-06-20/

Sargent, M., M. James, A. Evans, L. Bilyana, E. Nemeth and S. Dalzell. 2020. *Tracking and Disrupting the Illicit Antiquities Trade with Open Source Data.* RAND Corporation: Santa Monica CA.

Shelley, L., I. 2020. Illicit Trade and Terrorism. *Perspectives on Terrorism* August 2020, 14(4): 7–20.

Shorouk News. 27 February 2013. Theft of Libyan objects. Viewed 30 August 2022. https://tinyurl.com/57p9v4af

Smuggling antiquities from Mosul to Syria, *Taghrib News*, 21 May 2018. Viewed 30 August 2022. https://tinyurl.com/2ehjzfc4

Swan, S. BBC News. 23 June 2020. Facebook bans 'loot-to-order' antiquities trade. Viewed 30 August 2022. https://www.bbc.com/news/world-middle-east-53140615

Swedish Police Authority. 2019. *Swedish market for cultural objects from war and conflict zones: A risk analysis.* Published by The Swedish Police Authority. Stockholm. Viewed 30 August 2022. https://www.raa.se/app/uploads/2020/02/Swedish-market-for-cultural-objects-from-war-and-conflict-zones-A-risk-analysis.pdf

Syrianpc. 26 April 2021. Smugglers in Syria. Viewed 30 August 2022. https://tinyurl.com/2p9hdtt2

Temino, I.R., A. Yanez, S.J. Villar, A.R. Mateo, J.R. Rus, J.S. Alvarez and A.L. Berdonces. 2018. Forensic Archaeometry Applied to Antiquities Trafficking: The Beginnings of an Investigation at the Frontiers of Knowledge. *Arts* 7(4): 98. Viewed 30 August 2022. https://www.mdpi.com/2076-0752/7/4/98

Terrill, W.A. 2017. *Antiquities destruction and illicit sales as sources of ISIS funding and propaganda.* Strategic Studies Institute, US Army War College.

The Antiquities Coalition, Washington, DC. Viewed 30 August 2022. https://theantiquitiescoalition.org/antiquities-coalition-releases-cultural-piracy-mapping-antiquities-seizures-around-the-globe/ https://theantiquitiescoalition.org/multimedia-resources/interactive-maps/ https://www.prnewswire.com/news-releases/antiquities-coalition-releases-culture-under-threat-mapping-resource-300251043.html

The Carabinieri. Viewed 30 August 2022. www.carabinieri.it

UNESCO. UNESCO and Partners Demonstrate Space Technologies for Monitoring World Heritage. Viewed 30 August 2022. https://whc.unesco.org/en/news/293

UNESCO. Basic Actions concerning Cultural Objects being offered for Sale over the Internet. Viewed 30 August 2022. https://en.unesco.org/sites/default/files/basic-actions-cultural-objects-for-sale_en.pdf

UNESCO. UNESCO Database of National Cultural Heritage Laws. Viewed 30 August 2022. http://www.unesco.org/culture/en/natlaws/db/database_glossary_e_2009.pdf

UNESCO. Legal and practical measures against illicit trafficking in cultural property: UNESCO handbook. Viewed 30 August 2022. https://unesdoc.unesco.org/ark:/48223/pf0000146118
UNESCO. Mali and UNESCO receive symbolic reparation on behalf of international community for destruction of Timbuktu's mausoleums. 30 March 2021. Viewed 30 August 2022. https://whc.unesco.org/en/news/2268
UNESCO. UNESCO mission confirms plunder of Mallawi Museum. Viewed 30 August 2022. https://en.unesco.org/news/unesco-mission-confirms-plunder-mallawi-museum
UNESCO. Looting of museums and warehouses in Syria. Viewed 30 August 2022. https://www.unesco.org/en/node/66281
UNESCO. Curbing the spoils of war. Viewed 30 August 2022. https://en.unesco.org/courier/october-december-2017/curbing-spoils-war
UNESCO. UNESCO - WCO Model Export Certificate. Viewed 30 August 2022. http://www.wcoomd.org/-/media/wco/public/global/pdf/topics/enforcement-and-compliance/activities-and-programmes/cultural-heritage/model-export-certificate_-unseco_wco.pdf?la=en
UNESCO. List of National Cultural Heritage Laws. Viewed 30 August 2022. https://en.unesco.org/cultnatlaws/list
UNESCO. About the Convention on the Protection of the Underwater Cultural Heritage. Viewed 30 August 2022. https://en.unesco.org/underwater-heritage/2001
UNESCO. Convention Concerning the Protection of the World Cultural and Natural Heritage. Viewed 30 August 2022. https://whc.unesco.org/en/conventiontext/
UNESCO. Iraq Antiquities Law. Viewed 30 August 2022. https://en.unesco.org/sites/default/files/ir_law55200_engtno.pdf
UNESCO. Kuwait Antiquities Law. Viewed 30 August 2022. https://en.unesco.org/sites/default/files/kuw_decree_11_law_antiquities_engtof.pdf
UNESCO. Lebanese Antiquities Law. Viewed 30 August 2022. https://en.unesco.org/sites/default/files/lebanon_law37_2008_araorof.pdf
UNESCO. 'Return & Restitution' Intergovernmental Committee. Viewed 30 August 2022. https://en.unesco.org/fighttrafficking/icprcp
UNESCO. Saudi Antiquities Law. Viewed 30 August 2022. https://en.unesco.org/sites/default/files/saudi_herlaw14_entof
UNESCO. Syria Antiquities Law. Viewed 30 August 2022. https://en.unesco.org/sites/default/files/sy_antiquitieslaw1963_engtof.pdf
UNESCO. The UNESCO 1970 Convention. Viewed 30 August 2022. https://en.unesco.org/fighttrafficking/1970
UNESCO. 1954 Hague Convention for the Protection of Cultural Property in the Event of Armed Conflict. https://unesdoc.unesco.org/ark:/48223/pf0000379633
UNESCO. 1954 Hague Convention for the Protection of Cultural Property in the Event of Armed Conflict and its two (1954 and 1999) Protocols Status of Ratification. Viewed 30 August 2022. https://en.unesco.org/protecting-heritage/convention-and-protocols/1954-convention
United Nations Security Council Resolutions 2199 (February 2015) and 2253 (December 2015). Viewed 30 August 2022. https://unesdoc.unesco.org/ark:/48223/pf0000244857

UNESCO and the European Union join forces with lawyers, police and customs officers to curb illicit trafficking in cultural property. Viewed 30 August 2022. https://en.unesco.org/news/unesco-and-european-union-join-forces-lawyers-police-and-customs-officers-curb-illicit

UNIDROIT Morocco has ratified the 1995 UNIDROIT Convention will enter into force for Morocco on 1 February 2023. Viewed 28 August 2022. https://www.unidroit.org/morocco-accedes-to-the-1995-unidroit-convention-on-stolen-or-illegally-exported-cultural-objects/

UNIDROIT Status. Viewed 30 August 2022. https://www.unidroit.org/instruments/factoring/status/

UNIDROIT The International Institute for the Unification of Private Law (UNIDROIT). Viewed 30 August 2022. https://www.unidroit.org/about-unidroit/overview/

UNIDROIT Model Provisions on State Ownership of Undiscovered Cultural Objects. Viewed 30 August 2022. https://unidroit.org/english/documents/2012/study70a/s-70a-intro-ef.pdf

UNIDROIT Membership. Viewed 30 August 2022. https://www.unidroit.org/about-unidroit/membership-old/

UNIDROIT 1995 Convention. UNIDROIT Convention on Stolen or Illegally Exported Cultural Objects. Viewed 30 August 2022. https://www.unidroit.org/instruments/cultural-property/1995-convention/

United Nations. 26 February 2015. Iraq: UNESCO outraged over terrorist attack against Mosul Museum. Viewed 30 August 2022. https://news.un.org/en/story/2015/02/492082-iraq-unesco-outraged-over-terrorist-attack-against-mosul-museum

United Nations. United Nations Convention against Transnational Organized Crime and the Protocols Thereto. Viewed 30 August 2022. https://www.unodc.org/unodc/en/organized-crime/intro/UNTOC.html

United Nations. Treaty Collection. Viewed 30 August 2022. https://treaties.un.org/pages/showDetails.aspx?objid=08000002801170ec

United Nations. UN Resolutions on ECOSOC 2008. Viewed 30 August 2022. https://www.un.org/development/desa/dspd/un-resolutions-on-ecosoc-2008.html

United Nations Office on Drugs and Crime (UNODC). Libya Antiquities Law. Viewed 30 August 2022. https://sherloc.unodc.org/cld/uploads/res/document/lby/law-no-3-of-1994-on-cultural-property-protection_html/libya_cltherlaw_94_arorof.pdf

United Nations Office on Drugs and Crime (UNODC). Qatar Antiquities Law. Viewed 30 August 2022. https://sherloc.unodc.org/cld/uploads/res/document/qat/law-no-2-of-1980_html/qatar_aw_2_1980_arabe_orof.pdf

United Nations Office on Drugs and Crime (UNODC). Model treaty for the prevention of crimes that infringe on the cultural heritage of peoples in the form of movable property. Viewed 30 August 2022. https://www.unodc.org/documents/treaties/organized_crime/Model_Treaty.pdf

United Nations Office on Drugs and Crime (UNODC). 2013. Transnational Organized Crime in West Africa- Smuggling of Migrants from West Africa to Europe. Viewed 30 August 2022. https://www.unodc.org/toc/es/reports/TOCTAWestAfrica.html

United Nations Office on Drugs and Crime (UNODC). 2019. Opiate trafficking along the early stages of the Balkan route. Viewed 30 August 2022. https://www.unodc.org/documents/data-and-analysis/Studies/IFF_report_2015_final_web.pdf

UrdoPoint. 2 October 2018. Viewed 30 August 2022. https://tinyurl.com/24zwd7p8

U.S. Embassy in Libya. United States and Libya Sign Cultural Property Protection Agreement – February 23, 2018. Viewed 30 August 2022. https://2017-2021.state.gov/united-states-and-libya-sign-cultural-property-protection-agreement/index.html

World Customs Organization (WCO). 2016: *Illicit Trade Report*. Viewed 30 August 2022. www.wcoomd.org/-/media/wco/public/global/pdf/topics/enforcement-and-compliance/activities-and-programmes/illicit-trade-report/itr_2016_en.pdf?db=web

World Customs Organization (WCO). Cultural Heritage Programme. Viewed 30 August 2022. http://www.wcoomd.org/en/topics/enforcement-and-compliance/activities-and-programmes/cultural-heritage-programme.aspx

Yan, V. 2018. Saga of Beit Beirut, A museum struggles to remember civil war. Published by: The New Humanitarian. Peacebuilding Deeply. Viewed 30 August 2022. https://deeply.thenewhumanitarian.org/peacebuilding/articles/2018/07/18/saga-of-beit-beirut-a-museum-struggles-to-remember-civil-war

Youm 7. 16 July 2018. Seizure of 116 archaeological objects. Viewed 30 August 2022. https://tinyurl.com/4y8v4z2k

Ypagency. 20 February 2018. Detention of smugglers in Iraq. Viewed 30 August 2022. https://tinyurl.com/yphej25m

Annex 2

List of Antiquities Laws in Arab States

Links viewed 30 August 2022

Algeria

Antiquities were regulated by means of the Decree. No. 69-82 of June 1969, which was replaced by the **Law No. 98-04 of June 15, 1998,** on the protection of the cultural heritage.[1]

Bahrain

Decree **Law No. 11 of 1995 regarding the Protection of Antiquities**,[2] nullified the old Bahrain Antiquities Law of 1970, amended by Decree Law No (17) of 1985.

Comoros

Law No. 94-022 / AF on the protection of the national cultural heritage (Loi No.94-022/AF portant protection du patrimoine culturel national) was adopted on June 27, 1994.[3]

Djibouti

Not available.

Egypt

Egypt made amendments to Antiquities Law No.117 of 1983 through **Law No. 91 of 2018.**[4]

Iraq

Law No. 55 of Antiquities and Heritage of 2002.[5]

1 https://tinyurl.com/ce49cdes

2 https://sherloc.unodc.org/cld/uploads/res/document/decree-law-regarding-the-protection-of-antiquities-english_html/Decree_Law_No._11_Regarding_the_Protection_of_Antiquities_1995_English.pdf

3 https://sherloc.unodc.org/cld/uploads/res/document/loi-n-94-022-portant-protection-du-ptrimoine-culturel-national_html/comores_loi94022_freorof.pdf

4 https://sherloc.unodc.org/cld/uploads/res/document/egy/2018/_91_2018_117_1983_html/_91_2018_.pdf

5 https://en.unesco.org/sites/default/files/ir_law55200_araorof.pdf

Jordan

Antiquities in Jordan are regulated by **Law of Antiquities No. 21 for the year 1988**, as amended by **Law No. 23 for the year 2004.**[6]

Kuwait

Antiquities in Kuwait are regulated by **Princely Decree N.11 of 1960** on antiquities.[7]

Lebanon

Antiquities in Lebanon are regulated by **Order N.166 relating to regulations on antiquities of 1933.**

After the civil war in Lebanon, in accordance with **Decision No.8 of 1988**[8] and Decision **No. 8 of 1990** on import and export permits, Lebanon suspended all import and export of antiquities unless permitted by the Directorate General of Antiquities and stopped all permanent export of antiquities.[9]

Law No. 37 of 2008 regarding Cultural Property was an updating of the old law.[10]

Libya

Libya adopted Law No. 2 of 1983 Concerning Archaeological Monuments, Museums, and Documents. Then that law was replaced by **Law No. 3 of 1994 on Cultural Property Protection.**[11]

Mauritania

Antiquities are protected by Law No. 2005-046 in the year 2005 on the protection of tangible cultural heritage (https://tinyurl.com/2p8uucme).[12]

On May 14, **2019, Law No. 024-2019** annulled the law of 2005.

---

[6] https://sherloc.unodc.org/cld/uploads/res/document/law-of-antiquities_html/Law_of_Antiquities-1-_jordan.pdf

[7] https://en.unesco.org/sites/default/files/kuw_decree_11_law_antiquities_engtof.pdf

[8] https://en.unesco.org/sites/default/files/liban_decision1988_araorof.pdf

[9] https://en.unesco.org/sites/default/files/liban_decision1990_araorof.pdf

[10] https://en.unesco.org/sites/default/files/lebanon_law37_2008_araorof.pdf

[11] https://sherloc.unodc.org/cld/uploads/res/document/lby/law-no-3-of-1994-on-cultural-property-protection_html/libya_cltherlaw_94_arorof.pdf

[12] https://sherloc.unodc.org/cld/uploads/res/document/mrt/loi-2005-046_html/mauritanie_loi2005046_freorof.pdf

Morocco

Antiquities are regulated by **Dahir [Decree] No. 1-06-102 of June 15, 2006** promulgating law no. 19-05 relating to the **conservation of historical monuments and sites, inscriptions, objects of art and antiquity** (*Dahir n° 1-06-102 du 15 juin 2006 portant promulgation de la loi n° 19-05 relative à la conservation des monuments historiques et des sites, des inscriptions, des objets d'art et d'antiquité*).[13]

Oman

Antiquities are protected by the **Sultan's Decree No. 6/80 on the National Heritage Protection Law 1980.**[14]

Palestine

Palestine has been administered by various powers: the Ottoman Empire, the British Mandate, Jordan, Egypt and Israel. In the Gaza Strip, antiquities are governed by **British law No. 51 of 1929 on antiquities.** In the West Bank, they are governed by **Jordanian law No. 51 of 1966.** Since 1994, heritage in the occupied territories has been governed by the legislative acts that were in force before 5 June 1967.[15]

Qatar

In Qatar, antiquities are regulated by **Law No. 2 of 1980 Concerning Antiquities.**[16]

Saudi Arabi

Antiquities in Saudi Arabia are regulated by the **Law of Antiquities, Museums and Urban Heritage Regulations 1972.**[17]

Somalia

There is no legislation.

[13] https://sherloc.unodc.org/cld/uploads/res/document/mar/decret-15-juin-2006_html/maroc_decret106102_2006_freorof.pdf
[14] https://sherloc.unodc.org/cld/uploads/res/document/omn/law-on-the-protection-of-national-cultural-heritage_html/cultural_heritage_protection_law.pdf
[15] Fraoua. R. 2012. Legislative and institutional measures to combat trafficking in cultural property in Arab States. Paris. Viewed 24 May 2022. https://en.unesco.org/sites/default/files/fraoua_en.pdf
[16] https://sherloc.unodc.org/cld/uploads/res/document/qat/law-no-2-of-1980_html/qatar_aw_2_1980_arabe_orof.pdf
[17] https://en.unesco.org/sites/default/files/saudi_herlaw14_entof

Sudan

The Law on the Protection of cultural Heritage of 1999[18] replaced the previous Antiquities Law of 1952.

Syria

During the French Mandate in Syria (1920-1946), antiquities belonged to the authority of the French High Commissioner, by means of the Services of Antiquities in both Syria and Lebanon. In 1926, Law No. 651 was ratified. It was based on the agreement between France and Britain on the prohibition of importation of archaeological items, unless they had proper certification form the country of origin.[19] Since **1963, the Law of Antiquities and its Amendments 1999**[20] has regulated issues of cultural heritage.

Tunisia

Antiquities in Tunisia are protected by **Law No. 94-35 of February 24, 1994 relating to the code of archaeological heritage, historical heritage and the heritage of traditional arts** (*Loi No. 94-35 du 24 février 1994 relative au code du patrimoine archéologique, historique et des arts traditionnels*).[21]

United Arab Emirates

Antiquities were regulated by means of **Antiquities and Excavations Law No. 8 of 1970.**[22]

Then **Sharjah Antiquities Law No. 1 of 1992**[23] entered into force.

Federal Decree-Law No. 2 of 2017 deals with the immunity of foreign cultural objects from seizure and confiscation.[24]

Antiquities are also regulated by **Federal Law No. 11 of 2017 Concerning Antiquities.**[25]

---

[18] https://sherloc.unodc.org/cld/uploads/res/document/law-on-the-protection-of-cultural-heritage-of-1999_html/Law_on_Protection_of_cultural_Property_of_99-Arabic.pdf

[19] Al Khabour, A. 2018. Il ruolo della Legge sulle Antichità Siriane per la protezione del patrimonio culturale fino allo scoppio della guerra civile in Siria nel 2011, in: *Astarté: Estudios del Oriente Próximo y el Mediterráneo. Vol. 1,* pp.1-13. UCO Press, Editorial Universidad de Córdoba, Spain. Viewed 24 May 2022. *https://www.uco.es/ucopress/ojs/index.php/astarte/article/view/11480*

[20] https://en.unesco.org/sites/default/files/sy_antiquitieslaw1963_engtof.pdf

[21] https://sherloc.unodc.org/cld/uploads/res/document/tun/loi-no-94-35-relative-au-code-du-patrimoine_html/tn_actarchaehisthrtgetradarts1994_fretof.pdf

[22] https://sherloc.unodc.org/cld/uploads/res/document/are/antiquities-law-abu-dhabi_html/uae_loi_antiquite_fouilles_araorof1617.pdf

[23] https://sherloc.unodc.org/cld/uploads/res/document/are/antiquities-law-sharjah_html/uae_sharjah_antiquitieslaw1992_arborof.pdf

[24] https://sherloc.unodc.org/cld/uploads/res/document/are/2017/_2_2017__html/_2017.pdf

[25] https://sherloc.unodc.org/cld/uploads/res/document/are/2016/_11_2017__html/_2017.pdf

Yemen

Law No. 8 of 1997 amends some articles of Republican Decree Law No. 21 of 1994 on antiquities.[26]

[26] https://sherloc.unodc.org/cld/uploads/res/document/antiquities-law_html/yemen-Antiquities_Law_ar_1997.pdf

Annex 3

Seizures of antiquities in Arab States

Links viewed 24 May 2022

Algeria

1.

Country	Algeria
City	Algiers
Date	22/10/2014
Number of artifacts	2037
Description	During the first nine months of 2014, 2037 antiquities were reserved by the National Gendarmerie. They were able to reserve 1827 coins, an ancient device for examining diamonds, precious stones and a bronze ring dating back to The Roman period.
Estimated value USD	na
Source	Algerian Radio.
Source link	https://www.radioalgerie.dz/news/ar/article/20141022/17413.html

2.

Country	Algeria
City	Ain Sefra, Naama
Date	10/04/2016
Number of artifacts	500
Description	500 objects, fossils, Ottoman sward and coins dating back to the Numidian (202 BC- 46) and Ottoman periods.
Estimated value USD	na
Source	Algerian Radio.
Source link	https://www.radioalgerie.dz/news/ar/article/20160410/74121.html

3.

Country	Algeria
City	na
Date	18/04/2021 (between 2005 and 2020)
Number of artifacts	27000
Description	During Between 2005 and 2020, 27000 antiquities and art works were reserved by the National Gendarmerie. Between 2016 and 2020, 25772 antiquities were recovered.
Estimated value USD	na
Source	Echaab newsletter.
Source link	https://tinyurl.com/29u44by2

4.

Country	Algeria
City	Oran
Date	12/01/2021
Number of artifacts	103
Description	Two Egyptian statues, one statue of African goodness, 97 coins: 87 silver coins dated back to the Alaouite Dynasty (17th century and after), two golden objects dated to the Aghlabids (800-909), coins and necklace dated to Roman period, two marble stones, and ancient book.
Estimated value USD	na
Source	Ennahar newsletter
Source link	https://tinyurl.com/yfruam56

5.

Country	Algeria
City	Oum el-Bouaghi
Date	10/02/2021
Number of artifacts	2
Description	The police of the village of Oum el-Bouaghi in collaboration with the INTERPOL reserved two objects: one Egyptian Pharaonic statue made form ivory and a precious stone (Lonsdaleite diamond).
Estimated value USD	na
Source	El Maouid newsletter
Source link	https://tinyurl.com/mr2zb2nu

6.

Country	Algeria
City	Batna
Date	09/03/2020
Number of artifacts	291
Description	291 antiquities were reserved, 288 coins date back to the Roman period, two ceramics and one ancient sward.
Estimated value USD	na
Source	Echorouk newsletter
Source link	https://tinyurl.com/bdz2ywer

7.

Country	Algeria
City	Tebessa, Guelma
Date	17/05/2010
Number of artifacts	35

Description	Networks for smuggling coral. The National Gendarmerie reserved 35 items, including ahead of Pharaonic statue made of copper, another statue made of bronze, and 28 bronze and one silver coins.
Estimated value USD	na
Source	Djazairees news
Source link	https://www.djazairess.com/eloumma/11547

8.

Country	Algeria
City	na
Date	17/05/2013
Number of artifacts	10445
Description	Between 2000 and 2010, 10445 antiquities were reserved by the National Gendarmerie. They are: 7111 antiquities in 2006, 917 antiquities in 2007, 1489 in 2008 and 916 items between 2009 and 2010.
Estimated value USD	na
Source	Almaghrib today newsletter
Source link	https://www.almaghribtoday.net/317/10-10

9.

Country	Algeria
City	Tindouf, Tamanrasset, Souk Ahras, Béchar, Bettioua and Ain Sefra
Date	09/05/2018
Number of artifacts	1030
Description	Between 2016 and 2018, 1030 antiquities were reserved by the National Gendarmerie in the west of the country. They are smuggled to: Tindouf, Tamanrasset, Souk Ahras, Béchar. In Ain Sefra, they were able to reserve 247 items including coins dated to Roman and Ottoman periods, 100 precious stones, and ancient necklace. Besides, in Bechar, they reserved 198 items made of gold, silver, bronze, and ivory. The Police could recover in the city of Bettioua a statue that was exposed at the entrance of the Museum of Oran.
Estimated value USD	na
Source	el Bilad newspaper
Source link	https://tinyurl.com/yfvcy96f

10.

Country	Algeria
City	Oum el-Bouaghi
Date	02/12/2020
Number of artifacts	1

Description	In Oum el-Bouaghi, the National Gendarmerie reserved a statue made of bronze, looted from Mila. The statue represents an amputee, left-handed woman holding in her right hand an anchor for a ship, fixed on a hollow base, and her right leg resting on a book next to a ball. The statue is dated back to 1870-1915.
Estimated value USD	na
Source	Ennahar News
Source link	https://tinyurl.com/5y5c2zp8

11.

Country	Algeria
City	Tebessa, el Tarf, Souk Ahras
Date	13/11/2016
Number of artifacts	7
Description	Between January and November 2016, 7 antiquities were reserved by the National Gendarmerie. They are statues dating back to The Roman period.
Estimated value USD	na
Source	Vitaminedz News
Source link	https://tinyurl.com/394pxkvh

12.

Country	Algeria
City	Beni Slimane
Date	28/01/2020
Number of artifacts	294
Description	One ancient sward and 293 coins were reserved by the National Gendarmerie. The coins dating back to the Spanish presence in Algeria.
Estimated value USD	na
Source	Masdar news
Source link	https://tinyurl.com/466fsc9z

13.

Country	Algeria
City	Oum el-Bouaghi
Date	23/11/2020
Number of artifacts	100
Description	100 antiquities were reserved by the National Gendarmerie. They include 67 coins and 33 archaeological items.
Estimated value USD	na
Source	el Bilad News
Source link	https://tinyurl.com/47xsesny

14.

Country	Algeria
City	Batna
Date	01/09/2020
Number of artifacts	5020
Description	5022 antiquities were reserved by the National Gendarmerie.
Estimated value USD	na
Source	Algérie Presse Service
Source link	https://tinyurl.com/ph86cvsy

15.

Country	Algeria
City	Bordj Bou Arréridj
Date	29/11/2020
Number of artifacts	92
Description	The security services of Bordj Bou Arreridj state managed to retrieve 90 stolen antique coins, in addition to two art works of copper metal and a pendant of silver.
Estimated value USD	na
Source	Algérie Presse Service
Source link	https://tinyurl.com/bdzdpcmb

16.

Country	Algeria
City	Jijel
Date	23/06/2021
Number of artifacts	more than 700
Description	More than 700 antiquities were reserved by the National Gendarmerie.
Estimated value USD	na
Source	Akher saa News
Source link	https://tinyurl.com/36b94xj7

17.

Country	Algeria
City	Mila
Date	23/01/2021
Number of artifacts	195
Description	195 antiquities were reserved by the National Gendarmerie. They include 67 Numidian coins.
Estimated value USD	na
Source	Fibladi News
Source link	https://www.youtube.com/watch?v=FcDfr5Xj7WE https://tinyurl.com/bdfzbfpu

18.

Country	Algeria
City	Constantine
Date	22/07/2020
Number of artifacts	2351
Description	2351 antiquities were reserved by the National Gendarmerie. They are coins dated back to the Roman period.
Estimated value USD	na
Source	Algerie Presse Service
Source link	https://www.youtube.com/watch?v=qn0Uov1AtEA

19.

Country	Algeria
City	Skikda
Date	23/02/2021
Number of artifacts	770
Description	A bag inside which were found four small cardboard boxes containing 770 coins. Also, these coins are antiques of unknown historical period, three antique bracelets and an antique belt clasp, probably of bronze metal.
Estimated value USD	na
Source	Ennahar Online
Source link	https://tinyurl.com/3pz6fxcj

20.

Country	Algeria
City	Jijel
Date	30/06/2018
Number of artifacts	69
Description	The Antiquities Protection Department managed to retrieve 69 artifacts dating back to the Phoenician and Roman periods and some to prehistoric times.
Estimated value USD	na
Source	Djazairess
Source link	https://tinyurl.com/ydmpe3kd

Egypt

1.

Country	Egypt
City	Alexandria
Date	5/1/2018
Number of artifacts	11
Description	Customs authorities thwarted an attempt to smuggle archaeological coins of different sizes and forms, dating back to the Muhammad Ali dynasty's reign of Egypt. Among those coins was the 'red serrated edge millime' of the King Farouk era.
Estimated value USD	na
Source	Egypt Independent
Source link	https://www.egyptindependent.com/borg-al-arab-airport-authorities-thwart-smuggling-attempt-archaeological-coins/

2.

Country	Egypt
City	Damietta
Date	7/1/2018
Number of artifacts	116
Description	116 artifacts seized at the port by the port authorities. Items had been looted over the last few years.
Estimated value USD	na
Source	Youm7; Arabic Sputnik
Source link	https://tinyurl.com/4y8v4z2k

3.

Country	Egypt
City	Cairo
Date	8/1/2018
Number of artifacts	83
Description	A total of 83 pieces were confiscated by the police. Among the 83 antiquities recovered were 53 ancient Greek and Roman coins.
Estimated value USD	na
Source	Egypt Today
Source link	https://tinyurl.com/3tabuuns

4.

Country	Egypt
City	Giza
Date	12/18/2014
Number of artifacts	7
Description	The police of the Antiquities Investigation Department seized a dealer while he was trading 7 pieces of antiquities worth 10 million pounds in Al-Badrasheen area in Giza
Estimated value USD	1398464
Source	Youm 7
Source link	https://tinyurl.com/2p8m4uvc

5.

Country	Egypt
City	Dashur
Date	5/13/2015
Number of artifacts	3
Description	The items include three pieces of suspected antiquities, a 20 cm basalt statue in the form of Horus on a base carved in Pharaonic, a stone of the head of a king, a 35-cm-long basalt stone on a 25-cm-long base and 40 cm high with inscriptions in the ancient Egyptian language.
Estimated value USD	na
Source	Shorouk News
Source link	https://tinyurl.com/22ymxnrr

6.

Country	Egypt
City	Fayoum
Date	12/19/2014
Number of artifacts	359
Description	The General Administration of the Tourism and Antiquities Police of the Fayoum Security Directorate successfully seized 359 pharaonic statues in different sizes, dating back to the Pharaonic era, inside the residence of an employee in the Sennoras region.
Estimated value USD	na
Source	Youm 7
Source link	https://tinyurl.com/bdhu4kmu

7.

Country	Egypt
City	Beni Suef
Date	10/28/2014
Number of artifacts	14
Description	An investigation by the Antiquities Police in Beni Suef seized two statues and pieces of beads suspected of being found inside a farmer's house in a village in the center of Ehansia in the west of the province. The items include a round shaped bangle and 13 pieces of beads of different sizes and shapes.
Estimated value USD	na
Source	Almesryoon
Source link	https://tinyurl.com/aw44w32k

8.

Country	Egypt
City	Minya
Date	9/1/2017
Number of artifacts	18
Description	Security forces arrested a resident of Abu Qirqas for attempting to traffic a 12-cm-long Ushapati statue, six bronze coins, two amulets of lanterns, and seven pieces of small bead.
Estimated value USD	na
Source	Youm7
Source link	https://tinyurl.com/2p96rtvn

9.

Country	Egypt
City	Asyut
Date	2/1/2019
Number of artifacts	126
Description	15 Pharaonic figurines and 111 ancient Greek coins were seized by Tourism and Antiquities police from a house in Asyut.
Estimated value USD	na
Source	Egypt Today
Source link	https://tinyurl.com/3wa5dm9s

10.

Country	Egypt
City	Sohag
Date	9/27/2014
Number of artifacts	1
Description	Colonel Ahmed Refaat, head of the Antiquities and Tourism Investigation Department in Sohag, under the supervision of Major General Mumtaz Fathi, director of the General Department of Archaeological Investigation, and Major General Alaa Sabaai, Head of Antiquities Investigation, managed to seize an ancient basalt statue in the possession of a Sohag employee. The statue is 50 centimeters tall with a queen holding her right hand, the key to life, and the left under the chest, topped by a crown with inscriptions and drawings in pharaonic language.
Estimated value USD	33576
Source	Alfawd News
Source link	https://tinyurl.com/mv3wpau9

11.

Country	Egypt
City	Fayoum
Date	12/09/2014
Number of artifacts	30
Description	The security services managed to seize 30 archaeological objects in Fayoum.
Estimated value USD	na
Source	elbalad.news
Source link	https://tinyurl.com/bdfja9s7

12.

Country	Egypt
City	Aswan
Date	3/15/2015
Number of artifacts	3
Description	A 40 cm pottery vessel, an ancient pillar base and some fragments of pottery vessels and cylindrical artifacts were seized by the Tourism and Antiquities Police.
Estimated value USD	na
Source	Gate Ahram
Source link	https://tinyurl.com/msbzdzra

13.

Country	Egypt
City	Alexandria Port
Date	21/02/2020
Number of artifacts	21000
Description	Smuggling 21 thousand Egyptian antiquities to Italy. The full story of the artist Boutros Ghali
Estimated value USD	na
Source	Al Ain news
Source link	https://tinyurl.com/yf4jmvbf

14.

Country	Egypt
City	Cairo
Date	30/06/2021
Number of artifacts	201
Description	Alaa Hassanein uses a warehouse in Cairo to hide the artifacts he obtains through archaeological excavations, in preparation for smuggling and selling them to antiquities dealers abroad, in several ways, whether through ports or airports. Antiquities dealers and smugglers work to hide antiquities in several ways to keep them away from the eyes of the security services. Among the most prominent smuggling methods for recently seized antiquities is the smuggling of antiquities inside clothing bags, or through containers of import and export companies.
Estimated value USD	na
Source	Yom 7
Source link	https://tinyurl.com/4fsb99z5

15.

Country	Egypt
City	Cairo
Date	28/03/2021
Number of artifacts	3
Description	Within the framework of the efforts of the Ministry of Interior's agencies to combat crime, especially the intensification of traffic in police departments and stations nationwide, a security force affiliated to the Roads and Ports Security Department's Investigation Unit, designated to observe the security situation in the May 15 Police Department of the Cairo Security Directorate, managed to arrest two people one of them holds a foreign nationality, while they were riding in a car (the first driving), and three stone pieces were found in it, suspected of being antiquities.
Estimated value USD	na
Source	Yom 7
Source link	https://tinyurl.com/mr8vce3n

16.

Country	Egypt
City	Cairo
Date	26/12/2020
Number of artifacts	85
Description	The head of the Central Administration of Ports and Archaeological Units in Egyptian Ports said that the seizures were placed in magic pockets in a parcel that was sent to the United States of America through the mail.
Estimated value USD	na
Source	Yom 7
Source link	https://tinyurl.com/2an6m4tn

17.

Country	Egypt
City	Qalyubia (Cairo)
Date	22/12/2020
Number of artifacts	1
Description	The criminal investigation services in Qalyubia arrested five persons, including three doctors during the exchange of a statue suspected to be antiquity in one of the neighborhoods of the city of Obour.
Estimated value USD	na
Source	Yom 7
Source link	https://tinyurl.com/4eedz2ua

18.

Country	Egypt
City	Cairo
Date	04/11/2020
Number of artifacts	400
Description	They were going to sell the seized items to a person in the Abu al-Matamir area for an amount of (one million dollars).
Estimated value USD	1000000
Source	Yom 7
Source link	https://tinyurl.com/2v4n9u4y

19.

Country	Egypt
City	Cairo
Date	01/09/2020
Number of artifacts	4
Description	The security services succeeded in seizing four suspected antiquities in the possession of five persons in Qalyubia, as part of the Ministry of Interior's efforts to combat crime.

Estimated value USD	na
Source	Yom 7
Source link	https://tinyurl.com/5n9acw4y

20.

Country	Egypt
City	Alexandria Port
Date	29/08/2020
Number of artifacts	253
Description	Efforts to combat antiquities smuggling have succeeded in seizing a case of smuggling 253 pieces of 'paper and coins dating back to different eras'
Estimated value USD	na
Source	Yom 7
Source link	https://tinyurl.com/3srs2en5

21.

Country	Egypt
City	Minya
Date	07/08/2020
Number of artifacts	32
Description	A person was arrested in Minya for possessing 32 antiquities for the purpose of trafficking, they are Greek and Roman objects.
Estimated value USD	na
Source	Yom 7
Source link	https://tinyurl.com/3abbprcy

22.

Country	Egypt
City	Sharqia Governorate
Date	3/07/2020
Number of artifacts	406
Description	406 artifacts were found in the defendant's possession, consisting of '402 pieces of limestone ushabti statues dating back to the era of the Old Pharaonic Kingdom and 4 pots with a height of approximately 30 cm of limestone.'
Estimated value USD	na
Source	Yom 7
Source link	https://tinyurl.com/5n735pex

23.

Country	Egypt
City	Fayoum
Date	06/05/2020

Number of artifacts	20
Description	Confiscating of 20 suspected antiquity pieces, consisting of (16) pieces of a gold coin with pressed inscriptions on both sides, and two scarabs with hieroglyphic inscriptions, the first with dimensions (7 cm x 5 cm) and the second with dimensions (5 cm x 3 cm) and two statues of a human head with two gilded bases, both 10 cm high and (11 cm x 6 cm).
Estimated value USD	na
Source	Yom 7
Source link	https://tinyurl.com/bdcttwx6

24.

Country	Egypt
City	Cairo
Date	24/12/2017
Number of artifacts	329
Description	The Egyptian Ministry of Antiquities announced the seizure of 329 ancient coins, before they were smuggled to France through Cairo International Airport, east of the capital. The ministry said, in a statement, that 'the Antiquities Ports Unit at Cairo Airport managed to seize the coins with an Egyptian passenger, heading to France.'
Estimated value USD	na
Source	Anatolu Agency
Source link	https://tinyurl.com/yu42mpjb

25.

Country	Egypt
City	Safaga port
Date	12/09/2017
Number of artifacts	21
Description	Egypt thwart the smuggling of 21 ancient coins dating back to the Ottoman era. The objects were on its way to Saudi Arabia through the seaport of 'Safaga' in the east of the country
Estimated value USD	na
Source	Anatolu Agency
Source link	https://tinyurl.com/7rsxafy8

26.

Country	Egypt
City	Alexandria
Date	24/05/2018
Number of artifacts	30

Description	Egyptian authorities thwarted the smuggling of 30 ancient coins dating back to the Greco-Roman era. The archaeological unit at the customs of the Alexandria seaport (north), suspected the antiquity of 30 coins, and a committee was formed comprising a group of specialists to examine the pieces.
Estimated value USD	na
Source	Anatolu Agency
Source link	https://tinyurl.com/ms3p34w2

27.

Country	Egypt
City	Cairo
Date	28/05/2018
Number of artifacts	68
Description	Egyptian authorities thwarted the smuggling of 68 ancient coins dating back to the Ottoman era. A woman was arrested by the security of Cairo International Airport, she was in the possession of a passenger on her way to the Emirates
Estimated value USD	na
Source	Anatolu Agency
Source link	https://tinyurl.com/yf67uy4v

28.

Country	Egypt
City	Cairo
Date	28/03/2013
Number of artifacts	200
Description	Attempt to smuggle 'collectibles' belonging to Abdel Nasser to the Emirates The Egyptian Ministry of Antiquities revealed that it had thwarted an attempt to smuggle 'rare personal belongings' of the ex-president Gamal Abdel Nasser to the United Arab Emirates.
Estimated value USD	na
Source	Anatolu Agency
Source link	https://tinyurl.com/53hp9tkb

29.

Country	Egypt
City	Cairo
Date	10/03/2017
Number of artifacts	150
Description	150 Palestinian antique coins seized inside an Israeli parcel at Cairo Airport.
Estimated value USD	na
Source	Anatolu Agency
Source link	https://tinyurl.com/59xw99cy

30.

Country	Egypt
City	Meniya
Date	30/03/2020
Number of artifacts	113
Description	Thwarting the smuggling of antiquities deal in Minya, including 113 Pharaonic, Greek and Roman pieces.
Estimated value USD	na
Source	Youm 7
Source link	https://tinyurl.com/ekzex57n

31.

Country	Egypt
City	Aswan airport
Date	24/04/2019
Number of artifacts	35
Description	Aswan has launched an investigation with four Britons who were caught trying to smuggle antiquities by private plane from Aswan International Airport. Passenger inspection men at Aswan International Airport, were able to seize a statue and pottery.
Estimated value USD	na
Source	Masrawy
Source link	https://tinyurl.com/4j5au7pp

Iraq

1.

Country	Iraq
City	Mosul
Date	06/06/2018
Number of artifacts	2000
Description	Antiquities looted from the Mosul Museum were found in the house of a Daesh member. Daesh militants destroyed and stole items left in the museum's collection in 2014. The Museum of Mosul once held around 2000 artifacts.
Estimated value USD	na
Source	Kurdistan24
Source link	https://tinyurl.com/mpp9skst

2.

Country	Iraq
City	Kirkuk
Date	17/02/2018
Number of artifacts	na
Description	Iraqi security forces on Saturday announced they had arrested two people who were trying to smuggle at least 13 million USD worth of ancient artifacts from Kirkuk Province to Turkey. The relics included priceless ancient Assyrian, Akkadian, Babylonian, Persian, and Roman artifacts.
Estimated value USD	13000000
Source	Kurdistan24
Source link	https://www.kurdistan24.net/en/story/14783-Iraqi-forces-foil-%2413M-plot-to-smuggle-ancient-artifacts-from-Kirkuk-to-Turkey

3.

Country	Iraq
City	Baghdad
Date	7/09/2018
Number of artifacts	29
Description	The Minister of Tourism and Antiquities Brigade Samism received 29 artifacts dating back to different historical periods by the Iraqi Journalists Syndicate Muayad al-Lami, was found and bought by journalist Faleh Hassan Fathallah.
Estimated value USD	na
Source	Alsumaria
Source link	https://tinyurl.com/6km2mkn2

4.

Country	Iraq
City	Dhi Qar Governorate
Date	17/10/2019
Number of artifacts	na
Description	Iraq thwarts antiquities smuggling operation and arrests those involved in it, according to the Public Integrity Commission in Dhi Qar Governorate, in the south of the country.
Estimated value USD	na
Source	Anadolu Agency
Source link	https://tinyurl.com/3u2x2m69

5.

Country	Iraq
City	Nineveh Governorate
Date	11/11/2020
Number of artifacts	40
Description	Iraqi security thwarted antiquities smuggling operation in Nineveh Governorate, and arrested the smugglers, according to the Iraqi Interior Ministry. In a statement, the ministry said that the internal affairs detachments managed to thwart the smuggling of antiquities in one of the regions of the 'Nineveh' governorate, noting that 'the gang that tried to smuggle these antiquities from Iraq towards Syria throughout Mosul. The objects included archaeological manuscripts, coins and seals.
Estimated value USD	na
Source	Amena monitor
Source link	https://tinyurl.com/3jm6yb52

6.

Country	Iraq
City	Baghdad
Date	22/06/2021
Number of artifacts	1
Description	The security forces in the 15th Brigade in the Baghdad Operations Command, in a qualitative operation, arrested a gang of antiquities smuggling consisting of four accused and seized an archaeological book belonging to one of the monotheistic religions
Estimated value USD	na
Source	Annahar
Source link	https://tinyurl.com/4see3d4s

7.

Country	Iraq
City	Baghdad
Date	04/08/2018
Number of artifacts	800
Description	Investigation of smugglers involved in the theft and sale of 800 antiquities in Baghdad The Rusafa Investigation Court in Baghdad, which is specialized in issues of integrity and economic crime, ratified the testimonies of three defendants who were seized in possession of 800 antique metal objects.
Estimated value USD	na
Source	Nahrain net
Source link	https://tinyurl.com/8bjyevuu

8.

Country	Iraq
City	Mosul
Date	21/05/2018
Number of artifacts	3
Description	Seizures of three artifacts and a collection of manuscripts, papers and books. The smuggler confessed to trying to smuggle these pieces to the Syrian border to be sold to international antiquities dealers.
Estimated value USD	na
Source	Taghrib news
Source link	https://tinyurl.com/2ehjzfc4

9.

Country	Iraq
City	Mosul
Date	29/02/2018
Number of artifacts	10
Description	Several antiquities were seized from the gang's possession, including six seals, a piece bearing ancient Hebrew writings, and a stone weighing two kg in the city of Mosul. According to a security source, several precious antiquities date back to prehistoric times, and some of them date back to the Sumerian period. The source added to local media that one of the pieces belonged to the Hammurabi obelisk and a piece bearing ancient Hebrew inscriptions, noting that the value of these pieces was estimated at more than 10 million dollars.
Estimated value USD	10000000
Source	Yp agency
Source link	https://tinyurl.com/yphej25m

10.

Country	Jordan
City	Jerash
Date	8/26/2014
Number of artifacts	20
Description	The media center in the Directorate of Public Security said that days ago, the employees of the Preventive Security Department in the North received information about the possession of large quantities of antiquities inside their home in order to sell them. In addition to various ancient manuscripts, ancient coins and ancient Islamic artifacts as well as various glassware and pottery.
Estimated value USD	na
Source	Alrai
Source link	https://tinyurl.com/253tb34t

11.

Country	Jordan
City	Irbid
Date	16/09/2014
Number of artifacts	thousands
Description	Security forces seized thousands of artifacts along with unregistered weapons from a warehouse.
Estimated value USD	na
Source	Khaberni
Source link	https://tinyurl.com/4rzuee43

12.

Country	Jordan
City	Al Karama
Date	11/11/2004
Number of artifacts	430
Description	Authorities discovered in a vehicle at the Al Karama border crossing, included sculptures, ceramic dishes and glass lanterns of different sizes and shapes.
Estimated value USD	na
Source	Gulf News
Source link	https://tinyurl.com/yrbjs8r3

13.

Country	Jordan
City	Jaber crossing border
Date	13.02.2021
Number of artifacts	3
Description	Customs at the Jordanian 'Jaber' border crossing with Syria were able to thwart the smuggling of 3 artifacts of white limestone to Syria, which is a vineyard dating back to the Byzantine era. According to a statement issued by the Jordanian Customs Department, the artifacts were seized at the Jaber border crossing with Syria
Estimated value USD	na
Source	Art Arabic
Source link	https://tinyurl.com/4m2esefs

14.

Country	Jordan
City	Zarqa and Amman
Date	12-01-2020
Number of artifacts	163

Description	Preventive Security dealt with two cases of possession of antiquities for sale. Two people were arrested in possession of two statues believed to be antiquities in the capital, and the second in Zarqa Governorate, they had161 coins believed to be antiques.
Estimated value USD	na
Source	Alwakeel news
Source link	https://tinyurl.com/mtptj3h2

15.

Country	Jordan
City	Allenby Bridge
Date	11/12/2018
Number of artifacts	53
Description	The Israeli authorities thwarted the smuggling of antiquities in a vehicle carrying an Israeli number plate coming from Jordan via the King Hussein Bridge (Allenby Bridge). It indicated that a vehicle was in Jordan and heading to the occupied territories, and was driven by a woman, and inside it was found antiques, in addition to jewelry, distributed in different parts inside the vehicle.
Estimated value USD	na
Source	Khaberni news
Source link	https://tinyurl.com/pj8waca4

16.

Country	Jordan
City	Irbid
Date	22/09/2013
Number of artifacts	3
Description	The Public Security Directorate in Jordan announced that it had thwarted the sale and smuggling of three basalt statues dating back to the Roman and Byzantine eras.
Estimated value USD	na
Source	Alarabiya net
Source link	https://tinyurl.com/bddztstu

17.

Country	Jordan
City	Aqaba port
Date	25-12-2016
Number of artifacts	340
Description	Shaaban Abdel-Gawad, General Supervisor of the Department of Recovered Antiquities at the Ministry of Antiquities, said that the ministry received 340 artifacts dating back to different eras from the ancient Egyptian civilization, after they were seized by Jordanian customs in the Jordanian port of Aqaba.
Estimated value USD	na

Source	Gate ahram
Source link	https://tinyurl.com/475muv52

Kuwait

1.

Country	Kuwait
City	Kuwait
Date	08/10/2018
Number of artifacts	1
Description	Kuwait returns 'smuggled' rare Pharaonic artifact to Egypt
Estimated value USD	na
Source	Arabtimesonline
Source link	https://tinyurl.com/59a6c3wx

2.

Country	Kuwait
City	Kuwait
Date	26/09/2019
Number of artifacts	5
Description	Customs authorities at Kuwait International Airport thwarted an attempt to smuggle pharaonic antiquities coming from the Egyptian Luxor Airport. The Kuwaiti newspaper 'Al-Anbaa' reported that the National Council for Culture, Arts and Letters to investigate the issue of smuggled antiquities by confirming that they are real and not fake. The newspaper quoted the General Administration of Customs as saying that it intends to return the seized antiquities, numbering five pieces, to the Egyptian authorities.
Estimated value USD	na
Source	Alanba news
Source link	https://tinyurl.com/3srxea83

3.

Country	Kuwait
City	Kuwait
Date	25/11/2020
Number of artifacts	9
Description	According to a statement issued by the 'Customs', it was suspected that personal belongings were shipped from Egypt via air freight, and by searching them, they found objects suspected to be smuggled Pharaonic antiquities.
Estimated value USD	na
Source	Alanba news
Source link	https://tinyurl.com/329crdk8

Lebanon

1.

Country	Lebanon
City	Beirut
Date	5/9/2015
Number of artifacts	6000
Description	Syria's state news agency quoted an archaeology official as saying that authorities have confiscated and reclaimed 6000 looted antiquities trafficked by smugglers outside the country. The head of the General Directorate of Antiquities and Museums, Ahmad Deeb, said Friday that the materials include 69 antiquities and eight mosaics that were retrieved from Lebanon.
Estimated value USD	
Source	Culture Crime News
Source link	https://tinyurl.com/2t9642pb

2.

Country	Lebanon
City	Tyros
Date	03/09/2016
Number of artifacts	1
Description	Ancient artifact smugglers arrested in south Lebanon
Estimated value USD	
Source	Culture Crime News
Source link	https://news.culturecrime.org/entry/star2016ancient-artifac.html

3.

Country	Lebanon
City	Tipoli
Date	03/012/2015
Number of artifacts	na
Description	Report suggests Daesh is smuggling antiquities through Lebanon. It revealed that a recently arrested IS member had confessed to being related to the owner of a butcher shop in the northern city of Tripoli, and that the meat shipments received from Syria are not limited to the products he sells in his shop. The shipments also include narcotic pills, smuggled artifacts, and gold.
Estimated value USD	
Source	Al Bawaba
Source link	https://tinyurl.com/2p8zej3j

4.

Country	Lebanon
City	Beirut
Datc	23/02/2020
Number of artifacts	60
Description	Beirut airport authorities seized 60 artifacts hidden in bags of travelers who were heading to Australia on a flight for the Emirates 'Etihad' airline. The agency stated that the inspections detachment of the Internal Security Forces company at the airport seized these artifacts in the possession of two passengers of the Emirates plane, who were heading to Australia via Abu Dhabi.
Estimated value USD	
Source	Alarabiya
Source link	https://tinyurl.com/532znyen

Libya

1.

Country	Libya
City	Tripoli (Mitiga International Airport)
Date	07/08/2017
Number of artifacts	580
Description	A security force affiliated with the Libyan Government of National Accord (GNA) has landed 580 antique silver pieces dating back to the Roman period in the possession of a citizen at Mitiga Airport in the capital, Tripoli, which she said was in the process of smuggling them. The collection consisted mostly of ceramic Hellenistic grave goods: 10 lamps of different shapes and sizes, 10 amphorae with different shapes and sizes, 10 pots (three of which have lids), a small fragrance bottle made of alabaster, a set of pottery, and a small piece of limestone that is part of a mural. The pieces are consistent with the funerary goods found in the Greek tombs in one of the ancient cities in east Libya, dating to between the 5th and the late 3rd century B.CE.
Estimated value USD	
Source	Anatolu Agency
Source link	https://tinyurl.com/4rs958zh

2.

Country	Libya
City	As Sallūm and Musaid crossing border
Date	25/05/2017
Number of artifacts	35
Description	The Tourism and Antiquities Police arrested an accused of trafficking in antiquities through the Salloum port of trafficking in some smuggled antiquities from Libya entered the country illegally.

Estimated value USD	
Source	Anatolu Agency
Source link	https://tinyurl.com/2ayc2bsd

Mauritania

1.

Country	Mauritania
City	Gogui frontier cross
Date	na
Number of artifacts	na
Description	During the last war in Mali, 'some manuscripts were looted and burned, but at a limited level, particularly in the city of Timbuktu.'
Estimated value USD	
Source	Elwatan
Source link	https://tinyurl.com/ytws3j5n

Morocco

1.

Country	Morocco
City	Erfoud
Date	02/03/2017
Number of artifacts	1
Description	Local people who dig every part of the earth in search of white fossils, dating back millions of years. Paris: Auction house retracts its sale of a 'looted' dinosaur skeleton from Morocco.
Estimated value	450000 Euros
Source	France 24
Source link	https://tinyurl.com/sj9tp4ra

Oman

1.

Country	Oman
City	Muscat
Date	01/12/2017
Number of artifacts	na
Description	Oman also reported more cases in 2018 than in 2017
Estimated value USD	na
Source	WCO Illicit Trade Report 2018. World Customs Organization

Source link	www.wcoomd.org/-/media/wco/public/global/pdf/topics/enforcement-and-compliance/activities-and-programmes/illicit-trade-report/itr_2016_en.pdf?db=web

Palestine/Israel

1.

Country	Palestine/Israel
City	Jerusalem
Date	6/1/2018
Number of artifacts	91
Description	Egypt is to receive 91 ancient artefact which were illegally smuggled from thc country from Israel.
Estimated value USD	na
Source	Middle East Monitor
Source link	https://tinyurl.com/5n64h7d6

2.

Country	Palestine/Israel
City	West Bank
Date	7/1/2018
Number of artifacts	2571
Description	The Palestinian Authority police arrested two people who were transferring 2571 ancient artefacts from the neighborhood of Halhoul to the city of Hebron.
Estimated value USD	na
Source	Middle East Monitor
Source link	https://tinyurl.com/2p8bxdj3

3.

Country	Palestine/Israel
City	Area C
Date	2015
Number of artifacts	20000
Description	In 2015, the volume of seizures entered into the records of the Ministry of Tourism and Antiquities was estimated at approximately 20000 pieces.
Estimated value USD	na
Source	Almonitor
Source link	https://tinyurl.com/2tvk3apx

4.

Country	Palestine/Israel
City	Area C
Date	2016

Number of artifacts	2400
Description	In 2016, the volume of seizures entered into the records of the Ministry of Tourism and Antiquities was estimated at approximately 2400 pieces, most of which are from 'C' areas.
Estimated value USD	na
Source	Almonitor
Source link	https://tinyurl.com/2tvk3apx

5.

Country	Palestine/Israel
City	Nablus
Date	16/03/2017
Number of artifacts	1
Description	The Palestinian police thwarted an attempt to smuggle and sell an antique statue from the city of Nablus in the northern West Bank outside the country.
Estimated value USD	na
Source	Almonitor
Source link	https://tinyurl.com/2tvk3apx

6.

Country	Palestine/Israel
City	Jenin
Date	05/03/2017
Number of artifacts	1
Description	Jenin Governorate. Also on March 5, the police seized an ancient 2500-year-old windmill, which was found inside the house of a citizen.
Estimated value USD	na
Source	Almonitor
Source link	https://tinyurl.com/2tvk3apx

7.

Country	Palestine/Israel
City	Bethlehem
Date	6/1/2018
Number of artifacts	na
Description	The police of the Palestinian Authority in the city of Bethlehem, in the southern occupied West Bank, said that they thwarted, on Sunday, an attempt to sell and smuggle archaeological materials, and a statue in the form of a Pharaonic man dating back to the Bronze Age was seized. A statue in the form of a pharaonic man believed to be archaeological and dating back to the Bronze Age, 20 centimeters long, with ancient Pharaonic inscriptions on it, in addition to shiny crystals suspected to be pure gold weighs 30 grams.
Estimated value USD	na

Source	Qusdpress
Source link	https://tinyurl.com/2ce994d7

8.

Country	Palestine/Israel
City	Rafah Border Crossing
Date	25/11/2020
Number of artifacts	4
Description	The Crossings and Ports Control Department of the Police General Investigations Department in Gaza announced, on Wednesday, that it had thwarted an attempt to smuggle four artifacts through the Rafah border crossing between the Strip and Egypt.
Estimated value USD	na
Source	Paltoday
Source link	https://tinyurl.com/57vswbn6

9.

Country	Palestine/Israel
City	Betlehem
Date	09/02/2019
Number of artifacts	310
Description	The Bethlehem Governorate police failed an operation smuggling historical artifacts and arrested a person who tried to smuggle them out of the Palestinian territories. It contains 310 different relics of ancient coins and rings dating back to various eras.
Estimated value USD	na
Source	Ramallah News
Source link	https://tinyurl.com/bdcnxbc6

10.

Country	Palestine/Israel
City	Betlehem
Date	20/07/2011
Number of artifacts	23
Description	19 antique coins dating back to different eras, they include a black ball-like seal with an engraving of an angel carrying a cupid crossbow believed to be archaeological, dating back to the Greek period, and an antique coin 'Menorah' bearing an engraving of a candlestick. Police seized a rare bronze statue of 26 cm in length and 5 cm in width with open hands of a standing woman carrying a crown on her head and a ring in one of her ears, estimated to be 3000 years old and valued at about $50000, and a deer-skin manuscript in ancient Hebrew size 33cm x 17cm.
Estimated value USD	50000
Source	Alduds
Source link	https://tinyurl.com/2s7mjm6v

11.

Country	Palestine/Israel
City	Gaza
Date	12/08/2020
Number of artifacts	na
Description	The General Investigations of the Gaza Police seized valuable archaeological items that were in the possession of a group of antiquities smugglers, they were on their way to smuggle them across the border fence to Israel.
Estimated value USD	na
Source	Alray
Source link	https://tinyurl.com/mwzv4nz7

Qatar

1.

Country	Qatar
City	Doha
Date	01/12/2009
Number of artifacts	5
Description	The authorities in Switzerland reported finding a trove of antiquities in 2013. The recovered artefacts included five pieces from Yemen, which had transited through Qatar before arriving in Switzerland in 2009 and 2010. The items were stored at Geneva Freeport and discovered as part of a routine Customs inspection.
Estimated value USD	
Source	WCO Illicit Trade Report 2018. World Customs Organization
Source link	www.wcoomd.org/-/media/wco/public/global/pdf/topics/enforcement-and-compliance/activities-and-programmes/illicit-trade-report/itr_2016_en.pdf?db=web

Saudi Arabia

1.

Country	Saudi Arabi
City	Douba (Tabuk)
Date	10/01/2018
Number of artifacts	1599
Description	Saudi Customs at the port of Duba seized 1509 cultural objects, including antique coins and religious crosses. The objects were hidden in the storage compartment of a vehicle, were moving from Turkey via Saudi Arabia, with the final destination of Kuwait
Estimated value USD	na
Source	Antiquities Coalition
Source link	https://tinyurl.com/2p8zffbz

2.

Country	Saudi Arabi
City	Riyadh
Date	07/01/2018
Number of artifacts	6
Description	Six rare artifacts, some dating back to pre-Islamic eras have been handed over to the Saudi Commission for Tourism and National Heritage (SCTH) by a Saudi citizen.
Estimated value USD	na
Source	Arab News
Source link	https://tinyurl.com/y7jxpbbr

3.

Country	Saudi Arabi
City	Badr
Date	07/01/2016
Number of artifacts	2763
Description	Sa Saudi Customs seized 2763 pieces of ancient coins which dated back to the Pharaonic periods, which were concealed in secret compartments in an SUV arriving from Egypt.
Estimated value USD	na
Source	WCO Illicit Trade Report 2016. World Customs Organization
Source link	www.wcoomd.org/-/media/wco/public/global/pdf/topics/enforcement-and-compliance/activities-and-programmes/illicit-trade-report/itr_2016_en.pdf?db=web

4.

Country	Saudi Arabi
City	Riyadh
Date	07/01/2016
Number of artifacts	1321
Description	Archaeological objects dating back to the Graeco-Roman Period of Egypt and 109 Ushabti faience statues.
Estimated value USD	na
Source	WCO Illicit Trade Report 2016. World Customs Organization
Source link	www.wcoomd.org/-/media/wco/public/global/pdf/topics/enforcement-and-compliance/activities-and-programmes/illicit-trade-report/itr_2016_en.pdf?db=web

5.

Country	Saudi Arabi
City	Mecca
Date	09/11/2019
Number of artifacts	na

Description	The Saudi security services overthrew a Turkish person who tried to smuggle the antiquities of the Two Holy Mosques. According to the newspaper, the security authorities in the Holy Capital were able to arrest a 'Turkish' foreigner who tried to steal some of the antiquities in the Exhibition of the Two Holy Mosques Architecture, which is affiliated with the General Presidency for the Affairs of the Grand Mosque and the Prophet's Mosque.
Estimated value USD	na
Source	Al bayan.
Source link	https://tinyurl.com/y54xpe2d

Sudan

1.

Country	Sudan
City	Khartoum
Date	01/04/2021
Number of artifacts	40
Description	The Anti-Smuggling General Department managed to thwart a smuggling operation of 40 rare antiquities, in the capital, Khartoum.
Estimated value USD	na
Source	Ultra Sudan
Source link	https://tinyurl.com/2p94pezh

2.

Country	Sudan
City	Atbara
Date	30/12/2013
Number of artifacts	40
Description	The Sudanese security authorities have thwarted the smuggling of Sudanese antiquities near the city of Atbara, north of the Sudanese capital, Khartoum. The Sudanese police said that they had thwarted the smuggling of eight Sudanese artifacts near the city of Atbara, 400 km north of Khartoum.
Estimated value USD	na
Source	Skynewsarabia
Source link	https://tinyurl.com/252s4t5y

3.

Country	Sudan
City	Atbara
Date	29/12/2013
Number of artifacts	9

Description	The Anti-Smuggling Department of the General Administration of Customs, Anti-Smuggling Branch enabled to thwart an attempt to smuggle nine antiquities in Atbara. They are rare pieces that have no parallel in the museum, and they date back to the period of the Napatan Kingdom, which dates to the eighth century BC. They include a bronze mirror with writing on it, bronze and alabaster pots, pottery flasks, in addition to a set of beads made of precious stones.
Estimated value USD	na
Source	Customs Authority
Source link	https://tinyurl.com/3d6x2du7

4.

Country	Sudan
City	Atbara
Date	30/05/2016
Number of artifacts	3
Description	The Sudanese police reported that they were able to thwart an attempt to smuggle antiquities represented by a 150-centimeter-long skeleton and two ancient pottery pieces dating back to the post-Meroitic period, according to the preliminary report of the Antiquities Committee. The Sudan News Agency quoted government officials on Sunday that the anti-smuggling police in the Atbara area managed to thwart the smuggling attempt after coordination between the competent authorities.
Estimated value USD	na
Source	Altahjyeer news
Source link	https://tinyurl.com/4yvj65cb

Syria

1.

Country	Syria
City	Daraa
Date	10/1/2018
Number of artifacts	14
Description	According to the Syrian Arab news Agency (SANA), Roman columns with an ornament, pieces of basaltic sculptures and copper and glass bottles, all of which are of great cultural value, were among the antiquities which were due to be smuggled to Jordan.
Estimated value USD	na
Source	Urdu Point; Arabic Sputnik News; Arabic RT
Source link	https://tinyurl.com/24zwd7p8

2.

Country	Syria
City	Palmyra (Tadmur)
Date	3/19/2015
Number of artifacts	120
Description	The General Directorate of Syrian Antiquities and Museums announced that it had recovered 120 artifacts after being looted from historic sites in Palmyra. It is estimated that the number of stolen artifacts from the museums of Raqqa and Deir Atiya exceeds 1500 objects. According to official information that some of them are still inside Syria.
Estimated value USD	na
Source	Alwasat
Source link	https://tinyurl.com/bdh3rwdz

3.

Country	Syria
City	Tartus
Date	9/1/2015
Number of artifacts	18
Description	Ancient coins dating back to 3000 years, a golden ring and an old dagger hidden by a passenger in a public car heading for Lebanon.
Estimated value USD	na
Source	Sana
Source link	https://www.sana.sy/?p=276312

4.

Country	Syria
City	Daraa
Date	10/1/2018
Number of artifacts	14
Description	According to the Syrian Arab news Agency (SANA), Roman columns with an ornament, pieces of basaltic sculptures and copper and glass bottles, all of which are of great cultural value, were among the antiquities to be smuggled to Jordan.
Estimated value USD	na
Source	Antiquities Coalition
Source link	https://theantiquitiescoalition.org/multimedia-resources/interactive-maps/

5.

Country	Syria
City	Raqqa
Date	12/24/2017
Number of artifacts	200

Description	Mostly potter, but also includes metal and stone tools and clay dolls.
Estimated value USD	na
Source	Antiquities Coalition
Source link	https://theantiquitiescoalition.org/multimedia-resources/interactive-maps/

6.

Country	Syria
City	Daraa
Date	26/07/2021
Number of artifacts	42
Description	The competent authorities in Daraa thwarted an attempt to smuggle dozens of antiquities out of Syria.
Estimated value USD	na
Source	The limited Times
Source link	https://newsrnd.com/news/2021-07-26-the-competent-authorities-in-daraa-thwart-an-attempt-to-smuggle-antiquities-out-of-syria.SklXa-Q3Ad.html

7.

Country	Syria
City	Daraa
Date	01/10/2018
Number of artifacts	5
Description	An attempt to smuggle antiquities from Syria to Jordan.
Estimated value USD	na
Source	Al-Rai newspaper
Source link	https://tinyurl.com/mrybte3a

8.

Country	Syria
City	Deir ez-Zor.
Date	24/01/2019
Number of artifacts	1
Description	An attempt to smuggle antiquities from Deir Ez-Zor, Syria, an archaeological painting dating back to the Roman era from the countryside of the governorate across the border with Iraq to smuggle it out of Syria
Estimated value USD	na
Source	Xeber news
Source link	https://tinyurl.com/bdddpuhk

9.

Country	Syria
City	Tartus
Date	27/04/2021
Number of artifacts	150
Description	The security authorities seized more than 150 antique in the possession of several antiquities' dealers in the countryside of Tartous Governorate, western Syria. 15 persons were possessing more than 150 antiquities, and the authorities confiscated all the pieces, which contain rare and valuable pieces. The confiscated pieces included gold, silver and bronze coins, in addition to statues, gold rings and earrings, and a number of other artifacts.
Estimated value USD	na
Source	Syrian Social Journalism
Source link	https://tinyurl.com/bdcpftec

10.

Country	Syria
City	Bab al Hawa.
Date	15/06/2021
Number of artifacts	2533
Description	The Turkish Custom seized 8 boxes of ancient coins at the Bab al-Hawa border crossing. They are 308 Hellenistic coins, 2016 Roman period and 209 Byzantine. Turkish authorities replaced the objects at the Hatay Museum. Previously, Turkish authorities detained 93 persons involved in antiquities trafficking after smuggling in 30 provinces in Turkey.
Estimated value USD	na
Source	Syria 24
Source link	https://tinyurl.com/avk2rj7f

Tunisia

1.

Country	Tunisia
City	Ben Arous
Date	6/1/2018
Number of artifacts	32
Description	The National Security and police district of Ben Arous seized 32 priceless artifacts.
Estimated value USD	na
Source	Antiquities Coalition
Source link	https://theantiquitiescoalition.org/multimedia-resources/interactive-maps/

2.

Country	Tunisia
City	Tunisia
Date	19/01/2016
Number of artifacts	607
Description	In total, 591 antiquities (vases, glass utensils, lamps) dating from the Ottoman era and 16 paintings by Tunisian painters were seized, and the value of this seizure amounts to more than four million dinars, according to the Ministry.
Estimated value USD	1715118
Source	Webdo
Source link	https://tinyurl.com/4hsjmucd

3.

Country	Tunisia
City	Sousse
Date	2/28/2017
Number of artifacts	663
Description	Security forces dismantled a network of archeological artefacts following the arrest of four people and the discovery of 663 old pieces
Estimated value USD	na
Source	Webdo
Source link	https://tinyurl.com/yckmz85d

4.

Country	Tunisia
City	Essouassi
Date	3/1/2016
Number of artifacts	2
Description	Three individuals were arrested in possession of two archaeological artifacts
Estimated value USD	na
Source	Jawhara
Source link	https://tinyurl.com/y29w7rub

5.

Country	Tunisia
City	Sfax
Date	1/1/2014
Number of artifacts	920
Description	An individual is arrested at Sfax airport in possession of 920 antique coins with the intention of selling them in Europe
Estimated value USD	na

Source	Antiquities Coalition
Source link	https://theantiquitiescoalition.org/multimedia-resources/interactive-maps/

6.

Country	Tunisia
City	Sbiba
Date	3/1/2017
Number of artifacts	312
Description	A total of 308 fake archeological pieces and 4 other originals were seized after a tense ruffle by police officers to two suspects in the weekly Sbiba market.
Estimated value USD	na
Source	African Manager
Source link	https://tinyurl.com/3x99hv96

7.

Country	Tunisia
City	Kasserine
Date	1/1/2017
Number of artifacts	1035
Description	Tunisian police found hundreds of pieces of stone, clay, metal artifacts and antiques coins while raiding a house in the northwest of the country. The Interior Ministry said in a statement that it had discovered 20 pieces of stone and clay, 15 different kinds of metal, and about 1000 coins.
Estimated value USD	na
Source	Al Manar
Source link	https://tinyurl.com/34wdapmj

8.

Country	Tunisia
City	Tunisia
Date	3/1/2018
Number of artifacts	170
Description	Some 170 archeological coins were seized by the customs officers of the Ras Jedir and the brigade at the El Guitoun checkpoint. The seizure operation, carried out on 29 March 2018, an investigation of a vehicle of a foreigner, with the intention of smuggling them to Libya through the border point of Ras Jedir.
Estimated value USD	na
Source	Antiquities Coalition
Source link	https://theantiquitiescoalition.org/multimedia-resources/interactive-maps/

9.

Country	Tunisia
City	El Kef
Date	23/12/2020
Number of artifacts	2050
Description	The National Security Forces in the Tajrouine region, in the El Kef governorate, northwest of Tunisia, arrested a gang that specialized in stealing treasures and antiquities. According to Tunisian local media, the number of antiquities confiscated amounted to 2050 rare pieces, the value of which is approximately one million Tunisian dinars.
Estimated value	1000000 dinars
Source	Akhbarelyom
Source link	https://tinyurl.com/2jpnh4h9

10.

Country	Tunisia
City	Tunisia
Date	08/01/2021
Number of artifacts	2
Description	In mid-December, the Criminal Cases Sub-Department of the Judicial Police Department, following a house search in the Ibn Khaldun neighborhood, was able to seize a manuscript of historical value made of leather written in Hebrew with a liquid of gold water, in addition to a large sword of white metal, and experts from the Institute confirmed The National Heritage that the book is original and acquires great historical value and is written on thin leather.
Estimated value USD	na
Source	Qposts
Source link	https://tinyurl.com/yav7jw8t

11.

Country	Tunisia
City	Fouchana
Date	24/10/2020
Number of artifacts	3
Description	Seizure of two Hebrew manuscripts, each exceeding 10 meters in length, and a wooden box decorated and engraved in the Hebrew language dedicated to preserving the manuscripts.
Estimated value USD	na
Source	Tunisienumerique News
Source link	https://tinyurl.com/2z98hrcj

12.

Country	Tunisia
City	Tunisia
Date	25/12/2020
Number of artifacts	1
Description	One Hebrew manuscript.
Estimated value USD	na
Source	Ministry of Interior
Source link	https://tinyurl.com/58xwws2x

13.

Country	Tunisia
City	Sousse
Date	31/10/2020
Number of artifacts	5
Description	Five manuscripts in Hebrew have been reserved
Estimated value USD	na
Source	Ministry of Interior
Source link	https://tinyurl.com/ycxwb6xy

14.

Country	Tunisia
City	Frontier Tunisia and Libya
Date	19/12/2020
Number of artifacts	More than 8
Description	A copy of the Torah 'completely preserved', which was copied by hand in special ink on the skin of a bull measuring 37 meters in length, and it contained all parts of the Torah in its five books. This version was described as 'a remarkable and unique one in the world'. Also, among the seizures were 'six volumes and ancient Hebrew manuscripts, which a trafficking network operating between Tunis and Bizerte (north) and Libya tried to sell for 1.5 million Tunisian dinars (470000 euros),' according to what the Tunisian Ministry of the Interior revealed in early 2019. They also included Seized funeral furniture and religious books
Estimated value	470000 Euros
Source	Alwasat News.
Source link	https://tinyurl.com/3npskf84

15.

Country	Tunisia
City	Mohamedia is a town in Ben Arous Governorate, Tunisia.
Date	28/09/2019
Number of artifacts	3

Description	A patrol of the National Guard Research and Inspection Team in Muhammadiyah arrested 4 people on charges of excavating antiquities. They had a metal detector and antiques, including a jar, a lamp, and a tablet for a book of the Qur'an.
Estimated value USD	na
Source	Nessma Tv
Source link	https://tinyurl.com/5ddxu4fa

16.

Country	Tunisia
City	Gafsa
Date	08/04/2017
Number of artifacts	3
Description	The Research and Inspection Team of the National Guard in Gafsa was able to arrest a person who sells antiquities, and the two pieces were seized in his house.
Estimated value USD	na
Source	Nessma Tv
Source link	https://tinyurl.com/aehnwbe8

17.

Country	Tunisia
City	Monastir Governorate
Date	28/12/2017
Number of artifacts	2
Description	The National Security District in Maknin, Monastir Province, managed to unveil a network specialized in promoting antiquities, and arrested two of its members, and seized two antiquities (one in the form of a rectangular panel about 60 cm long and 20 cm wide, carved with figures of humans and animals, and the second piece is a small yellow stone human head statue).
Estimated value	10000 Euro
Source	Nessma Tv
Source link	https://tinyurl.com/mwwpbtwa

18.

Country	Tunisia
City	Majaz al Bab
Date	08/01/2018
Number of artifacts	2
Description	Two archaeological objects.
Estimated value USD	na
Source	Nessma Tv
Source link	https://tinyurl.com/5n8dzjs7

19.

Country	Tunisia
City	Tunisia
Date	23/03/2018
Number of artifacts	3
Description	The National Security and police seized three archaeological objects
Estimated value USD	na
Source	Nessma Tv
Source link	https://tinyurl.com/2p9d6dw6

20.

Country	Tunisia
City	Béja
Date	21/12/2016
Number of artifacts	13
Description	Agents of the National Guard Center in the Delegation of Tibar in Beja seized 13 artifacts that were in a cafe.
Estimated value USD	na
Source	Nessma Tv
Source link	https://tinyurl.com/ys7yheyr

21.

Country	Tunisia
City	Gafsa
Date	01/12/2016
Number of artifacts	4
Description	The special team of the regional regiment for maintaining order in Gafsa enabled the arrest of three people in a Fiat car in the Sidi Ahmed Zarrouk area, in their possession four ancient statues, intended to sell for 200000 dinars.
Estimated value	200000 dinars
Source	Nessma Tv
Source link	https://tinyurl.com/4d7pa8e5

22.

Country	Tunisia
City	Gaâfour
Date	08/11/2016
Number of artifacts	27
Description	The units affiliated to the National Guard area in Qaafour, Siliana, managed to seize 27 Roman artifacts.
Estimated value USD	na
Source	Nessma Tv

Source link	https://tinyurl.com/5zu5mkar

23.

Country	Tunisia
City	Ben Arous
Date	10/03/2017
Number of artifacts	1
Description	Tunisian authorities seize a rare manuscript of the Torah, it dates back to the 15th century AD. The manuscript, carved in special ink, on the skin of a calf, is 37 meters long and 47 centimeters wide. It was presented to specialists in the Hebrew language, who said that it contains all parts of the Torah in its five books, namely Genesis, Exodus, Leviticus, and the Book of Leviticus. Number and Deuteronomy, in its first old version, that is, before arranging and organizing these books in the form that the Torah became in its current version. Al-Shaibani added, 'The font in which this manuscript was written is used only in writing antiquities with sacred contents, especially the Torah and its religious interpretations.' He continued: 'The skin on which the manuscript was written is of a special kind, where, one month before the birth of the cow, the fetus is extracted and flayed, and after that the writing is done on its skin, which lasts hundreds of years, according to experts from the National Heritage Institute.' Al-Shaibani stressed, 'This piece is priceless,' expecting that 'their financial value will be very large.' He pointed out that 'the phenomenon of smuggling, looting, vandalizing and trafficking antiquities in illegal ways has spread widely in the country, especially after the 2011 revolution, and specialized networks and gangs are involved in it.' For his part, the spokesman for the Tunisian Ministry of Interior, Yasser Mesbah, said that 'the insurance on this manuscript was estimated at four million and 500 thousand million euros ten years ago, according to Tunisian experts.'
Estimated value	4500000 Euro
Source	Anatolu Agency
Source link	https://tinyurl.com/4z6tsvxh

United Arab Emirates

1.

Country	United Arab Emirates
City	Sharjah
Date	11/01/2017
Number of artifacts	354
Description	Egypt has recovered 354 archaeological objects that were seized by authorities in the United Arab Emirates.
Estimated value USD	na
Source	Arab news
Source link	https://tinyurl.com/bdhu5tbu

2.

Country	United Arab Emirates
City	Abu Dhabi
Date	18/10/2018
Number of artifacts	na
Description	Abu Dhabi Police, Brigadier General Dr. Rashid Burshid, said that after following-up and investigation of the group's movements, it was confirmed that the gang members possessed antiques, including manuscripts, daggers, precious stones and ancient coins. They tried to sell for high sums of money.
Estimated value USD	na
Source	Emarat al youm
Source link	https://www.emaratalyoum.com/local-section/accidents/2016-10-18-1.938144

Yemen

1.

Country	Yemen
City	Aden
Date	08/10/2018
Number of artifacts	12
Description	Port officials in Aden seized a shipment of antiques that is suspected to be part of what the Yemeni government says is looting of the country's heritage by Houthis to fund their insurgency. The consignment of eight objects seized last week arrived by lorry from Sanaa, the rebel-held capital, on its way to an address in Djibouti, according to the Col Shallal Al Shoubagi of the harbor security force.
Estimated value USD	na
Source	The National news
Source link	https://tinyurl.com/2p8un8cb

2.

Country	Yemen
City	Sanaa
Date	01/12/2016
Number of artifacts	110
Description	Five seizures of antiquities were reported by the Yemeni Customs authorities to the WCO in 2016. These seizures resulted in the retention of over 110 individual cultural objects, including statues, coins, and calligraphy pieces.
Estimated value USD	na
Source	WCO Illicit Trade Report 2018. World Customs Organization
Source link	www.wcoomd.org/-/media/wco/public/global/pdf/topics/enforcement-and-compliance/activities-and-programmes/illicit-trade-report/itr_2016_en.pdf?db=web

3.

Country	Yemen
City	Sanaa
Date	12/10/2006
Number of artifacts	7
Description	The Yemeni security services at Sanaa Airport and the Antiquities Smuggling Department of the Yemeni General Authority for Antiquities thwarted an attempt to smuggle seven antiquities dating back to the Shebaan era. Yemeni security sources told the Yemeni News Agency that the antiquities were seized in a diplomatic bag belonging to one of the foreign embassies operating in Yemen, and it was intended to be smuggled abroad through a shipping company.
Estimated value USD	na
Source	Saudi Press Agency
Source link	https://tinyurl.com/2p8jz4xt